CAMBRIDGE LIBRARY COLLECTION

Books of enduring scholarly value

Education

This series focuses on educational theory and practice, particularly in the context of eighteenth- and nineteenth-century Europe and its colonies, and America. During this period, the questions of who should be educated, to what age, to what standard and using what curriculum, were widely debated. The reform of schools and universities, the drive towards improving women's education, and the movement for free (or at least low-cost) schools for the poor were all major concerns both for governments and for society at large. The books selected for reissue in this series discuss key issues of their time, including the 'appropriate' levels of instruction for the children of the working classes, the emergence of adult education movements, and proposals for the higher education of women. They also cover topics that still resonate today, such as the nature of education, the role of universities in the diffusion of knowledge, and the involvement of religious groups in establishing and running schools.

The Educational Writings of John Locke

John Locke (1632–1704) is widely regarded as one of the most influential of the Enlightenment philosophers. This volume, edited by J. W. Adamson and published as a second edition in 1922, contains two of John Locke's essays concerning education; *Some Thoughts Concerning Education* (1693) and *Of the Conduct of the Understanding* (1706). *Some Thoughts Concerning Education* expands on Locke's pioneering theory of mind by explaining how to educate a child using three complementary methods: the development of a healthy body; the formation of a virtuous mind; and the pursuit of an academic curriculum including the emerging sciences, mathematics and languages. *Of the Conduct of the Understanding* continues the theme of the earlier essay by describing how to develop rational thought. For over a century after the publication of these essays, John Locke's views on education were considered authoritative, and his work was translated into almost all major European languages.

T0370743

Cambridge University Press has long been a pioneer in the reissuing of out-of-print titles from its own backlist, producing digital reprints of books that are still sought after by scholars and students but could not be reprinted economically using traditional technology. The Cambridge Library Collection extends this activity to a wider range of books which are still of importance to researchers and professionals, either for the source material they contain, or as landmarks in the history of their academic discipline.

Drawing from the world-renowned collections in the Cambridge University Library, and guided by the advice of experts in each subject area, Cambridge University Press is using state-of-the-art scanning machines in its own Printing House to capture the content of each book selected for inclusion. The files are processed to give a consistently clear, crisp image, and the books finished to the high quality standard for which the Press is recognised around the world. The latest print-on-demand technology ensures that the books will remain available indefinitely, and that orders for single or multiple copies can quickly be supplied.

The Cambridge Library Collection will bring back to life books of enduring scholarly value (including out-of-copyright works originally issued by other publishers) across a wide range of disciplines in the humanities and social sciences and in science and technology.

The Educational
Writings of John Locke

Edited by John William Adamson

CAMBRIDGE
UNIVERSITY PRESS

CAMBRIDGE UNIVERSITY PRESS

Cambridge, New York, Melbourne, Madrid, Cape Town, Singapore,
São Paolo, Delhi, Dubai, Tokyo, Mexico City

Published in the United States of America by Cambridge University Press, New York

www.cambridge.org
Information on this title: www.cambridge.org/9781108010177

This edition first published 1922
This digitally printed version 2010

ISBN 978-1-108-01017-7 Paperback

THE EDUCATIONAL WRITINGS OF
JOHN LOCKE

CAMBRIDGE UNIVERSITY PRESS
C. F. CLAY, Manager
LONDON : FETTER LANE, E.C. 4

NEW YORK : THE MACMILLAN CO.
BOMBAY ⎫
CALCUTTA ⎬ MACMILLAN AND CO., Ltd.
MADRAS ⎭
TORONTO   THE MACMILLAN CO. OF
CANADA, Ltd.
TOKYO : MARUZEN-KABUSHIKI-KAISHA

1 Mens Sana in Corpore Sano
is a short but full description of a hap
py state in y^s world these two thing[s]
more to wish for & he y^t wants either
of them is but little y^e bett^r for any thing
else Mens happynesse or misery is
most part of their own making. He
whose minde directs not wisely will nev^r
take ye right way, & he whose body is cra
zy & feeble will never be able to mart[ch]
in it. I confesse there are some mens
constitutions of body & minde soe vigo
rous & well framed by nature y^t they
need not much assistance from others
but by ye strength of their naturall genius
are from their Cradles carried towards
w^t is Excellent & by ye vigour of their
Constitutions are able to doe wonders But
these examples are but few, & I thinke

Facsimile page of the original draft of
Some Thoughts concerning Education.

THE EDUCATIONAL WRITINGS

OF

JOHN LOCKE

EDITED BY

JOHN WILLIAM ADAMSON
PROFESSOR OF EDUCATION IN THE UNIVERSITY OF LONDON

CAMBRIDGE
AT THE UNIVERSITY PRESS
1922

First published 1912.
Second edition 1922.

PREFACE

THE educational writings of an author who died more than two centuries ago may be thought to possess an interest little more than antiquarian at the present day. Unfortunately, the historical study of education, as commonly pursued, serves to confirm rather than to correct such a supposition, since it frequently diverts the student from the development which has taken place in the actual application of educational ideas, and transfers his attention to the biographies, personal opinions, or mere *obiter dicta* of individual men and women, whose influence upon homes, schools, universities, or administration has been either small or quite negligible.

But there have been men and women whose lives or writings or both combined have exerted great influence upon the course of events; the educational situation of the present is to be understood in its completeness only by reference to the past as embodied in their work. John Locke is of the number. He was profoundly dissatisfied with education as practised in his own day, and his criticisms throw light on the aims and methods of the schools of the late seventeenth century. But his writings also shaped the theory and practice of his immediate successors outside his own country, particularly in France and Germany. His principles and methods still live, as witness some of the most recent changes of scholastic procedure. The present volume attempts to make clear his position amongst the various influences which have shaped the real history of education.

The educational writings of John Locke are of more than professional interest; indeed, their more obvious appeal is to the parent and the young man who consciously sets himself the task of "self-education." But the reader, whether lay or professional, is apt to find the longer treatise somewhat prolix and encumbered by repetitions, while the *Conduct of the Understanding* was not revised by its author. In the present work, the provision of cross-references and the selection of the first edition of *Some Thoughts* as the basal text have, it is hoped, secured an arrangement of Locke's exposition convenient for the purposes of study.

J. W. A.

CONTENTS

CHRONOLOGICAL TABLE

1632. John Locke, born at Wrington, Somerset, August 29.

1646–52. At Westminster School.

1652–67. At Christ Church, Oxford. B.A. 1656. M.A. 1658. Senior student, tutor, teacher of Greek and of rhetoric. First continental tour 1665. M.B. 1674.

1668. Locke, a Fellow of the Royal Society.

1667–84. Member of the household of Lord Ashley (first Earl of Shaftesbury 1672). Guardian to Ashley's grandson (third Earl) 1674–83. 1675–79: Locke in France. 1684: Expelled from his studentship at Christ Church by desire of Charles II.

1683–89. Exile in Holland. Locke's letters on the education of Clarke's son.

1689–1704. Commissioner of Appeals.

1690. *An Essay concerning Human Understanding* published.

1693. *Some Thoughts concerning Education* published.

1695–1700. Locke, a Commissioner of Trade and Plantations.

1695. Third edition of *Some Thoughts*, enlarged; Coste's French translation (fifth edition 1744).

1697. *Of the Conduct of the Understanding* begun. Memorandum proposing Poor Law reform and the institution of "Working Schools."

1698. Fourth edition of *Some Thoughts*.

1704. Locke died at Oates, High Laver, Essex, October 28. Oates was his home from 1691 onwards.

1706. *Of the Conduct of the Understanding* published in *The Works of Mr. John Locke*.

1714. First edition of Locke's Collected Works published.

THE EDUCATIONAL WRITINGS
OF JOHN LOCKE

INTRODUCTION

THE most general charge brought by its contemporaries against the school-room of the seventeenth century was that it failed to adapt its ideals to the profound changes which were becoming manifest in social life. Throughout Europe the school maintained the cosmopolitan type of instruction which was the natural correlative of the medieval Church and Empire. It ignored, or affected to ignore, the spirit of nationalism which was everywhere manifest; consequently, it taught no modern languages, and made no open and avowed use of modern history, literature, or geography. It admitted grudgingly a little commercial arithmetic amongst its studies, as a concession to the same demand which, at a later date, caused schools to offer teaching in shorthand or typewriting; and this was in the age of Descartes and Isaac Newton. Of modern science, then come to the birth, and of the widespread readiness to carry observation and experiment into the realm of "Nature," the school took no account.

It is true that the "new philosophy" was not yet sufficiently advanced, elaborated, and systematized to be made an agent of education. Sprat, in his *History of the Royal Society* (1667) deprecated the notion that the new body would encroach upon the work of the universities, seeing that its studies were unsuited to undergraduates.

But the extension of the bounds of knowledge was obvious, and many shared Bacon's enthusiastic belief in the possibility of greater achievements to come. Outside the schools the monopoly of knowledge and wisdom which had once been conceded to the ancients was gradually breaking down, in consequence of the newer methods of inquiry, directed by a spirit which cared little for the pretensions of authority. With Bacon the newer men were ready to urge that *they* were the ancients; the assertion carried with it a claim for the official recognition of modern studies, and the hope of insuring "the relief of man's estate" carried the new method into every field of investigation.

In spite of changed circumstances, the schools preserved unaltered the traditional course of much Latin, some Greek, and, far less frequently, some Hebrew; the learning of the great biblical scholars had effected an entrance where the new philosophy had failed. We must not, of course, think of the Latin of the seventeenth-century school as we think of a "subject" in a modern curriculum—that is, as a single branch of knowledge lying within well-defined boundaries. But the greater part of a boy's school-life was devoted to the formal side of the study of Latin, the memorizing of the grammar book (in Latin) during the earlier years, and rhetorical training in prose and verse during the later.

As part of the new order of things, domestic comfort was more generally enjoyed and appreciated, and a greater refinement in manners and in taste followed. Nevertheless, the schools retained a roughness of life and of behaviour which had become an anachronism; and boys left home for school at an age which, to-day, would find them in the Kindergarten. Eton and Westminster were the most noted English schools of Locke's day; he was a boy at the latter when Busby was in his prime. "Westminsters" became a byword for turbulence and worse, and the savagery of the Eton "ram-hunt" survived for nearly half a century after Locke's death. The novelists and essayists of the early eighteenth century

frequently attribute the unpopularity of schools to the
fears of weakly indulgent mothers; a more convincing
explanation may be found in the contrast between the
life of the home and that of the boarding-school.[1]

Throughout the seventeenth century the schools continued to lose their hold upon the socially distinguished
class, and the process was accelerated as the studies and
manners of school-boys departed more widely from its
social ideals. The schools imparted "learning," and
learning was something of a trade, unsuitable to men of
position or of affluence. Referring to her son, Colin, a
Westminster boy, Lady Caithness writes, in 1692 : "Som
says the Scool he is at is mo proper for to breed up
youths for Church men than any other station; I supos
my sons inclination will not be for that post." [2] Owners
of great estates frequently educated their sons at home
under a private tutor ; and the fashion spread amongst
country gentlemen. Fielding's " Squire Western " in
Tom Jones (1749) embodies the failure of the system;
contemporary evidence shows the failure was not uncommon. But its success produced the accomplished
virtuoso and man of the world, whose powers had been
stimulated and strengthened by a residence of two or
three years in one of the Inns of Court, where he found
access to good society, the sojourn in London being
followed by a prolonged tour in France and Italy.

The domestic part of this education was a survival
from the Middle Ages, when the knight's training
customarily began by an apprenticeship, first as page,
next as squire, in the household and service of some
great noble, or prince. Here the novice learned the
management of his horse and weapons, practised
bodily exercises, and acquired such social accomplishments as dancing and music; the ladies of the house
grounded him in good manners whilst he served as

[1] On this point, see *Some Thoughts*, etc., sec. 70.
[2] Sargeaunt, *Annals of Westminster School*, p. 289. *Cf.*
Some Thoughts, sec. 94 : " A great part of the learning now in
fashion," etc.

4 JOHN LOCKE

page. The Renascence added a new element, the admiration of letters and a desire for the knowledge to be got from books. The combination of the medieval tradition with these newer aspirations found expression in a series of books which expounded the "doctrine of courtesy," as the education of the prince, nobleman, and gentleman came to be called. Castiglione's *Courtier*, the most celebrated of the books of courtesy, is also the earliest (1516-1528) ; amongst English courtesy books are Sir Thomas Elyot's *The Governour* (1531), Henry Peacham's *The Compleat Gentleman* (1622), Jean Gailhard's book bearing a similar title (1678), and Stephen Penton's *The Guardian's Instructor* (1688).[1] Milton's *Of Education* (1644) and Locke's *Some Thoughts concerning Education* and *Of the Conduct of the Understanding* are written from a very similar standpoint. The main principles of this new type of education are stated by Montaigne, particularly in the essays, *De l'Institution des Enfants* and *Du Pedantisme* (1580).

The kind of education advocated in these books was beyond the resources of the school; and, though instruction in the many branches of knowledge which it required could in Locke's day be had in Oxford and Cambridge, mainly from private teachers, the official course of university education was quite unlike it. In France, private enterprise, or munificence, opened "academies" which were expressly intended to educate after the pattern of the doctrine of courtesy; and these late sixteenth and early seventeenth century institutions had many German imitators. Persistent attempts were made throughout the seventeenth century to establish academies of a like kind in England, but they all failed. Milton wrote the tractate already mentioned to advocate the foundation of an academy, which would make it needless for Englishmen to seek courtly breeding in a foreign land.

The academies laid great stress upon the value of

[1] Locke seems to have had the books of Gailhard and Penton by him when he wrote *Some Thoughts*.

modern studies, especially in languages and history; physical exercises, dancing, music, and social amenities generally were integral parts of their course. The seventeenth-century amateur commonly cherished some form of handwork as a hobby; and hobbies were taught in great variety in some of the academies.[1] The essentially useful character of a study was thought to be no bar to its adoption in the training of one who was to lead a public life; on the other hand, the academies made little account of exact scholarship, which they were apt to stigmatize as pedantry. They agreed with Locke in placing " learning " last and least, when compared with virtue, prudence, and good manners. Further, they agreed with him in acting upon a truth which is too often ignored in the present day, that education is a process by no means conducted in schools and universities alone, that mere school-work, as commonly understood, cannot by itself educate.

The writers on courtesy and the founders of the academies fully recognized that there are other forms of excellence than the purely intellectual; and, since expense presented no great difficulty to their pupils, they tried to frame a curriculum as varied as human capacity itself. The influence exercised by the doctrine of courtesy, thus expounded, upon later educational theory and practice has not been at all adequately realized; it is significant that France and Germany, the early homes of the academies, modernized their courses of study long before such a change was adopted by England, where academies never flourished.

Locke's place in educational history cannot be appreciated by attending only to his educational writings, or to the march of events in his own country. During the eighteenth century there was much theorizing concerning education in France and Germany, followed by attempts, more or less successful, to translate theory into practice. At the root of most of this theorizing lay the conceptions belonging to Locke's philosophy, particularly as this is

[1] *Cf. Some Thoughts*, secs. 201-209.

set forth in *An Essay concerning Human Understanding*,
a book which, after nearly twenty years of intermittent
labour, was published in 1690.

The leading problem proposed in the *Essay* is an inquiry
"into the original [origin], certainty, and extent of human
knowledge." Waiving the metaphysical considerations
which that inquiry suggests, and starting from the observable phenomena of consciousness, Locke treats his
problem as primarily a psychological one, a question as
to the origin of mind-content, or, in his own phrase, " of
Ideas." His first conclusion is that the child's mental
condition at birth is appropriately figured by "white
paper, void of all characters,"[1] or, as it was afterwards
expressed in *Some Thoughts*, "wax to be moulded and
fashioned as one pleases."[2] Amongst other things the
similes were intended to deny that man is born in possession of an equipment of general principles which
spontaneously reveal themselves as occasion offers. "It
is an established opinion amongst some men that there
are in the understanding certain innate principles, some
primary notions, κοιναὶ ἔννοιαι,[3] characters as it were
stamped upon the mind of man, which the soul receives
in its very first being and brings into the world with it."[4]
Against this established opinion Locke maintained his
figure of the blank sheet or *tabula rasa ;* ideas as they
existed in an individual mind were the consequence of
that mind's individual history. Experience is the writer
who covers the blank sheet with characters, the sculptor
who moulds the wax into well-defined shapes.

"Whence comes [the mind] by that vast store which
the busy and boundless fancy of man has painted on it

[1] *Essay*, ii., chap. i., sec. 2.

[2] Sec. 216. Locke is inconsistent in his use of this simile, which
attributes everything to nurture, nothing to Nature. A comparison
of passages shows that Locke was disposed to magnify the effects of
nurture above those of Nature, without entirely ignoring the latter.
Compare the following: *Conduct*, secs. 2 and 4; and *Some
Thoughts*, secs. 66, 101, 139, 176.

[3] Thoughts common to all men.

[4] *Essay*, i., chap. ii., sec. 1.

with an almost endless variety? Whence has it all the materials of reason and knowledge? To this I answer in one word, from experience; in that all our knowledge is founded, and from that it ultimately derives itself. Our observation, employed either about external sensible objects, or about the internal operations of our minds, perceived and reflected on by ourselves, is that which supplies our understandings with all the materials of thinking. These two are the fountains of knowledge, from whence all the ideas we have, or can naturally have, do spring. First, our senses, conversant about particular sensible objects, do convey into the mind several distinct perceptions of things, according to those various ways wherein those objects do affect them [*i.e.* the senses]. . . . This great source of most of the ideas we have, depending wholly upon our senses and derived from them to the understanding, I call Sensation. Secondly, the other fountain from which experience furnisheth the understanding with ideas, is the perception of the operations of our own mind within us, as it is employed about the ideas it has got; which operations when the soul comes to reflect on and consider, do furnish the understanding with another set of ideas which could not be had from things without; and such are perception, thinking, doubting, believing, reasoning, knowing, willing, and all the different actings of our own minds; which we being conscious of and observing in ourselves, do from these receive into our understandings as distinct ideas, as we do from bodies affecting our senses. This source of ideas every man has wholly in himself; and though it be not sense, as having nothing to do with external objects, yet it is very like it, and might properly enough be called internal sense. But as I call the other Sensation, so I call this Reflection."[1]

The dissociation from metaphysics, and the experimental origin assigned to mental development and con-

[1] *Essay*, ii., chap. i., secs. 2-4. It will be remarked that mental representations, processes, and states are all covered by the one name—Ideas.

tent in these and in similar passages of the *Essay*, became the basis of the modern study of psychology, which
may be said to date from the publication of that work;
the comparative method, which plays a conspicuous part
in the study to-day, is anticipated in principle by the
casual though frequent references which Locke there
makes to the mental processes of children,[1] of savages,
and of idiots.   Although he is careful to assign two
"fountains" to experience—namely, sensation and reflection—the stress of Locke's exposition falls to excess upon
the first-named, and it is therefore not surprising that he
is sometimes regarded as the originator of a sensationalist
rather than an experiential psychology.   The misinter-
pretation is the easier on account of the confusion between
ideas, processes, and states for which Locke is himself
responsible; the later eighteenth-century educational
theorists for the most part assume a purely sensationalist
origin for the whole mental life.

One of the most characteristic features of the *Essay* is
its uncompromising attitude towards dogmatism and the
construction of abstract systems generally; its method
demands a close adherence to reality, and full allowance
for the results of concrete thinking.   The claims of
authority are confronted by the assertion of the absolute
necessity for independence of mind.   "Not that I want
a due respect to other men's opinions; but after all the
greatest reverence is due to truth; and I hope it will not
be thought arrogance to say, that perhaps we should
make greater progress in the discovery of rational and
contemplative knowledge, if we sought it in the fountain
and made use rather of our own thoughts than other
men's to find it; for I think we may as rationally hope
to see with other men's eyes as to know by other men's
understandings.   So much as we ourselves consider and
comprehend of truth and reason, so much we possess of
real and true knowledge.   The floating of other men's

---

[1] The reader will also note the frequent occurrence in *Some
Thoughts* of anecdotes of children—*e.g.*, secs. 78, 166, 178, and in
the dedication to Clarke.

opinions in our brains makes us not one jot the more knowing, though they happen to be true. What in them was science is in us but opiniatrety,[1] whilst we give up our assent only to reverend names, and do not, as they did, employ our own reason to understand those truths which gave them reputation."[2]

Locke is here asserting the sufficiency of reason for the discovery of truth, and the obligation of each individual mind to employ reason for that purpose, two principles, rationalism and individualism, which made great play in the life of the eighteenth century, and especially in the prevalent conceptions respecting education. Locke thus became the prophet of rationalism and the originator of teaching which proved to be a greater solvent than he at all realized. He himself was a convinced believer in the truth of revealed religion, and, amongst other writings on the subject, produced in 1695 an *Essay on the Reasonableness* [characteristic word !] *of Christianity as delivered in the Scriptures*, which became an object of controversy to some of the orthodox. Yet the principles of the *Essay on Human Understanding* were a principal cause of the subsequent English deism, and of that attitude towards all assertions of the supernatural which has marked French thought since the time of Locke's admirer and disciple, Voltaire. Indeed, Locke's discussion of the problem of knowledge, owing to its fundamental incompleteness, leads straight to the conclusion that the problem is unanswerable, that certainty is unattainable, and that scepticism on all subjects is the only consistent position open to the philosopher. The *Essay* does not indeed go so far as this, although a sceptical temper is not without illustration in its pages. "But whilst we are destitute of senses acute enough to discover the minute particles of bodies and to give us ideas of their mechanical affections, we must be content to be ignorant of their properties and ways of operation ; nor can we be assured about them

---

[1] *I.e.*, obstinate adherence to one's own opinion.
[2] *Essay*, i., chap. iv., sec. 23. *Cf. Conduct*, sec. 24.

any farther than some few trials we make are able to reach. *But whether they will succeed again another time we cannot be certain.* This hinders our certain knowledge of universal truths concerning natural bodies, and our reason carries us herein very little beyond particular matter of fact. And therefore I am apt to doubt how far soever human industry may advance useful and experimental philosophy in physical things, scientifical will be still out of our reach."[1] This inherent scepticism was evident from the first to some of Locke's opponents, though not to all ; it became manifest a generation after Locke's death in the teaching of David Hume, and in that form aroused Kant to controvert it.

The influence of Descartes upon French thought did not yield at once to the philosophy of the Englishman who supplanted him. " It took more than twenty years to sell off the first edition of the French translation [of the *Essay*], but from 1723 to 1758 editions followed one another in rapid succession at intervals of about six years.[2] Voltaire had been a serious student of Bacon, Locke, and Newton during his exile in this country, from 1726 to 1729 ; in 1734 Europe received the result of his studies in the *Lettres sur les Anglais*. Locke's teaching was also made familiar in foreign philosophical circles by Condillac's *Origine des Connaissances humaines* (1746) and *Traité des Sensations* (1754). From this period onwards the sensationalist element of Locke's psychology speedily made its way abroad, till it became the philosophical creed of the French and German "intellectuals," thus giving a new and much more extended lease of life to doctrines which were not complete novelties to the countrymen of Montaigne, Bayle, and Fontenelle.

It is true that the half-century between the accession of Frederick the Great in 1740 and the death of Joseph II. of Austria is usually known by the German name " die

[1] *Essay*, iv., chap. iii., secs. 25-26. *Cf. Some Thoughts*, secs. 190, 193.
[2] Fowler's *Locke*, p. 7.

Aufklärung," the Enlightenment; but the master ideas of this Age of Reason are those of Locke as interpreted by the French Rationalists. Locke pokes fun at the definition, " Homo, animal rationale," but the phrase admirably expresses one of his firmest convictions.[1] A combination of the experiential psychology with philanthropic sentiment and the belief in man's essential rationality was bound to issue in schemes of educational change; if all men are initially equal (one *tabula rasa* is like all the others) and subsequent differences are due solely to experience, then education, a beneficent form of experience, is capable of effecting unlimited reform in those submitted to it.

Two of the most remarkable educational treatises of the eighteenth century, Rousseau's *Émile* (1762) and the *Essai d'Éducation Nationale* (1763) of La Chalotais, adopt Locke's teaching on the genesis of mental content and apply it to their theme. The differences between the educational doctrines of Locke and Pestalozzi (1746-1827) are greater than the agreements; but the latter's most distinctive principle of method is merely an explicit statement of Locke's implied canon, that teaching should be based on first-hand experience. All these thinkers emphasized the truth that educational purposes and processes must wait on mental development, and not on aims and methods foreign to it. In Locke's philosophical teaching is found the source of the principles so frequently repeated since his time, that the sense-organs of children should be exercised in school, that learners should follow the path marked by discoverers, and that they should be habituated to objects and to processes rather than to names and words.

Locke's professedly educational writings have proved much less influential on the great scale than has his philosophy; yet they touch the present condition of English education more closely. They include one or two brief tracts and some letters of advice, whose substance is incorporated, either in the great *Essay* or

[1] *Cf. Some Thoughts*, secs. 31, 33, 122 *ad fin.*

in his two educational treatises.   The fragment on
" Study,"[1] written in Locke's journal during his French
tour (November, 1675, to April, 1679), shows him medi-
tating upon themes which he treated at length in the
Conduct and in the *Essay.   Some Thoughts concerning
Reading and Study for a Gentleman*[2] is chiefly interesting as a summary of a fireside conversation taken down
from Locke's dictation.   Its general statements present
nothing new to the reader of the two books on education
to be noticed immediately.   Locke here recommends
authors or books upon oratory, morals, politics, history,
law, geography, travel, chronology, dictionaries or books
of reference, and *belles lettres*, the last division containing nothing purely English.   As a writer on education,
Locke's fame rests upon *Some Thoughts concerning
Education*, first published in 1693, and the incomplete
and unrevised *Of the Conduct of the Understanding*,
which first appeared in the posthumous edition of
Locke's works published in 1706.

In April, 1697, Locke wrote as follows to William
Molyneux : "I have lately got a little leisure to think of
some additions to my book [the *Essay*] against the next
edition, and within these few days have fallen upon a
subject that I know not how far it will lead me.   I have
written several pages on it, but the matter, the farther I
go, opens the more upon me, and I cannot yet get sight
of any end of it.   The title of the chapter will be ' Of
the Conduct of the Understanding,' which, if I shall
pursue as far as I imagine it will reach, will, I conclude,
make the largest chapter of my *Essay*."[3]   The short
treatise was written to serve as a manual of self-instruc-
tion, which should do for young men what, in Locke's
opinion, the customary text book of logic quite failed to
do for the undergraduate.   From that point of view it
has lost none of its vitality.

[1] Lord King, *Life and Letters of Locke*, 1858, pp. 92 *ff*.   See
also Quick's edition of *Some Thoughts concerning Education*
p. 191.
[2] Locke, *Works*, 1812, vol. iii.   [3] *Works*, 1812, vol. x., p. 407.

The *Conduct* is complementary to *Some Thoughts,* and is therefore indispensable to an understanding of Locke's ideas respecting education. In the latter book Locke is at times overshadowed by his authorities, and his attention is challenged by conventional standards. But in the *Conduct* he is entirely himself; the one problem is, how best to cultivate the rational element in man, a problem with which Locke conceived neither schoolmasters nor tutors have much concern, since it can only be effectively taken in hand when their reign is ended. As a gentleman's vade-mecum, the *Conduct,* especially when read in conjunction with the later sections of *Some Thoughts,*[1] may be fairly ranked amongst the long line of English " courtesy " books.

Although *Some Thoughts concerning Education* now ranks as one of the few English classics on its theme, its author did not regard it, originally at least, as a deliberately planned or exhaustive work. "While I was in Holland, I employed some leisure hours in writing letters to a friend to help him in the training of his little boy. The treatise that has grown out of these has been translated into French and Dutch."[2] The sojourn in Holland here mentioned is the period of exile which Locke suffered between August or September, 1683, and February, 1689, when he returned in Queen Mary's train. The "friend" is the Edward Clarke, subsequently M.P. for Taunton, to whom *Some Thoughts* is dedicated. At the request of friends, the letters were transformed into the "treatise" and published early in 1693. The book reached its fourth edition in 1699, and the sixth appeared in the year following the author's death. As early as 1695 Pierre Coste produced a French translation, which ran through five editions at least; a Dutch version was issued in 1698, a Swedish translation followed in 1709, and there were translations into German (1729, 1787) and Italian (1763, fifth edition 1782). The demand for the book amongst the educated classes was met by

---

[1] *E.g.,* secs. 94, 141-143, 185-187, 193, 196-199, 201-204, 206-216.
[2] Locke to Thoynard, March, 1698. See p. 21 below.

the version in French, the then common language of the Continent; the other translations were for the benefit of a less instructed, but more numerous, class of readers.

Some Thoughts no doubt is indebted to its author's experience as a teacher at Oxford, and as superintendent of the third Earl of Shaftesbury's education;[1] it owes much more to his reading, thought, and general knowledge of men and affairs. The conception of education and the methods of realizing it which are stated in *Some Thoughts* are also to be found in Montaigne's *Essais,* more particularly in the two essays already named. The array of parallel passages from the two writers, reprinted from F. A. Arnstaedt's *François Rabelais,* by Quick in his edition of *Some Thoughts,* is entirely misleading. The references to the *Thoughts* in this list are gathered from Coste's later translations, where they are not advanced as exhausting the parallels; and since Coste in his later editions divided the text into chapters and renumbered the sections, a comparison of the *Essais* and any English edition of *Some Thoughts* with the help of Arnstaedt's lists, only serves to throw doubt on Locke's debt to the French writer. But this laborious mode of comparison is quite unnecessary to anyone who considers the general attitude of both writers to their subject, the objects which they set before themselves, and the means adopted to attain them. Isolated passages, thoughts, and phrases only serve to confirm a proposition which a more general survey renders obvious enough. That Locke was an advocate for an extended and modernized course of studies is so evident that the topic will not be further pressed.[2]

From the standpoint of method the most striking features of *Some Thoughts* are the insistence on the educational function of play,[3] the part assigned to utility

[1] See Fox Bourne, *The Life of John Locke,* vol. i., pp. 422, 423.
[2] See sec. 169 *ff.*
[3] See secs. 130, 152-154, and compare Montaigne, *Essay on Custom* (bk. i., chap. 22) : " We should note that children's games are not games; we ought to regard them as their most serious occupations."

in determining the choice of studies, and the principle that the learning of young children should be acquired by the active employment of the organs of sense rather than through information supplied by books or teachers. It is a cardinal principle with both Montaigne and Locke that the child should not be *compelled* to learn.[1] Extravagant as the statement seems, there is reason behind it, and its later application to practice makes it necessary to give it attention.

His knowledge of the current school practice taught Locke that the child's special aptitudes and capacities were ignored by the curriculum, his rote-memory was overtaxed by things which yielded little spontaneous interest, and he was made to labour against the grain by fear of the rod. Learning was imposed arbitrarily, and therefore tended to become irksome. Locke realized that no really effective learning could take place till the pupil's will had been evoked, and he knew that no motive could give greater stimulus than the desire to learn, while learning itself cannot be done by proxy. The principle involved is one which filled so great a place in Froebel's theory of method,[2] and which made play so prominent an instrument of his practice. Locke was not so inexperienced as to believe that all objects are equally successful in arousing spontaneous interest, and he recognized that children must sometimes be required to attend to things which do not possess intrinsic charm. Even so he remains true to principle, and advises the teacher to prepare the way in these cases by recalling to the pupil's mind suitable ideas or by appealing to his "likes" and "dislikes."[3] Still, it must be admitted that Locke does not help us much by direct recommendation to get the

[1] See *Some Thoughts*, secs. 72-74, 84, 103, 123, 128, 148, 149, 167, 202; for the hint of a sounder principle, see secs. 126, 127.

[2] " Regarded in the light of their origin and first principles, education, instruction, and doctrine must of necessity be passive, following — guarding, merely, and sheltering — not prescribing, determining, encroaching."—Froebel, *The Education of Human Nature*, i. 7 (1826).

[3] *Cf. Some Thoughts*, secs. 74, 126, 127.

boy to adopt the maxim, "Duty for duty's sake." He probably thought it beyond the reach of the child, and trusted to the general character of the training given to implant it later and in due course. But Locke's statement of this sound principle was open to misconstruction, and it was, in fact, perverted by later writers, like Basedow, who made learning synonymous with amusement, and therefore thought it necessary to coax and wheedle children into learning. The doctrine of interest often suffers the same perversion to-day, and the perversion is made to excuse modes of instruction whose tendency is wholly mischievous. Not amusement nor distraction, but the desire to effect some cherished purpose is the strongest motive that can move the learner.

Locke's advocacy of the principle of utility had a similar result. "I think that the time and pains allotted to serious improvements should be employed about things of most use and consequence, and that too in the methods the most easy and short."[1] This reads like a platitude until we ponder on the words "use" and "consequence," and require examples of the short and easy methods contemplated. Basedow inferred that every subject of study and *every part of a subject* which could not be turned to practical account should be discarded by the school-master. In his recommendations respecting the education of a prince, he advises the omission of algebra and theology, but includes dancing and riding as useful arts indispensable to a sovereign. The Latin taught in Basedow's institute at Dessau was "current Latin," indistinguishable from the canine sort. There was no instruction in Greek; "we already have one learned tongue too many." The studies retained were those which Locke calls "real knowledge." Handwork had a place in the school exercises; but, practically useful though it was, it came into conflict with Basedow's other touchstone of method, amusement, and ended by being employed as a form of punishment.

Extravagances such as these combined with Basedow's

[1] *Some Thoughts*, sec. 197.

incapacity for managing men, or institutions, brought his work to an end long before his death. Yet he stimulated an interest in public education which was already vigorous amongst the princes and statesmen of Germany and Northern Europe. His experiments won the approval of Kant, and he was the adviser of Zedlitz, the minister who reformed Prussian education, and of Rochow, the "Prussian Pestalozzi." Basedow was therefore one of the most influential persons in the sphere of public education during the second half of the eighteenth century, and thus became a channel by which Locke affected the educational theory and practice of Germany.[1]

Notwithstanding his championship of "real knowledge" and his contempt for "words," most of Locke's directions of the practical sort relate to the study of language. He gives excellent advice respecting the way in which a boy may be trained to write and speak the mother tongue. The best modern practice is but an elaboration of what stands written in *Some Thoughts*.[2]

On the other hand, if we were to base our judgment on that book alone, we should say that in 1693 England possessed no literature worthy of the name. Two English writers only are singled out for mention as authors whose works should be read. Ralph Cudworth bears a name which is still honourably associated with English philosophy; but Chillingworth, a controversial divine praised by Locke as a model of logical thinking, is now almost forgotten.[3] When one remembers Locke's scorn for the "poetic vein"[4] and the sourness of his regard for the fine arts, it is scarcely surprising that, in a work on the educa-

[1] Johann Bernhard Basedow (1724-1790) opened the first Philanthropinum at Dessau in 1774 in order to carry out principles of education enunciated by Comenius, Locke, and La Chalotais. Schools in imitation of it were opened in other parts of Germany and in Switzerland, but the Philanthropinist movement was a failure owing to its extravagances of principle and practice.

[2] Secs. 168, 171, 172, and particularly 189. Most of Locke's recommendations on the teaching of foreign languages, Latin included, have reappeared in later educational history.

[3] *Some Thoughts*, secs. 188, 193.

[4] *Ibid.*, sec. 174; but *cf. Conduct*, sec. 4.

tion of an English gentleman, there is no reference to
Shakspere, Spenser, or Milton. The brief *Some Thoughts
concerning Reading and Study for a Gentleman* names
more than eighty writers or works, mostly foreign; but
none of these great names is included, though *Don Quixote*
is ranked as unequalled amongst "all the books of fiction."
Locke apparently failed to see that English literature in
his day afforded that very knowledge of life to which he
attached the highest importance. He seems to have been
by constitution deficient in appreciation for imaginative
work, when he was not suspicious that its tendency was
irrational.

The practical teacher will endorse what is said in
Some Thoughts respecting the exercise of rote-memory
(sections 175-176), and the best mode of sustaining a
pupil's attention (section 167) : Locke here anticipates
and expresses concisely much of the best writing on
these topics. Although he says nothing directly concerning the education of girls, the references to them
which occur in sections 6 and 9 seem susceptible of a
wider application, and they incline one to believe that
Locke did not entirely approve the custom of his day
which gave girls an inferior education to that given to
boys. The charge of want of sympathy with women is
not sustained by our knowledge of Locke's private life;
it is certain that he speaks with respect when alluding
to cultivated women, and governesses appear in his pages
as capable persons who compare very favourably indeed
with professional schoolmasters.[1]

There is no question in *Some Thoughts* of the instruction of great numbers of the people; it deals not with
popular education, but with the breeding of children
destined to occupy positions of social prominence. Yet
it was impossible that Locke, writing on such a subject,
should restrict himself to a narrow outlook, and so frequently are his remarks of general application that his
main purpose in writing the book is often forgotten by
his readers.

[1] *Cf. Some Thoughts*, secs. 168, 177, 189.

What his views were with respect to the education of the very poor can be learned on reference to his memorandum on reform of the Poor Law, drawn up in 1697, when he was " a commissioner of trade and plantations."[1] It must be remembered that this was written before the foundation of the Charity Schools, which, in the eighteenth century, demonstrated the feasibility of a system of popular schools under central direction and local management. Locke's proposal was in effect one for the general adoption in rural districts of the workhouse " schools " which had existed in some town parishes since the middle of the seventeenth century. To these "working schools" Locke would send daily all pauper children between the ages of three and fourteen, there to be taught "spinning or knitting, or some other part of the woollen manufacture, unless in countries where the place shall furnish other materials fitter for the employment of such poor children." Each child should receive an allowance of bread and, in winter, " a little warm water-gruel "; it is estimated that the proceeds of a child's labour will in the course of years cover the expense of his, or her, teaching and partial maintenance. The only form of instruction mentioned in the memorandum (other than that given in teaching the child to perform his manual task) is religious instruction, obtained by being " obliged to come constantly to church every Sunday, along with their schoolmasters or dames, whereby they may be brought into some sense of religion." This very exiguous course of instruction completely accords with the proposition asserted in section 19 of the *Conduct* ; "for a man to understand fully the business of his particular calling in the commonwealth and of religion, which is his calling as he is a man in the world, is usually enough to take up his whole time." It is for the person of leisure to go farther.[2]

[1] Printed in Fox Bourne's *Life of John Locke*, vol. ii., pp. 377 ff.
[2] *Conduct*, sec. 7 (" Those methinks, who, by the industry," etc.), the last paragraph of that section, and sec. 8.

BOOKS ON LOCKE AND HIS PERIOD

Life of Locke:
  H. R. Fox Bourne: *The Life of John Locke*, London, 1876.
  T. Fowler: *Locke*, in "English Men of Letters" Series.
  A. C. Fraser: *Locke*, in "Philosophical Classics," *circa* 1890.
  E. Fechner: *John Locke*, Stuttgart, 1898.
  Ch. Bastide: *John Locke*, Paris, 1907.
The Works of John Locke, in ten volumes, London, 1812 and 1823.
A. C. Fraser, editor: *An Essay concerning Human Understanding*,
    Oxford, 1894.
R. H. Quick: *Some Thoughts concerning Education*, Cambridge,
    1880, etc.
Evan Daniel: *Some Thoughts concerning Education*, London, 1880.
T. Fowler: Locke's *Conduct of the Understanding*, Oxford, 1880, etc.
P. Villey: *L'influence de Montaigne sur les idées pédagogiques de Locke
    et de Rousseau*, Paris, 1911.
E. A. Thiele: *Montaigne und Locke, ihre Stellung zur Erziehung zur
    Selbsttätigkeit*, Leipzig, 1920.
E. Taglialatela: *Giovanni Locke, Educatore, studio critico*, Rome, 1920.
History of Education during the Period covered by the Introduction:
  W. H. Woodward: *Studies in Education during the Renaissance,
    1400–1600*.
  J. W. Adamson: *Pioneers of Modern Education, 1600–1700*.
  Oxford Historical Society's Publications, *Collectanea*, first series,
    Oxford, 1885.
  J. W. Adamson: "Education" (1660–1750), in *Cambridge History
    of English Literature*, vol. ix.
  A. Pinloche: *La Reforme de l'Education en Allemagne au 18ᵉ Siècle*,
    Paris, 1889.
  W. Rein: *Encyklopädisches Handbuch der Pädagogik*, vol. i., *sub
    vocibus* "Aufklärung" and "Basedow."
  Foster Watson: *The English Grammar Schools to 1660*, Cambridge,
    1908.
  Foster Watson: *The Beginnings of the Teaching of Modern Subjects
    in England*, 1909.

SOME THOUGHTS CONCERNING EDUCATION

THE text here followed is that of the first edition, supplemented by passages from later editions which are historically interesting, or of special educational value at the present time: such passages are enclosed in square brackets. Summaries of insertions in later editions are here printed in italic type. Sections 3–28 deal with the care of health; modern medical opinion does not endorse all their recommendations, and they are therefore represented here by Locke's summary, sections 29, 30. The sections are numbered as in the latest editions, for convenience of reference. It has not been thought advisable to retain the original spelling and punctuation.

Locke's original draft, which extends to sections 1 to 166 only, was acquired by the British Museum in 1913 from a descendant of Edward Clarke. It is Additional MS. 38,771, "Some Directions concerning ye Education of his son sent to his worthy Freind, Mr. Edward Clarke of Chipley, 1684." The manuscript contains one hundred pages, each measuring 4¼ inches by 3¼ inches. Apologizing for the "disjoynted parts" observable in "these papers," Locke continues, "I began them before my ramble this sommer about these provinces and thinking it convenient you should have them as soon as might be, I writ severall parts of them as stay gave me leasure and oportunity any where in my journey soe yt [that] great distance of place and time intervening between the severall parts often broke the thread of my thoughts and discourse and therefor you must not wonder if yt they be not well put togeather and yis must be my excuse for ye faults in ye method, order and connection."

TO
EDWARD CLARKE,
OF
CHIPLEY, Esq.;

SIR,

These Thoughts concerning Education, which now come abroad into the world, do of right belong to you, being written several years since for your sake, and are no other than what you have already by you in my letters. I have so little varied any thing, but only the order of what was sent you at different times, and on several occasions, that the reader will easily find, in the familiarity and fashion of the style, that they were rather the private conversation of two friends, than a discourse designed for public view.

The importunity of friends is the common apology for publications men are afraid to own themselves forward to. But you know I can truly say, that if some, who, having heard of these papers of mine, had not pressed to see them, and afterwards to have them printed, they had lain dormant still in that privacy they were designed for. But those whose judgment I defer much to, telling me, that they were persuaded, that this rough draft of mine might be of some use, if made more public, touched upon what will always be very prevalent with me: for I think it every man's indispensable duty, to do all the service he can to his country; and I see not what difference he puts between himself and his cattle, who lives without that thought. This subject is of so great concernment, and a right way of education is of so general advantage, that did I find my abilities answer my wishes, I should not have needed exhortations or importunities from others. However, the meanness of these papers, and my just distrust of them, shall not keep me, by the shame

of doing so little, from contributing my mite, when there
is no more required of me than my throwing it into the
public receptacle. And if there be any more of their size
and notions, who liked them so well, that they thought
them worth printing, I may flatter myself they will not
be lost labour to every body.

I myself have been consulted of late by so many, who
profess themselves at a loss how to breed their children,
and the early corruption of youth is now become so
general a complaint, that he cannot be thought wholly
impertinent, who brings the consideration of this matter
on the stage, and offers something, if it be but to excite
others, or afford matter for correction; for errors in
education should be less indulged than any. These, like
faults in the first concoction, that are never mended in the
second or third, carry their afterwards-incorrigible taint
with them through all the parts and stations of life.

I am so far from being conceited of anything I have here
offered, that I should not be sorry, even for your sake,
if some one abler and fitter for such a task would in a just
treatise of education, suited to our English gentry, rectify
the mistakes I have made in this, it being much more
desirable to me, that young gentlemen should be put into
(that which every one ought to be solicitous about) the
best way of being formed and instructed, than that my
opinion should be received concerning it. You will, however, in the meantime bear me witness, that the method
here proposed has had no ordinary effects upon a gentleman's son[1] it was not designed for. I will not say the good
temper of the child did not very much contribute to it; but
this I think you and the parents are satisfied of, that a contrary usage, according to the ordinary disciplining of

[1] A reference, perhaps, to Francis Cudworth Masham (b. 1686), son
of Sir Francis Masham, the owner of Oates, Locke's home from 1691.

children, would not have mended that temper, nor have brought him to be in love with his book, to take a pleasure in learning, and to desire, as he does, to be taught more than those about him think fit always to teach him.

But my business is not to recommend this treatise to you, whose opinion of it I know already; nor it to the world, either by your opinion or patronage. The well educating of their children is so much the duty and concern of parents, and the welfare and prosperity of the nation so much depends on it, that I would have every one lay it seriously to heart; and after having well examined and distinguished what fancy, custom, or reason advises in the case, set his helping hand to promote that way in the several degrees of men, which is the easiest, shortest, and likeliest to produce virtuous, useful, and able men in their distinct callings. Though that most to be taken care of is the gentleman's calling;[1] for if those of that rank are by their education once set right, they will quickly bring all the rest into order.

I know not whether I have done more than shewn my good wishes towards it in this short discourse; such as it is, the world now has it, and if there be any thing in it worth their acceptance, they owe their thanks to you for it. My affection to you gave the first rise to it, and I am pleased, that I can leave to posterity this mark of the friendship that has been between us. For I know no greater pleasure in this life, nor a better remembrance to be left behind one, than a long-continued friendship with an honest, useful, and worthy man, and lover of his country.

I am, Sir,

Your most humble and most faithful servant.

---

[1] A phrase reminiscent of such "courtesy" books as *The Gentleman's Calling* (1659), *The Lady's Calling*, *The Courtier's Calling*. See Introduction.

SOME THOUGHTS CONCERNING EDUCATION

1. A SOUND mind in a sound body, is a short but full description of a happy state in this world : he that has these two, has little more to wish for; and he that wants either of them, will be but little the better for any thing else. Men's happiness or misery is most part of their own making. He whose mind directs not wisely, will never take the right way ; and he whose body is crazy and feeble, will never be able to advance in it. I confess there are some men's constitutions of body and mind so vigorous and well framed by nature, that they need not much assistance from others, but by the strength of their natural genius, they are from their cradles carried towards what is excellent ; and, by the privilege of their happy constitutions are able to do wonders. But examples of these are but few ; and I think I may say that, of all the men we meet with, nine parts of ten are what they are, good or evil, useful or not, by their education. 'Tis that which makes the great difference in mankind. The little, and almost insensible impressions on our tender infancies, have very important and lasting consequences ; and there 'tis, as in the fountains of some rivers, where a gentle application of the hand turns the flexible waters into channels, that make them take quite contrary courses; and by this little direction, given them at first in the source, they receive different tendencies, and arrive at last at very remote and distant places.

2. *Health.*—I imagine the minds of children, as easily turned, this or that way, as water itself; and though this be the principal part, and our main care should be about the inside, yet the clay cottage is not to be

neglected. I shall therefore begin with the case, and consider first the health of the body, as that which perhaps you may rather expect, from that study I have been thought more peculiarly to have applied myself to;[1] and that also, which will be soonest dispatched, as lying, if I guess not amiss, in a very little compass.

Sections 3 to 28 treat of health. For reasons already given, they are replaced by the author's summary, section 30; but sections 6 and 9 are retained for their references to girls. See note on p. 21.

6. I have said *he* here, because the principal aim of my discourse is, how a young gentleman should be brought up from his infancy, which in all things will not so perfectly suit the education of daughters; though, where the difference of sex requires different treatment, 'twill be no hard matter to distinguish.

9. *Air.*—Another thing that is of great advantage to every one's health, but especially children's, is, to be much in the open air, and very little, as may be, by the fire, even in winter. By this he will accustom himself also to heat and cold, shine and rain; all which if a man's body will not endure, it will serve him to very little purpose in this world: and when he is grown up, it is too late to begin to use him to it: it must be got early and by degrees. Thus the body may be brought to bear almost anything. If I should advise him to play in the wind and sun without a hat, I doubt whether it could be borne. There would a thousand objections be made against it, which at last would amount to no more, in truth, than being sun-burnt. And if my young master be to be kept always in the shade, and never exposed to the sun and wind, for fear of his complexion, it may be a good way to make him a beau, but not a man of business.[2]

[1] *Cf.* sec. 29. Locke practised medicine at Oxford in 1667, and in London with his friend, Dr. Sydenham, between that year and 1670. Though commonly known as "Dr. Locke," he never proceeded beyond the M.B. degree.

[2] *I.e.*, a man of affairs.

And although greater regard be to be had to beauty in
the daughters, yet I will take the liberty to say, that the
more they are in the air, without prejudices to their faces,
the stronger and healthier they will be; and the nearer
they come to the hardships of their brothers in their
education, the greater advantage will they receive from
it all the remaining part of their lives.[1]

29. *Physic.*—This is all I have to trouble you with, concerning his management, in the ordinary course of his
health; and perhaps it will be expected from me, that I
should give some directions of physic, to prevent diseases:
for which, I have only this one very sacredly to be observed:
Never to give children any physic for prevention. The
observation of what I have already advised, will, I suppose, do that better than apothecary's drugs and medi-
cines. Have a great care of tampering that way, lest,
instead of preventing, you draw on diseases. Nor even
upon every little indisposition is physic to be given, or
the physician to be called to children; especially if he be
a busy man, that will presently fill their windows with
gally-pots, and their stomachs with drugs. It is safer
to leave them wholly to nature, than to put them into the
hands of one forward to tamper, or that thinks children
are to be cured in ordinary distempers, by anything but
diet, or by a method very little distant from it. It seeming suitable both to my reason and experience, that the
tender constitutions of children should have as little done
to them as is possible, and as the absolute necessity of the
case requires. A little cold-stilled red poppy-water, which
is the true surfeit-water, with ease and abstinence from
flesh, often puts an end to several distempers in the beginning, which, by too forward applications, might have
been made lusty diseases. When such a gentle treatment
will not stop the growing mischief, but that it will turn
into a formed disease, it will be time to seek the advice of
some sober and discreet physician. In this part, I hope,
I shall find an easy belief; and nobody can have a pretence to doubt the advice of one, who has spent some

[1] *Cf.* end of secs. 119 and 165.

time in the study of physic, when he counsels you not to be too forward in making use of physic and physicians.

30. And thus I have done with what concerns the body and health, which reduces itself to these few and easily observable rules. Plenty of open air, exercise, and sleep; plain diet, no wine or strong drink, and very little or no physic; not too warm and strait clothing; especially the head and feet kept cold, and the feet often used to cold water and exposed to wet.

31. *Mind.*—Due care being had to keep the body in strength and vigour, so that it may be able to obey and execute the orders of the mind: the next and principal business is, to set the mind right, that on all occasions it may be disposed to do nothing but what may be suitable to the dignity and excellency of a rational creature.

32. If what I have said in the beginning of this discourse be true, as I do not doubt but it is, viz. that the difference to be found in the manners and abilities of men, is owing more to their education than to any thing else; we have reason to conclude, that great care is to be had of the forming children's minds, and giving them that seasoning early, which shall influence their lives always after. For when they do well or ill, the praise or blame will be laid there: and when any thing is done untowardly, the common saying will pass upon them, that it is suitable to their breeding.

33 As the strength of the body lies chiefly in being able to endure hardships, so also does that of the mind. And the great principle and foundation of all virtue and worth is placed in this, that a man is able to deny himself his own desires, cross his own inclinations, and purely follow what reason directs as best, though the appetite lean the other way.

34. *Early.*—The great mistake I have observed in people's breeding their children has been, that this has not been taken care enough of in its due season; that the mind has not been made obedient to rules, and pliant to reason, when at first it was most tender, most easy to be bowed. Parents being wisely ordained by nature to

love their children, are very apt, if reason watch not that natural affection very warily; are apt, I say, to let it run into fondness.[1] They love their little ones, and 'tis their duty : but they often with them cherish their faults too. They must not be crossed, forsooth; they must be permitted to have their wills in all things; and they being in their infancies not capable of great vices, their parents think they may safely enough indulge their little irregularities, and make themselves sport with that pretty perverseness, which they think well enough becomes that innocent age. But to a fond parent, that would not have his child corrected for a perverse trick, but excused it, saying it was a small matter; Solon very well replied, 'Ay, but custom is a great one.'[2]

35. The fondling must be taught to strike, and call names; must have what he cries for, and do what he pleases. Thus parents, by humouring and cockering them when little, corrupt the principles of nature in their children, and wonder afterwards to taste the bitter waters, when they themselves have poisoned the fountain. For when their children are grown up, and these ill habits with them; when they are now too big to be dandled, and their parents can no longer make use of them as playthings; then they complain, that the brats are untoward and perverse; then they are offended to see them wilful, and are troubled with those ill humours, which they themselves inspired and cherished in them. And then, perhaps too late, would be glad to get out those weeds which their own hands have planted, and which now have taken too deep root to be easily extirpated. For he that has been used to have his will in every thing, as long as he was in coats, why should we think it strange that he should desire it, and contend for it still, when he is in breeches? Indeed, as he grows more towards a man, age shows his faults the more, so that there be few parents then so blind, as not to see them; few so insensible as

[1] *I.e.*, foolishness.
[2] Quoted by Montaigne in the essay, *De la Coustume*, i., chap. xxii.

not to feel the ill effects of their own indulgence. He
had the will of his maid before he could speak or go; he
had the mastery of his parents ever since he could prattle;
and why, now he is grown up, is stronger and wiser than
he was then, why now of a sudden must he be restrained
aud curbed? Why must he at seven, fourteen, or twenty
years old, lose the privilege which the parents' indulgence,
till then, so largely allowed him? Try it in a dog, or an
horse, or any other creature, and see whether the ill and
resty[1] tricks they have learned when young, are easily to
be mended when they are knit: and yet none of those
creatures are half so wilful and proud, or half so desirous
to be masters of themselves and others, as man.

36. We are generally wise enough to begin with them,
when they are very young, and discipline betimes those
other creatures we would make useful to us. They are
only our own offspring, that we neglect in this point;
and having made them ill children, we foolishly expect
they should be good men. For if the child must have
grapes, or sugar-plums, when he has a mind to them,
rather than make the poor baby cry, or be out of humour,
why, when he is grown up, must he not be satisfied too,
if his desires carry him to wine or women? They are
objects as suitable to the longing of one of more years,
as what he cried for, when little, was to the inclinations
of a child. The having desires suitable to the apprehensions and relish of those several ages, is not the fault;
but the not having them subject to the rules and restraints
of reason : the difference lies not in the having or not
having appetites, but in the power to govern, and deny
our selves in them. And he that is not used to submit
his will to the reason of others, when he is young, will
scarce hearken or submit to his own reason, when he is
of an age to make use of it. And what a kind of a man
such an one is like to prove, is easy to foresee.

*Section 37.—Parents, by example and incitement, com-
monly teach children to be violent, to love finery, to lie
and be gluttonous. Cf. Section 116.*

[1] Restive, restless.

38.[1] *Craving.*—It seems plain to me, that the principle of all virtue and excellency lies in a power of denying our selves the satisfaction of our own desires, where reason does not authorize them. This power is to be got and improved by custom, made easy and familiar by an early practice. If therefore I might be heard, I would advise, that, contrary to the ordinary way, children should be used to submit their desires, and go without their longings, even from their very cradles. The first thing they should learn to know, should be, that they were not to have anything, because it pleased them, but because it was thought fit for them. If things suitable to their wants were supplied to them, so that they were never suffered to have what they once cried for, they would learn to be content without it; would never with bawling and peevishness contend for mastery; nor be half so uneasy to themselves and others as they are, because from the first beginning they are not thus handled. If they were never suffered to obtain their desire by the impatience they expressed for it, they would no more cry for other things than they do for the moon.

39. I say not this, as if children were not to be indulged in any thing, or that I expected they should, in hanging sleeves, have the reason and conduct of counsellors. I consider them as children that must be tenderly used, that must play, and have playthings. That which I mean is, that whenever they craved what was not fit for them to have, or do, they should not be permitted it, because they were little and desired it: nay, whatever they were importunate for, they should be sure, for that very reason, to be denied. I have seen children at a table, who, whatever was there, never asked for anything, but contentedly took what was given them; and at another place, I have seen others cry for every thing they saw, must be served out of every dish, and that first too. What made this vast difference, but this; that one was accustomed to have what they called or cried for, the other to go without it? The younger they are, the less, I think,

[1] Sec. 37 in first edition.

are their unruly and disorderly appetites to be complied
with; and the less reason they have of their own, the
more are they to be under the absolute power and restraint
of those, in whose hands they are. From which I confess,
it will follow, that none but discreet people should be
about them. If the world commonly does otherwise, I
cannot help that : I am saying what I think should be;
which, if it were already in fashion, I should not need to
trouble the world with a discourse on this subject. But
yet I doubt not, but when it is considered, there will be
others of opinion with me, that the sooner this way is
begun with children, the easier it will be for them, and
their governors too. And that this ought to be observed
as an inviolable maxim, that whatever once is denied
them, they are certainly not to obtain by crying or
importunity ; unless one has a mind to teach them to be
impatient and troublesome, by rewarding them for it,
when they are so.

40. *Early.*—Those therefore that intend ever to govern
their children, should begin it whilst they are very little ;
and look that they perfectly comply with the will of their
parents. Would you have your son obedient to you, when
past a child ?   Be sure then to establish the authority of
a father, as soon as he is capable of submission, and can
understand in whose power he is. If you would have him
stand in awe of you, imprint it in his infancy ; and, as he
approaches more to a man, admit him nearer to your
familiarity : so shall you have him your obedient subject
(as is fit) whilst he is a child, and your affectionate friend
when he is a man. For methinks they mightily misplace
the treatment due to their children, who are indulgent
and familiar when they are little, but severe to them, and
keep them at a distance when they are grown up.   For
liberty and indulgence can do no good to children : their
want of judgment makes them stand in need of restraint
and discipline. And, on the contrary, imperiousness and
severity is but an ill way of treating men, who have reason
of their own to guide them, unless you have a mind to
make your children, when grown up, weary of you ; and

secretly to say within themselves, "When will you die, father?"[1]

41. I imagine every one will judge it reasonable, that their children, when little, should look upon their parents as their lords, their absolute governors; and, as such, stand in awe of them : and that, when they come to riper years, they should look on them as their best, as their only sure friends; and, as such, love and reverence them. The way I have mentioned, if I mistake not, is the only one to obtain this. We must look upon our children, when grown up, to be like ourselves, with the same passions, the same desires. We would be thought rational creatures, and have our freedom; we love not to be uneasy under constant rebukes and brow-beatings; nor can we bear severe humours, and great distance, in those we converse with. Whoever has such treatment when he is a man, will look out other company, other friends, other conversation, with whom he can be at ease. If therefore a strict hand be kept over children from the beginning, they will in that age be tractable, and quietly submit to it, as never having known any other : and if, as they grow up to the use of reason, the rigour of government be, as they deserve it, gently relaxed, the father's brow more smooth to them, and the distance by degrees abated, his former restraints will increase their love, when they find it was only a kindness to them, and a care to make them capable to deserve the favour of their parents, and the esteem of every body else.

42. Thus much for the settling your authority over your children in general. Fear and awe ought to give you the first power over their minds, and love and friendship in riper years to hold it : for the time must come, when they will be past the rod and correction; and then, if the love of you make them not obedient and dutiful, if the love of virtue and reputation keep them not in laudable courses, I ask, what hold will you have

---

[1] The thought occurs in Montaigne, ii., chap. viii., "On the affection of fathers for their children," with which these earlier sections of the *Thoughts* should be compared.

upon them, to turn them to it ?   Indeed, fear of having
a scanty portion, if they displease you, may make them
slaves to your estate, but they will be never the less ill
and wicked in private; and that restraint will not last
always, Every man must some time or other be trusted
to himself, and his own conduct; and he that is a good,
a virtuous, and able man, must be made so within.   And
therefore, what he is to receive from education, what is
to sway and influence his life, must be something put
into him betimes, habits woven into the very principles
of his nature; and not a counterfeit carriage, and dissembled outside, put on by fear, only to avoid the
present anger of a father, who perhaps may disinherit
him.

43. *Punishments.*—This being laid down in general, as
the course ought to be taken, 'tis fit we now come to
consider the parts of the discipline to be used, a little
more particularly.   I have spoken so much of carrying a
strict hand over children, that perhaps I shall be suspected of not considering enough, what is due to their
tender age and constitutions.   But that opinion will
vanish, when you have heard me a little farther.   For I
am very apt to think, that great severity of punishment
does but very little good; nay, great harm in education:
and I believe it will be found, that, *cæteris paribus,* those
children who have been most chastised, seldom make the
best men..   All that I have hitherto contended for, is,
that whatsoever rigour is necessary, it is more to be used
the younger children are; and having by a due application wrought its effect, it is to be relaxed, and changed
into a milder sort of government.

44. *Awe.*—A compliance and suppleness of their wills,
being by a steady hand introduced by parents, before
children have memories to retain the beginnings of it,
will seem natural to them, and work afterwards in them,
as if it were so, preventing all occasions of struggling or
repining.   The only care is, that it be begun early, and
inflexibly kept to, till awe and respect be grown familiar,
and there appears not the least reluctancy in the sub-

mission, and ready obedience of their minds. When this reverence is once thus established (which it must be early, or else it will cost pains and blows to recover it, and the more, the longer it is deferred), 'tis by it, mixed still with as much indulgence, as they make not an ill use of, and not by beating, chiding, or other servile punishments, [that] they are for the future to be governed as they grow up to more understanding.

45. That this is so, will be easily allowed, when it is but considered what is to be aimed at in an ingenuous education, and upon what it turns.

1. *Self-denial.*—He that has not a mastery over his inclinations, he that knows not how to resist the importunity of present pleasure or pain, for the sake of what reason tells him is fit to be done, wants the true principle of virtue and industry, and is in danger never to be good for any thing. This temper, therefore, so contrary to unguided nature, is to be got betimes; and this habit, as the true foundation of future ability and happiness, is to be wrought into the mind, as early as may be, even from the first dawnings of any knowledge or apprehension in children ; and so to be confirmed in them, by all the care and ways imaginable, by those who have the oversight of their education.

46. 2. *Dejected.*—On the other side, if the mind be curbed, and humbled too much in children; if their spirits be abased and broken much, by too strict an hand over them, they lose all their vigour and industry, and are in a worse state than the former. For extravagant young fellows, that have liveliness and spirit, come sometimes to be set right, and so make able and great men : but dejected minds, timorous and tame, and low spirits, are hardly ever to be raised, and very seldom attain to any thing. To avoid the danger that is on either hand, is the great art; and he that has found a way, how to keep up a child's spirit, easy, active, and free; and yet, at the same time, to restrain him from many things he has a mind to, and to draw him to things that are uneasy to him; he, I say, that knows how to reconcile these seem-

ing contradictions, has, in my opinion, got the true secret of education.

47. *Beating.*[1]—The usual lazy and short way by chastisement, and the rod, which is the only instrument of government that tutors generally know, or ever think of, is the most unfit of any to be used in education ; because it tends to both those mischiefs, which, as we have shown, are the Scylla and Charybdis, which, on the one hand or the other, ruin all that miscarry.

48. 1. This kind of punishment contributes not at all to the mastery of our natural propensity to indulge corporal and present pleasure, and to avoid pain at any rate, but rather encourages it ; and so strengthens that in us, which is the root of all vicious and wrong actions. For what motives, I pray, does a child act by, but of such pleasure and pain, that drudges at his book against his inclination, or abstains from eating unwholesome fruit, that he takes pleasure in, only out of fear of whipping ? He in this only prefers the greater corporal pleasure, or avoids the greater corporal pain ; and what is it, to govern his actions, and direct his conduct, by such motives as these ?   What is it, I say, but to cherish that principle in him, which it is our business to root out and destroy ?   And therefore I cannot think any correction useful to a child, where the shame of suffering for having done amiss does not work more upon him than the pain.

49. 2. This sort of correction naturally breeds an aversion to that which it is the tutor's business to create a liking to.   How obvious is it to observe, that children come to hate things liked at first, as soon as they come to be whipped, or chid, and teazed about them ?   And it is not to be wondered at in them, when grown men would not be able to be reconciled to any thing by such ways.   Who is there that would not be disgusted with any innocent recreation in itself indifferent to him, if he should with blows, or ill language, be haled to it, when he had no mind ?   Or be constantly so treated, for some

[1] *Cf.* Montaigne, ii., chap. viii.

circumstance in his application to it ? This is natural to be so. Offensive circumstances ordinarily infect innocent things which they are joined with : and the very sight of a cup, wherein any one uses to take nauseous physic, turns his stomach, so that nothing will relish well out of it, though the cup be never so clean and well-shaped, and of the richest materials.

50. 3. Such a sort of slavish discipline makes a slavish temper. The child submits, and dissembles obedience, whilst the fear of the rod hangs over him ; but when that is removed, and, by being out of sight, he can promise himself impunity, he gives the greater scope to his natural inclination, which by this way is not at all altered, but on the contrary heightened and increased in him ; and after such restraint, breaks out usually with the more violence. Or,

51. 4. If severity carried to the highest pitch does prevail, and works a cure upon the present unruly distemper, it is often bringing in the room of it a worse and more dangerous disease, by breaking the mind ; and then, in the place of a disorderly young fellow, you have a low-spirited, moped creature : who, however with his unnatural sobriety he may please silly people, who commend tame, unactive children because they make no noise, nor give them any trouble ; yet, at last, will probably prove as uncomfortable a thing to his friends, as he will be, all his life, an useless thing to himself and others.

52. *Rewards.*—Beating then, and all other sorts of slavish and corporal punishments, are not the discipline fit to be used in the education of those we would have wise, good, and ingenuous men ; and therefore very rarely to be applied, and that only in great occasions, and cases of extremity. On the other side, to flatter children by rewards of things that are pleasant to them, is as carefully to be avoided. He that will give to his son apples, or sugar-plums, or what else of this kind he is most delighted with, to make him learn his book, does but authorize his love of pleasure, and cocker up that

dangerous propensity, which he ought by all means to subdue and stifle in him. You can never hope to teach him to master it whilst you compound for the check you give his inclination in one place, by the satisfaction you propose to it in another. To make a good, a wise, and a virtuous man, it is fit he should learn to cross his appetite, and deny his inclination to riches, finery, or pleasing his palate, etc., whenever his reason advises the contrary, and his duty requires it. But when you draw him to do anything that is fit, by the offer of money; or reward the pains of learning his book, by the pleasure of a luscious morsel; when you promise him a lace-cravat, or a fine new suit, upon performance of some of his little tasks; what do you, by proposing these as rewards, but allow them to be the good things he should aim at, and thereby encourage his longing for them, and accustom him to place his happiness in them ? Thus people, to prevail with children to be industrious about their grammar, dancing, or some other such matter of no great moment to the happiness or usefulness of their lives, by misapplied rewards and punishments, sacrifice their virtue, invert the order of their education, and teach them luxury, pride, or covetousness, etc. For in this way, flattering those wrong inclinations, which they should restrain and suppress, they lay the foundations of those future vices, which cannot be avoided, but by curbing our desires, and accustoming them early to submit to reason.

53. I say not this, that I would have children kept from the conveniences or pleasures of life, that are not injurious to their health or virtue. On the contrary, I would have their lives made as pleasant, and as agreeable to them as may be, in a plentiful enjoyment of whatsoever might innocently delight them : provided it be with this caution, that they have those enjoyments only as the consequences of the state of esteem and acceptation they are in with their parents and governors ; but they should never be offered or bestowed on them, as the reward of this or that particular performance, that they show an

aversion to, or to which they would not have applied themselves without that temptation.[1]

54. But if you take away the rod on one hand, and these little encouragements, which they are taken with, on the other, How then (will you say) shall children be governed? Remove hope and fear, and there is an end of all discipline. I grant, that good and evil, reward and punishment, are the only motives to a rational creature; these are the spur and reins whereby all mankind are set on work and guided, and therefore they are to be made use of to children too. For I advise their parents and governors always to carry this in their minds, that they are to be treated as rational creatures.

55. Rewards, I grant, and punishments must be proposed to children, if we intend to work upon them. The mistake, I imagine, is that those that are generally made use of, are ill chosen. The pains and pleasures of the body are, I think, of ill consequence, when made the rewards and punishments, whereby men would prevail on their children: for they serve but to increase and strengthen those appetites which 'tis our business to subdue and master. What principle of virtue do you lay in a child, if you will redeem his desires of one pleasure by the proposal of another? This is but to enlarge his appetite, and instruct it to wander. If a child cries for an unwholesome and dangerous fruit, you purchase his quiet by giving him a less hurtful sweet-meat; this perhaps may preserve his health, but spoils his mind, and sets that farther out of order. For here you only change the object, but flatter still his appetite, and allow that must be satisfied: wherein, as I have showed, lies the root of the mischief: and till you bring him to be able to bear a denial of that satisfaction, the child may at present be quiet and orderly, but the disease is not cured. By this way of proceeding you

---

[1] Locke here proposes a real discipline of *moral* consequences, which Rousseau and Herbert Spencer afterwards perverted to a so-called discipline of natural consequences (see secs. 56-60, 72, 84, 107, 124).

foment and cherish in him, that which is the spring from whence all the evil flows, which will be sure on the next occasion to break out again with more violence, give him stronger longings, and you more trouble.

56. *Reputation.*—The rewards and punishments, then, whereby we should keep children in order, are quite of another kind; and of that force, that when we can get them once to work, the business, I think, is done, and the difficulty is over. Esteem and disgrace are, of all others, the most powerful incentives to the mind, when once it is brought to relish them.[1] If you can once get into children a love of credit, and an apprehension of shame and disgrace, you have put into them the true principle, which will constantly work, and incline them to the right. But it will be asked, How shall this be done?

I confess, it does not, at first appearance, want some difficulty; but yet I think it worth our while to seek the ways (and practise them when found) to attain this, which I look on as the great secret of education.

57. First, children (earlier perhaps than we think) are very sensible of praise and commendation. They find a pleasure in being esteemed and valued, especially by their parents, and those whom they depend on. If therefore the father caress and commend them, when they do well; show a cold and neglectful countenance to them upon doing ill; and this accompanied by a like carriage of the mother, and all others that are about them, it will in a little time make them sensible of the difference: and this, if constantly observed, I doubt not but will of itself work more than threats or blows, which lose their force, when once grown common, and are of no use when shame does not attend them; and therefore are to be forborne, and never to be used, but in the case hereafter-mentioned, when it is brought to extremity.

58. But, secondly, to make the sense of esteem or disgrace sink the deeper, and be of the more weight, other agreeable or disagreeable things should constantly

[1] See note, p. 180.

accompany these different states; not as particular
rewards and punishments of this or that particular
action, but as necessarily belonging to, and constantly
attending one, who by his carriage has brought himself
into a state of disgrace or commendation. By which
way of treating them, children may as much as possible
be brought to conceive, that those that are commended
and in esteem for doing well, will necessarily be beloved
and cherished by every body, and have all other good
things as a consequence of it. And, on the other side,
when any one by miscarriage falls into disesteem, and
cares not to preserve his credit, he will unavoidably fall
under neglect and contempt; and in that state, the want
of what ever might satisfy or delight him, will follow.
In this way the objects of their desires are made assist-
ing to virtue, when a settled experience from the beginning teaches children, that the things they delight in,
belong to, and are to be enjoyed by those only, who are
in a state of reputation. If by these means you can
come once to shame them out of their faults, (for besides
that, I would willingly have no punishment,) and make
them in love with the pleasure of being well thought on,
you may turn them as you please, and they will be in
love with all the ways of virtue.

59. The great difficulty here is, I imagine, from the
folly and perverseness of servants, who are hardly to be
hindered from crossing herein the design of the father
and mother. Children, discountenanced by their parents
for any fault, find usually a refuge and relief in the
caresses of those foolish flatterers, who thereby undo
whatever the parents endeavour to establish. When the
father or mother looks sour on the child, everybody else
should put on the same carriage to him, and nobody
give him countenance, till forgiveness asked, and a
contrary carriage restored him to his esteem and former
credit again. If this were constantly observed, I guess
there would be little need of blows or chiding: their
own ease and satisfaction would quickly teach children
to court commendation, and avoid doing that which they

found every body condemned, and they were sure to suffer for, without being chid or beaten. This would teach them modesty and shame; and they would quickly come to have a natural abhorrence for that which they found made them slighted and neglected by every body. But how this inconvenience from servants is to be remedied, I can only leave to parents' care and consideration. Only I think it of great importance; and that they are very happy, who can get discreet people about their children.

60. *Shame.*—Frequent beating or chiding is therefore carefully to be avoided; because it never produces any good, farther than it serves to raise shame and abhorrence of the miscarriage that brought it on them. And if the greatest part of the trouble be not sense that they have done amiss, and the apprehension that they have drawn on themselves the just displeasure of their best friends, the pain of whipping will work but an imperfect cure; it only patches up for the present, and skins it over, but reaches not to the bottom of the sore. Shame, then, and apprehension of displeasure, being that which ought alone to give a check and hold the reins, 'tis impossible but punishment should lose that efficacy, when it often returns. Shame has in children the same place as modesty in women, which cannot be kept, and often transgressed against. And as to the apprehension of displeasure in the parents, that will come to be very insignificant, if the marks of that displeasure quickly cease. And therefore I think parents should well consider, what faults in their children are weighty enough to deserve the declaration of their anger: but when their displeasure is once declared to a degree that carries any punishment with it, they ought not presently to lay by the severity of their brows, but to restore their children to their former grace with some difficulty; and delay till their conformity, and more than ordinary merit, make good their amendment. If this be not so ordered, punishment will be by familiarity but a thing of course; and offending, being punished and then forgiven, be as

natural and ordinary as noon, night, and morning, following one another.

61. *Reputation.*—Concerning reputation, I shall only remark this one thing more of it : that, though it be not the true principle and measure of virtue, (for that is the knowlege of a man's duty, and the satisfaction it is to obey his Maker, in following the dictates of that light God has given him, with the hopes of acceptation and reward), yet it is that which comes nearest to it : and being the testimony and applause that other people's reason, as it were, by common consent, gives to virtuous and well-ordered actions, is the proper guide and encouragement of children, till they grow able to judge for themselves, and to find what is right by their own reason.[1]

[62. *Praise should be given in public, blame in private.*]

63. *Childishness.*[2]—But if a right course be taken with children, there will not be so much need of the application of the common rewards and punishments, as we imagine, and as the general practice has established. For, all their innocent folly, playing, and childish actions are to be left perfectly free and unrestrained, as far as they can consist with the respect due to those that are present ; and that with the greatest allowance. If these faults of their age, rather than of the children themselves, were, as they should be, left only to time, and imitation, and riper years to cure, children would escape a great deal of misapplied and useless correction ; which either fails to overpower the natural disposition of their childhood, and so, by an ineffectual familiarity, makes correction in other necessary cases of less use ; or else if it be of force to restrain the natural gaiety of that age, it serves only to spoil the temper both of body and mind. If the noise and bustle of their play prove at any time inconvenient or unsuitable to the place or company they are in, (which can only be where their parents are,) a look or a word from the father or mother, if they have established the authority they should, will be enough

---

[1] Subject returned to in sec. 72 ; see also sec. 112.
[2] Sec. 61 in first edition.

either to remove or quiet them for that time. But this
gamesome humour, which is wisely adapted by nature to
their age and temper, should rather be encouraged, to
keep up their spirits, and improve their strength and
health, than curbed or restrained : and the chief art is to
make all that they have to do, sport and play too.

64. *Rules.*—And here give me leave to take notice of
one thing I think a fault in the ordinary method of education; and that is, the charging of children's memories,
upon all occasions, with rules and precepts, which
they often do not understand, and constantly as soon
forget as given. If it be some action you would have
done, or done otherwise; whenever they forget, or do it
awkwardly, make them do it over and over again, till
they are perfect; Whereby you will get these two
advantages : first, to see whether it be an action they
can do, or is fit to be expected of them; For sometimes
children are bid to do things, which, upon trial, they
are found not able to do ; and had need be taught and
exercised in, before they are required to do them. But
it is much easier for a tutor to command than to teach.
Secondly, another thing got by it will be this; that by
repeating the same action, till it be grown habitual in
them, the performance will not depend on memory, or
reflection, the concomitant of prudence and age, and not
of childhood; but will be natural in them. Thus, bowing
to a gentleman when he salutes him, and looking in his
face when he speaks to him, is by constant use as natural
to a well-bred man as breathing; it requires no thought,
no reflection. Having this way cured in your child any
fault, it is cured for ever : and thus one by one, you may
weed them out all, and plant what habits you please.

65. I have seen parents so heap rules on their children,
that it was impossible for the poor little ones to remember a tenth part of them, much less to observe them.
However, they were either by words or blows corrected
for the breach of those multiplied and often very impertinent[1] precepts. Whence it naturally followed, that

[1] Pointless.

the children minded not what was said to them; when it was evident to them, that no attention they were capable of, was sufficient to preserve them from transgression, and the rebukes which followed it.

Let therefore your rules to your son be as few as is possible, and rather fewer than more than seem absolutely necessary. For if you burden him with many rules, one of these two things must necessarily follow; that either he must be very often punished, which will be of ill consequence, by making punishment too frequent and familiar; or else you must let the transgressions of some of your rules go unpunished, whereby they will of course grow contemptible, and your authority become cheap to him. Make but few laws, but see they be well observed, when once made. Few years require but few laws; and as his age increases, when one rule is by practice well established, you may add another.

66. *Practice.*—But pray remember, children are not to be taught by rules, which will be always slipping out of their memories. What you think necessary for them to do, settle in them by an indispensable practice, as often as the occasion returns; and, if it be possible, make occasions. This will beget habits in them, which, being once established, operate of themselves easily and naturally, without the assistance of the memory. But here let me give two cautions: 1. The one is, that you keep them to the practice of what you would have grow into a habit in them by kind words and gentle admonitions, rather as minding them of what they forget, than by harsh rebukes and chiding, as if they were wilfully guilty. 2ndly. Another thing you are to take care of is, not to endeavour to settle too many habits at once, lest by variety you confound them, and so perfect none. When constant custom has made any one thing easy and natural to them, and they practise it without reflection, you may then go on to another.

[This method of teaching children by a repeated practice, and the same action done over and over again, under the eye and direction of the tutor, till they have got the habit of doing it well, and not by relying on rules trusted to their memories; has so many advantages, which way soever we consider it, that I cannot but wonder (if ill customs could be wondered at in any thing) how it could possibly be so much neglected. I shall name one more that comes now in my way. By this method we shall see, whether what is required of him be adapted to his capacity, and any way suited to the child's natural genius and constitution: for that too must be considered in a right education. We must not hope wholly to change their original tempers, nor make the gay pensive and grave; nor the melancholy sportive, without spoiling them. God has stamped certain characters upon men's minds, which, like their shapes, may perhaps be a little mended; but can hardly be totally altered and transformed into the contrary.

He, therefore, that is about children, should well study their natures and aptitudes, and see, by often trials, what turn they easily take, and what becomes them; observe what their native stock is, how it may be improved, and what it is fit for: he should consider what they want, whether they be capable of having it wrought into them by industry, and incorporated there by practice; and whether it be worth while to endeavour it. For, in many cases, all that we can do, or should aim at, is, to make the best of what nature has given, to prevent the vices and faults to which such a constitution is most inclined, and give it all the advantages it is capable of. Every one's natural genius should be carried as far as it could; but to attempt the putting another upon him, will be but labour in vain; and what is so plastered on, will at best sit but untowardly, and have always hanging to it the ungracefulness of constraint and affectation.]

67. *Manners.*—Manners, as they call it, about which children are so often perplexed, and have so many goodly exhortations made them, by their wise maids and governesses, I think, are rather to be learnt by example than rules; and then children, if kept out of ill company, will take a pride to behave themselves prettily, after the

fashion of others, perceiving themselves esteemed and commended for it. But if, by a little negligence in this part, the boy should not put off his hat, nor make legs very gracefully, a dancing-master would cure that defect, and wipe off all that plainness of nature, which the *à-la-mode* people call clownishness. And since nothing appears to me to give children so much becoming confidence and behaviour, and so to raise them to the conversation of those above their age, as dancing, I think they should be taught to dance, as soon as they are capable of learning it. For, though this consist only in outward gracefulness of motion, yet, I know not how, it gives children manly thoughts and carriage, more than any thing. But otherwise I would not have children much tormented about punctilios, or niceties of breeding. Never trouble yourself about those faults in them, which you know age will cure. And therefore want of well-fashioned civility in the carriage, whilst civility is not wanting in the mind (for there you must take care to plant it early), should be the parent's and tutor's least care, whilst they are young. If his tender mind be filled with a veneration for his parents and teachers, which consists in love and esteem, and a fear to offend them; and with respect and good-will to all people; that respect will of itself teach those ways of expressing it, which he observes most acceptable. Be sure to keep up in him the principles of good-nature and kindness; make them as habitual as you can, by credit and commendation, and the good things accompanying that state: and when they have taken root in his mind, and are settled there by a continued practice, fear not; the ornaments of conversation, and the outside of fashionable manners, will come in their due time.

Whilst they are young, any carelessness is to be borne with in children, that carries not with it the marks of pride or ill nature; but those, when they appear in any action, are to be corrected immediately, by the ways above mentioned; and what else remains like clownishness, or want of good breeding, time and observation will of itself reform in them, as they ripen in years, if they are bred in good company; but if in ill, all the rules in the world, all the correction imaginable, will not be able to polish them. For you must take this for a certain truth, that let them have what instructions you will, what teachers soever you please, that which will most influence their carriage, will be the company they converse with. Children (nay, and men too) do most by example. We are all a sort of chameleons, that still take a tincture from things near us: nor is it to be wondered at in children, who better understand what they see, than what they hear.[1]

68. *Company.*—I mentioned above, one great mischief that came by servants to children, when by their flatteries they take off the edge and force of the parents' rebukes, and so lessen their authority. And here is another great inconvenience, which children receive from the ill examples which they meet with, amongst the meaner servants. They are wholly, if possible, to be kept from such conversation : for the contagion of these ill precedents, both in civility and virtue, horribly infects children, as often as they come within reach of it. They frequently learn from unbred or debauched servants such language, untowardly tricks and vices, as otherwise they possibly would be ignorant of, all their lives.

69. 'Tis a hard matter wholly to prevent this mischief. You will have very good luck, if you never have a clownish or vicious servant, and if from them your children never get any infection. But yet, as much must be done towards it, as can be; and the children kept as much as may be in the company of their parents, and those to whose care they are committed. To this purpose, their being in their presence should be made easy to them : they should be allowed the liberties and freedom suitable to their ages, and not be held under unnecessary restraints, when in their parents' or governor's sight. If it be a prison to them, 'tis no wonder they should not like it. They must not be hindered from being children, or from playing, or doing as children, but from doing ill; all other liberty

[1] See sec. 146.

is to be allowed them. Next, to make them in love with the company of their parents, they should receive all their good things there, and from their hands. The servants should be hindered from making court to them, by giving them strong drink, wine, fruit, play-things, and other such matters, which may make them in love with their conversation.

70. Having named company, I am almost ready to throw away my pen, and trouble you no farther on this subject. For since that does more than all precepts, rules, and instructions, methinks 'tis almost wholly in vain to make a long discourse of other things, and to talk of that almost to no purpose. For you will be ready to say, What shall I do with my son? If I keep him always at home, he will be in danger to be my young master; and if I send him abroad, how is it possible to keep him from the contagion of rudeness and vice, which is so every where in fashion? In my house, he will perhaps be more innocent, but more ignorant, too, of the world, and being used constantly to the same faces, and little company will, when he comes abroad, be a sheepish or conceited creature.[1]

[I confess, both sides have their inconveniences. Being abroad, it is true, will make him bolder, and better able to bustle and shift amongst boys of his own age; and the emulation of school-fellows often puts life and industry into young lads. But till you can find a school, wherein it is possible for the master to look after the manners of his scholars, and can show as great effects of his care of forming their minds to virtue, and their carriage to good breeding, as of forming their tongues to the learned languages; you must confess, that you have a strange value for words, when preferring the languages of the ancient Greeks and Romans, to that which made them such brave men, you think it worth while to hazard your

---

[1] Fifteen lines follow, in which private is preferred to public education. The passage is replaced here by the much lengthier statement from a later edition, which elaborates the point (see Introduction).

son's innocence and virtue for a little Greek and Latin. For, as for that boldness and spirit, which lads get amongst their play-fellows at school, it has ordinarily such a mixture of rudeness, and an ill-turned confidence, that those misbecoming and disingenuous ways of shifting in the world must be unlearned, and all the tincture washed out again, to make way for better principles, and such manners as make a truly worthy man. He that considers how diametrically opposite the skill of living well, and managing, as a man should do, his affairs in the world, is to that malapertness, tricking, or violence, learnt among school-boys, will think the faults of a privater education infinitely to be preferred to such improvements; and will take care to preserve his child's innocence and modesty at home, as being nearer of kin, and more in the way of those qualities, which make an useful and able man. Nor does any one find, or so much as suspect, that that retirement and bashfulness, which their daughters are brought up in, makes them less knowing or less able women. Conversation, when they come into the world, soon gives them a becoming assurance; and whatsoever, beyond that, there is of rough and boisterous, may in men be very well spared too : for courage and steadiness, as I take it, lie not in roughness and ill breeding.

Virtue is harder to be got than a knowledge of the world; and if lost in a young man, is seldom recovered. Sheepishness and ignorance of the world, the faults imputed to a private education, are neither the necessary consequences of being bred at home; nor, if they were, are they incurable evils. Vice is the more stubborn, as well as the more dangerous evil of the two; and therefore, in the first place, to be fenced against. If that sheepish softness, which often enervates those, who are bred like fondlings at home, be carefully to be avoided, it is principally so for virtue's sake; for fear lest such a yielding temper should be too susceptible of vicious impressions, and expose the novice too easily to be corrupted. A young man, before he leaves the shelter of his father's house, and the guard of a tutor, should be fortified with resolution, and made acquainted with men, to secure his virtue; lest he should be led into some ruinous course, or fatal precipice, before he is sufficiently acquainted with the dangers of conversation, and has steadiness enough not to yield to every temptation. Were it not for this, a young man's bashfulness and ignorance in the world would not so much need an early care. Conversation would cure it in a great measure; or if that will not do it early enough, it is only a stronger reason for a good tutor at home. For, if pains be to be taken to give him a manly air and assurance betimes, it is chiefly as a fence to his virtue, when he goes into the world, under his own conduct.

It is preposterous, therefore, to sacrifice his innocency to the attaining of confidence, and some little skill of bustling for himself among others, by his conversation with ill-bred and vicious boys; when the chief use of that sturdiness and standing upon his own legs, is only for the preservation of his virtue. For if confidence or cunning come once to mix with vice, and support his miscarriages he is only the surer lost; and you must undo again, and strip him of that he has got from his companions, or give him up to ruin. Boys will unavoidably be taught assurance by conversation with men, when they are brought into it; and that is time enough. Modesty and submission, till then, better fits them for instruction; and therefore there needs not any great care to stock them with confidence beforehand. That which requires most time, pains, and assiduity, is to work into them the principles and practice of virtue and good breeding. This is the seasoning they should be prepared with, so as not easily to be got out again: this they had need to be well provided with. For conversation, when they come into the world, will add to their knowledge and assurance, but be too apt to take from their virtue; which therefore they ought to be plentifully stored with, and have that tincture sunk deep into them.

How they should be fitted for conversation, and entered into the world, when they are ripe for it, we shall consider in another place. But how any one's being put into a mixed herd of unruly boys, and then learning to wrangle at trap, or rook[1] at span farthing, fits him for civil conversation or business I do not see. And what qualities are ordinarily to be got from such a troop of play-fellows as schools usually assemble together, from parents of all kinds, that a father should so much covet it, is hard to divine. I am sure, he who is able to be at the charge of a tutor at home, may there give his son a more genteel carriage, more manly thoughts, and a sense of what is worthy and becoming, with a greater proficiency in learning into the bargain, and ripen him up sooner into a man, than any at school can do. Not that I blame the school-master in this, or think it to be laid to his charge. The difference is great between two or three pupils in the same house, and three or fourscore boys lodged up and down. For, let the master's industry and skill be ever so great, it is impossible he should have 50 or 100 scholars under his eye any longer than they are in the school together : nor can it be expected, that he should instruct them successfully in any thing but their books ; the forming of their minds and manners requiring a constant attention, and particular application to every single boy ; which is impossible in a numerous flock, and would be wholly in vain (could he have time to study and correct every one's particular defects and wrong inclinations) when the lad was to be left to himself, or the prevailing infection of his fellows, the greatest part of the four and twenty hours.

But fathers, observing that fortune is often most successfully courted by bold and bustling men, are glad to see their sons pert and forward betimes ; take it for a happy omen, that they will be thriving men, and look on the tricks they play their school-fellows, or learn from them, as a proficiency in the art of living, and making their way through the world. But I must take the liberty to say, that he that lays the foundation of his son's fortune in virtue and good breeding takes the only sure

[1] Cheat.

and warrantable way. And it is not the waggeries or
cheats practised among school-boys, it is not their roughness one to another, nor the well-laid plots of robbing an
orchard together, that make an able man; but the
principles of justice, generosity and sobriety, joined with
observation and industry, qualities which I judge school-
boys do not learn much of one another. And if a young
gentleman, bred at home, be not taught more of them
than he could learn at school, his father has made a very
ill choice of a tutor. Take a boy from the top of a
grammar-school, and one of the same age, bred as he
should be in his father's family, and bring them into
good company together; and then see which of the two
will have the more manly carriage, and address himself
with the more becoming assurance to strangers. Here I
imagine the school-boy's confidence will either fail or
discredit him; and if it be such as fits him only for the
conversation of boys, he had better be without it.

Vice, if we may believe the general complaint, ripens
so fast now-a-days, and runs up to seed so early in young
people, that it is impossible to keep a lad from the
spreading contagion, if you will venture him abroad in
the herd, and trust to chance, or his own inclination, for
the choice of his company at school. By what fate vice
has so thriven amongst us these few years past, and by
what hands it has been nursed up into so uncontrolled a
dominion, I shall leave to others to enquire. I wish that
those who complain of the great decay of Christian piety
and virtue everywhere, and of learning and acquired
improvements in the gentry of this generation, would
consider how to retrieve them in the next. This I am
sure, that, if the foundation of it be not laid in the education and principling of the youth, all other endeavours
will be in vain. And if the innocence, sobriety, and
industry of those who are coming up, be not taken care
of and preserved, it will be ridiculous to expect, that
those who are to succeed next on the stage, should abound
in that virtue, ability, and learning, which has hitherto
made England considerable in the world. I was going

to add courage, too, though it has been looked on as the
natural inheritance of Englishmen. What has been talked
of some late actions at sea,[1] of a kind unknown to our
ancestors, gives me occasion to say, that debauchery
sinks the courage of men; and when dissoluteness has
eaten out the sense of true honour, bravery seldom stays
long after it. And I think it impossible to find an
instance of any nation, however renowned for their valour,
who ever kept their credit in arms, or made themselves
redoubtable amongst their neighbours, after corruption
had once broken through, and dissolved the restraint of
discipline; and vice was grown to such a head, that it durst
show itself barefaced, without being out of countenance.

It is virtue then, direct virtue, which is the hard and
valuable part to be aimed at in education; and not a
forward pertness, or any little arts of shifting. All other
considerations and accomplishments should give way and
be postponed to this. This is the solid and substantial
good, which tutors should not only read lectures, and talk
of; but the labour and art of education should furnish
the mind with, and fasten there, and never cease till the
young man had a true relish of it, and placed his strength,
his glory, and his pleasure in it.

The more this advances, the easier way will be made
for other accomplishments in their turns. For he that is
brought to submit to virtue, will not be refractory, or
resty, in any thing that becomes him. And therefore I
cannot but prefer breeding of a young gentleman at
home in his father's sight, under a good governor, as
much the best and safest way to this great and main end
of education, when it can be had, and is ordered as it
should be. Gentlemen's houses are seldom without
variety of company: they should use their sons to all the

---

[1] This passage appeared in the third edition of 1695, but not in
the first edition. Possibly the reference is to the events of the
year 1695, and more especially to the conduct of the Marquis of
Carmarthen, who withdrew his fleet into Milford Haven, and left
our trade a prey to French cruisers and privateers (Burnet's *History
of his Own Times*, vi.).

strange faces that come there, and engage them in conversation, with men of parts and breeding, as soon as
they are capable of it.   And why those, who live in the
country, should not take them with them, when they make
visits of civility to their neighbours, I know not : this I
am sure, a father that breeds his son at home, has the
opportunity to have him more in his own company, and
there give him what encouragement he thinks fit ; and can
keep him better from the taint of servants, and the
meaner sort of people, than is possible to be done abroad.
But what shall be resolved in the case, must in great
measure be left to the parents, to be determined by their
circumstances and conveniences.   Only I think it the
worst sort of good husbandry, for a father not to strain
himself a little for his son's breeding ; which, let his condition be what it will, is the best portion he can leave
him.   But if, after all, it shall be thought by some, that
the breeding at home has too little company, and that at
ordinary schools, not such as it should be for a young
gentleman ; I think there might be ways found out to
avoid the inconveniences on the one side and the other.]

71. *Example.*—Having under consideration how great
the influence of company is, and how prone we are all,
especially children, to imitation, I must here take the
liberty to mind parents of this one thing, viz.   That he
that will have his son have a respect for him and his
orders, must himself have a great reverence for his son.
Maxima debetur pueris reverentia.[1]   You must do nothing
before him, which you would not have him imitate.   If
anything 'scape you,[2] which you would have pass for a
fault in him, he will be sure to shelter himself under your
example, and how then you will be able to come at him,
to correct it in the right way, I do not easily see.   And
if you will punish him for it, he cannot look on it as a
thing which reason condemns, since you practise it ; but
he will be apt to interpret it the peevishness and arbi-

---

[1] " The most scrupulous respect is due to boyhood " (Juvenal
Satires XIV., 47).
[2] *I.e.,* if you allow yourself to do anything.

trary imperiousness of a father, which, without any ground
for it, would deny his son the liberty and pleasures he
takes himself. Or if you would have it thought it is
a liberty belonging to riper years, and not to a child, you
add but a new temptation, since, you must always remember, that children affect to be men earlier than is thought:
and they love breeches, not for their cut or ease, but
because the having them is a mark or a step towards
manhood. What I say of the father's carriage before
his children, must extend itself to all those who have any
authority over them, or for whom he would have them
have any respect.

72. Thus all the actions of childishness, and un-
fashionable carriage, and whatever time and age will of
itself be sure to reform, being exempt from the discipline
of the rod, there will not be so much need of beating
children, as is generally made use of. To which, if we
add learning to read, write, dance, foreign language,
etc., as under the same privilege, there will be but very
rarely any occasion for blows or force in an ingenuous
education. The right way to teach them those things,
is, to give them a liking and inclination to what you
propose to them to be learned, and that will engage their
industry and application. This I think no hard matter
to do, if children be handled as they should be, and the
rewards and punishments above-mentioned be carefully
applied, and with them these few rules observed in the
method of instructing them.[1]

73. 1. *Task.*—None of the things they are to learn
should ever be made a burden to them, or imposed on
them as a task. Whatever is so proposed, presently
becomes irksome: the mind takes an aversion to it,
though before it were a thing of delight or indifferency.
Let a child be but ordered to whip his top at a certain
time every day, whether he has, or has not a mind to it;
let this be but required of him as a duty, wherein he
must spend so many hours morning and afternoon, and
see whether he will not soon be weary of any play at

[1] See secs. 43-61, 84, 107 (at end), 124.

this rate. Is it not so with grown men? What they do cheerfully of themselves, do they not presently grow sick of, and can no more endure, as soon as they find it is expected of them as a duty? Children have as much a mind to show that they are free, that their own good actions come from themselves, that they are absolute and independent, as any of the proudest of you grown men, think of them as you please.

74. 2. *Disposition.*—As a consequence of this, they should seldom be put upon doing even those things you have got an inclination in them to, but when they have a mind and disposition to it. He that loves reading, writing, music, etc., finds yet in himself certain seasons wherein those things have no relish to him; and, if at that time he forces himself to it, he only pothers and wearies himself to no purpose. So it is with children. This change of temper should be carefully observed in them, and the favourable seasons of aptitude and inclination be heedfully laid hold of, to set them upon anything.[1] By this means a great deal of time and tiring would be saved: for a child will learn three times as much when he is in tune, as he will with double the time and pains, when he goes awkwardly, or is dragged unwillingly to it. If this were minded as it should, children might be permitted to weary themselves with play, and yet have time enough to learn what is suited to the capacity of each age. And if things were ordered right, learning anything they should be taught, might be made as much a recreation to their play, as their play is to their learning. The pains are equal on both sides: nor is it that which troubles them, for they love to be busy, and the change and variety is that which naturally delights them. The only odds is, in that which we call play they act at liberty, and employ

---

[1] "In all pedagogy the great thing is to strike the iron while hot, and to seize the wave of the pupil's interest in each successive subject before its ebb has come" (William James, *Psychology*, "Briefer Course," chap. xxv.; on the doctrine of "Learning without Compulsion," see Introduction, p. 15).

their pains (whereof you may observe them never
sparing) freely; but what they are to learn, they are
driven to it, called on or compelled. This is that, that
at first entrance balks and cools them; they want their
liberty: get them but to ask their tutor to teach them,
as they do often their play-fellows, instead of this calling upon them to learn, and they being satisfied that
they act as freely in this, as they do in other things,
they will go on with as much pleasure in it, and it will
not differ from their other sports and play   By these
ways, carefully pursued, I guess a child may be brought
to desire to be taught any thing you have a mind he
should learn.   The hardest part, I confess, is with the
first or eldest; but when once he is set right, it is easy
by him to lead the rest whither one will.

75. *Task.*—Though it be past doubt, that the fittest
time for children to learn anything is when their minds
are in tune, and well disposed to it; when neither
flagging of spirit, nor intentness of thought upon something else, makes them awkward and averse; yet two
things are to be taken care of: 1. That these seasons
either not being warily observed and laid hold on as
often as they return; or else not returning as often as
they should (as always happens in the ordinary method
and discipline of education, when blows and compulsion
have raised an aversion in the child to the thing he is to
learn), the improvement of the child be not thereby
neglected, and so he be let grow into a habitual idleness, and confirmed in this indisposition.   2. That
though other things are ill learned when the mind is
either indisposed, or otherwise taken up; yet it is a
great matter, and worth our endeavours, to teach the
mind to get the mastery over itself; and to be able,
upon choice, to take itself off from the hot pursuit of
one thing, and set itself upon another with facility and
delight; or at any time to shake off its sluggishness, and
vigorously employ itself about what reason, or the
advice of another, shall direct.   This is to be done in
children, by trying them sometimes, when they are by

laziness unbent, or by avocation bent another way, and endeavouring to make them buckle to the thing proposed. If by this means the mind can get a habitual dominion over it self, lay by ideas or business, as occasion requires, and betake itself to new and less acceptable employments, without reluctancy or discomposure, it will be an advantage of more consequence than Latin, or logic, or most of those things children are usually required to learn.

76. *Compulsion.*—Children being more active and busy in that age, than [in] any other part of their life, and being indifferent to anything they can do, so they may be but doing, dancing and Scotch-hoppers[1] would be the same thing to them, were the encouragements and discouragements equal. But to things we would have them learn, the great and only discouragement I can observe, is, that they are called to it, 'tis made their business; they are teased and chid about it, and do it with trembling and apprehension; or, when they come willingly to it, are kept too long at it, till they are quite tired; all which intrenches too much on that natural freedom they extremely affect, and 'tis that liberty alone, which gives the true relish and delight to their ordinary play-games. Turn the tables, and you will find they will soon change their application; especially if they see the examples of others, whom they esteem and think above themselves. And if the things they see others do, be ordered so that they are persuaded it is the privilege of an age or condition above theirs, then ambition, and the desire still to get forward, and higher, and to be like those above them, will give them an inclination which will set them on work in a way wherein they will go on with vigour and pleasure, enjoying in it their dearly beloved freedom; which if it brings with it also the satisfaction of credit and reputation, I am apt to think there will need no other spur to excite their application and assiduity, as much as is necessary.[2] I

---

[1] Now known as "hop-scotch."

[2] *Cf.* secs. 103, 128, 129, 148, 149, 167, 202.

confess, there needs patience and skill, gentleness and attention, and a prudent conduct to attain this at first. But why have you a tutor if there needed no pains ? But when this is once established, all the rest will follow more easily, than in any more severe and imperious discipline. And I think it no hard matter, to gain this point; I am sure it will not be, where children have no ill examples set before them. The great danger therefore I apprehend, is only from servants and other ill-ordered children, or such other vicious or foolish people, who spoil children, both by the ill pattern they set before them in their own ill manners, and by giving them together, the two things they should never have at once ; I mean vicious pleasures, and commendation.

77. *Chiding.*—As children should very seldom be corrected by blows; so, I think, frequent, and especially, passionate chiding, of almost as ill consequence. It lessens the authority of the parents and the respect of the child; for I bid you still remember, they distinguish early between passion and reason : and as they cannot but have a reverence for what comes from the latter, so they quickly grow into a contempt of the former: or if it causes a present terror, yet it soon wears off ; and natural inclination will easily learn to slight such scare-crows, which make a noise, but are not animated by reason. Children being to be restrained by the parents only in vicious (which, in their tender years, are only a few) things, a look or nod only ought to correct them, when they do amiss : or, if words are sometimes to be used, they ought to be grave, kind, and sober, representing the ill or unbecomingness of the fault, rather than a hasty rating of the child for it, which makes him not sufficiently distinguish whether your dislike be not more directed to him than his fault.

78. *Obstinacy.*—I foresee here it will be objected to me : What then, will you have children never beaten nor chid for any fault ? This will be to let loose the reins to all kind of disorder. Not so much as is imagined, if a

right course has been taken in the first seasoning of their minds, and implanting that awe of their parents above-mentioned. For beating, by constant observation, is found to do little good, where the smart of it is all the punishment that is feared or felt in it; for the influence of that quickly wears out, with the memory of it. But yet there is one, and but one fault, for which, I think, children should be beaten; and that is obstinacy or rebellion. And in this, too, I would have it ordered so, if it can be, that the shame of the whipping, and not the pain, should be the greatest part of the punishment. Shame of doing amiss, and deserving chastisement, is the only true restraint belonging to virtue. The smart of the rod, if shame accompanies it not, soon ceases, and is forgotten, and will quickly, by use, lose its terror. I have known the children of a person of quality kept in awe, by the fear of having their shoes pulled off, as much as others by apprehension of a rod hanging over them. Some such punishment I think better than beating; for 'tis shame of the fault, and the disgrace that attends it, that they should stand in fear of, rather than pain, if you would have them have a temper truly ingenuous. But stubbornness and an obstinate disobedience must be mastered with force and blows:[1] for this there is no other remedy. Whatever particular action you bid him do, or forbear, you must be sure to see yourself obeyed; no quarter in this case, no resistance. For when once it comes to be a trial of skill, a contest for mastery betwixt you, as it is, if you command, and he refuses, you must be sure to carry it, whatever blows it costs, if a nod or words will not prevail; unless, for ever after, you intend to live in obedience to your son. A prudent and kind mother, of my acquaintance, was on such an occasion, forced to whip her little daughter, at her first coming home from nurse, eight times successively, the same morning, before she could master her stubbornness, and

[1] "Lying, and, in a less degree, obstinacy, seem to me to be those [childish actions] whose birth and progress should in every case alone be combated" (Montaigne, i., chap. ix., "On Liars").

obtain a compliance in a very easy and indifferent matter. If she had left off sooner, and stopped at the seventh whipping, she had spoiled the child for ever; and, by her unprevailing blows, only confirmed her refractoriness, very hardly afterwards to be cured: but wisely persisting, till she had bent her mind and suppled her will, the only end of correction and chastisement, she established her authority throughly in the very first occasions, and had ever after a very ready compliance and obedience in all things from her daughter. For, as this was the first time, so, I think, it was the last too she ever struck her.[1]

[2] This, if well reflected on, would make people more wary in the use of the rod and the cudgel; and keep them from being so apt to think beating the safe and universal remedy, to be applied at random, on all occasions. This is certain, however, if it does no good, it does great harm; if it reaches not the mind, and makes not the will supple, it hardens the offender; and whatever pain he has suffered for it, it does but endear to him his beloved stubbornness, which has got him this time the victory, and prepares him to contest and hope for it for the future. Thus, I doubt not but by ill-ordered correction, many have been taught to be obstinate and refractory, who otherwise would have been very pliant and tractable. For, if you punish a child, so as if it were only to revenge the past fault, which has raised your choler, what operation can this have upon his mind, which is the part to be amended? If there were no sturdy wilfulness of mind mixed with his fault, there was nothing in it that needed the severity of blows. A kind, or grave admonition would have been enough to remedy the faults of frailty, forgetfulness, or inadvertency, as much as they needed. But, if there were a perverseness in the will, if it were a designed, resolved disobedience, the punishment is not to be measured by the greatness or smallness of the matter wherein it appeared,

---

[1] The mother does not seem to have applied Locke's own caution: "Be sure that it is obstinacy, *and nothing else.*"

[2] Sec. 77 in first edition.

but by the opposition it carries, and stands in, to that respect and submission [that] is due to the father's orders, and must always be rigorously exacted, and the blows by pauses laid on, till they reach the mind, and you perceive the signs of a true sorrow, shame, and resolution of obedience. This, I confess, requires something more than setting children a task, and whipping them without any more ado, if it be not done, and done to our fancy. This requires care, attention, observation, and a nice study of children's tempers, and weighing their faults well, before we come to this sort of punishment. But is not that better, than always to have the rod in hand, as the only instrument of government; and, by frequent use of it, on all occasions, misapply and render inefficacious this last and useful remedy where there is need of it? For, what else can be expected, when it is promiscuously used upon every little slip, when a mistake in concordance, or a wrong position in verse, shall have the severity of the lash, in a well-tempered and industrious lad, as surely as a wilful crime in an obstinate and perverse offender? How can such a way of correction be expected to do good on the mind, and set that right, which is the only thing to be looked after; and, when set right, brings all the rest that you can desire along with it?

79. Where a wrong bent of the will wants not amendment, there can be no need of blows. All other faults, where the mind is rightly disposed, and refuses not the government and authority of the father or tutor, are but mistakes, and may often be overlooked; or, when they are taken notice of, need no other but the gentle remedies of advice, direction, and reproof; till the repeated and wilful neglect of those, shows the fault to be in the mind, and that a manifest perverseness of the will lies at the root of their disobedience. But when ever obstinacy, which is an open defiance, appears, that cannot be winked at or neglected, but must, in the first instance, be subdued and mastered; only care must be had, that we mistake not; and we must be sure it is obstinacy, and nothing else.

80. But since the occasions of punishment, especially

beating, are as much to be avoided as may be, I think it should not be often brought to this point. If the awe I spoke of be once got, a look will be sufficient in most cases. Nor indeed should the same carriage, seriousness or application be expected from young children as from those of riper growth. They must be permitted, as I said, the foolish and childish actions, suitable to their years, without taking notice of them; inadvertency, carelessness, and gaiety, is the character of that age. I think the severity I spoke of, is not to extend it self to such unseasonable restraints. Keep them from vice and vicious dispositions, and such a kind of behaviour in general will come, with every degree of their age, as is suitable to that age, and the company they ordinarily converse with; and as they grow in years, they will grow in attention and application. But that your words may always carry weight and authority with them, if it shall happen, upon any occasion, that you bid him leave off the doing of any even childish things, you must be sure to carry the point, and not let him have the mastery. But yet, I say, I would have the father seldom interpose his authority and command in these cases, or in any other, but such as have a tendency to vicious habits. I think there are better ways of prevailing with them; and a gentle persuasion in reasoning (when the first point of submission to your will is got) will most times do much better.

81. *Reasoning.*—It will perhaps be wondered, that I mention reasoning with children: and yet I cannot but think that the true way of dealing with them. They understand it as early as they do language; and, if I misobserve not, they love to be treated as rational creatures, sooner than is imagined. 'Tis a pride should be cherished in them, and, as much as can be, made the greatest instrument to turn them by.

But when I talk of reasoning, I do not intend any other, but such as is suited to the child's capacity and apprehension. Nobody can think a boy of three or seven years old, should be argued with, as a grown man.

Long discourses, and philosophical reasonings, at best, amaze and confound, but do not instruct, children. When I say therefore, that they must be treated as rational creatures, I mean, that you should make them sensible, by the mildness of your carriage, and the composure, even in your correction of them, that what you do is reasonable in you, and useful and necessary for them; and that it is not out of caprice, passion, or fancy, that you command or forbid them any thing. This they are capable of understanding; and there is no virtue they should be excited to, nor fault they should be kept from, which I do not think they may be convinced of: but it must be by such reasons as their age and understanding are capable of, and those proposed always in very few and plain words. The foundations on which several duties are built, and the fountains of right and wrong, from which they spring, are not, perhaps, easily to be let into the minds of grown men, not used to abstract their thoughts from common received opinions. Much less are children capable of reasonings from remote principles. They cannot conceive the force of long deductions : the reasons that move them must be obvious, and level to their thoughts, and such as may (if I may so say) be felt and touched. But yet, if their age, temper, and inclinations, be considered, they will never want such motives, as may be sufficient to convince them. If there be no other more particular, yet these will always be intelligible, and of force, to deter them from any fault, fit to be taken notice of in them, (*viz.*) that it will be a discredit and disgrace to them, and displease you.

82. *Examples.*—But, of all the ways whereby children are to be instructed, and their manners formed, the plainest, easiest, and most efficacious, is to set before their eyes the examples of those things you would have them do or avoid. Which, when they are pointed out to them, in the practice of persons within their knowledge, with some reflections on their beauty or unbecomingness, are of more force to draw or deter their imitation, than any discourses which can be made to them. Virtues and

5

vices can by no words be so plainly set before their understandings, as the actions of other men will show them, when you direct their observation, and bid them view this or that good or bad quality in their practice. And the beauty or uncomeliness of many things, in good and ill breeding, will be better learnt, and make deeper impressions on them, in the examples of others, than from any rules or instructions that can be given about them.

This is a method to be used, not only whilst they are young, but to be continued, even as long as they shall be under another's tuition or conduct. Nay, I know not whether it be not the best way to be used by a father, as long as he shall think fit, on any occasion, to reform any thing he wishes mended in his son; nothing sinking so gently and so deep, into men's minds, as example. And what ill they either overlook, or indulge in them themselves, they cannot but dislike, and be ashamed of, when it is set before them in another.

83. *Whipping.*—It may be doubted concerning whipping, when, as the last remedy, it comes to be necessary, at what times, and by whom it should be done: whether presently upon the committing the fault, whilst it is yet fresh and hot; and whether parents themselves should beat their children. As to the first, I think it should not be done presently, lest passion mingle with it and so, though it exceed the just proportion, yet it lose the authority; for even children discern when we do things in passion. But, as I said before, that has most weight with them, that appears sedately to come from their parents' reason; and they are not without this distinction.[1] Next, if you have any discreet servant capable of it, and has the place of governing your child (for if you have a tutor, there is no doubt) I think it is best the smart should come more immediately from another's hand, though by the parent's order, who should see it done; whereby the parent's authority will be preserved,[2] and the child's aversion for the pain it suffers rather be

---

[1] *I.e.*, this power of distinguishing.
[2] " Preferred " in text.

turned on the person that immediately inflicts it. For I would have a father seldom strike his child, but upon very urgent necessity, and as the last remedy: and then perhaps it will be fit to do it so that the child should not quickly forget it.

84. But, as I said before, beating is the worst, and therefore the last, means to be used in the correction of children; and that only in cases of extremity, after all gentler ways have been tried, and proved unsuccessful: which, if well observed, there will be very seldom any need of blows. For, it not being to be imagined that a child will often, if ever, dispute his father's present command in any particular instance; and the father not rigorously interposing his absolute authority in positive rules, concerning childish or indifferent actions, wherein his son is to have his liberty: nor concerning his learning or improvement wherein there is no compulsion to be used,[1] there remains only the prohibition of some vicious actions, wherein a child is capable of obstinacy, and consequently can deserve beating: and so there will be but very few occasions of that discipline to be used by any one, who considers well, and orders his child's education as it should be. For the first seven years, what vices can a child be guilty of, but lying, or some ill-natured tricks; the repeated commission whereof, after his father's direct command against it, shall bring him into the condemnation of obstinacy, and the chastisement of the rod? If any vicious inclination in him be, in the first appearance and instances of it, treated as it should be, first with your wonder, and then, if returning again a second time, discountenanced with the severe brow of the father, tutor, and all about him, and a treatment suitable to the state of discredit before-mentioned,[2] and this continued till he be made sensible and ashamed of his fault, I imagine there will be no need of any other correction, nor ever any occasion to come to blows. The necessity of such chastisement is usually the consequence

[1] See Introduction, p. 15.
[2] See secs. 53, 56-60, 72, 107, 124-129.

only of former indulgencies or neglects. If vicious inclinations were watched from the beginning, and the first irregularities which they caused corrected by those gentler ways, we should seldom have to do with more than one disorder at once, which would be easily set right without any stir or noise, and not require so harsh a discipline as beating. Thus, one by one, as they appeared, they might all be weeded out without any signs or memory that ever they had been there. But we letting their faults (by indulging and humouring our little ones) grow up till they are sturdy and numerous, and the deformity of them makes us ashamed and uneasy, we are fain to come to the plough and the harrow; the spade and the pick-ax must go deep to come at the roots, and all the force, skill, and diligence we can use, is scarce enough to cleanse the vitiated seed-plat overgrown with weeds, and restore us the hopes of fruits to reward our pains in its season.

85. This course, if observed, will spare both father and child the trouble of repeated injunctions, and multiplied rules of doing and forbearing. For I am of opinion, that of those actions which tend to vicious habits (which are those alone that a father should interpose his authority and commands in), none should be forbidden children till they are found guilty of them. For such untimely prohibitions, if they do nothing worse, do at least so much towards teaching and allowing them, that they suppose that children may be guilty of them, who would possibly be safer in the ignorance of any such faults. And the best remedy to stop them, is, as I have said, to show wonder and amazement at any such action as hath a vicious tendency, when it is first taken notice of in a child. For example, when he is first found in a lie, or any ill-natured trick, the first remedy should be, to talk to him of it as a strange, monstrous matter, that it could not be imagined he would have done; and so shame him out of it.

86. It will be ('tis like) objected, That whatever I fancy of the tractableness of children, and the prevalency

of those softer ways of shame and commendation ; yet there are many, who will never apply themselves to their books, and to what they ought to learn, unless they are scourged to it. This I fear is nothing but the language of ordinary schools and fashion, which have never suffered the other to be tried as it should be, in places where it could be taken notice of. Why, else, does the learning of Latin and Greek need the rod, when French and Italian needs it not ? Children learn to dance and fence without whipping : nay, arithmetic, drawing, etc., they apply themselves well enough to, without beating : which would make one suspect that there is something strange, unnatural, and disagreeable to that age, in the things required in Grammar-Schools, or the methods used there, that children cannot be brought to, without the severity of the lash, and hardly with that too ; or else that it is a mistake, that those tongues could not be taught them without beating.

87. But let us suppose some so negligent or idle, that they will not be brought to learn by the gentle ways proposed ; for we must grant, that there will be children found of all tempers, yet it does not thence follow, that the rough discipline of the cudgel is to be used at all. Nor can any one be concluded unmanageable by the milder methods of government, till they have been throughly tried upon him ; and, if they will not prevail with him to use his endeavours, and do what is in his power to do, we make no excuse for the obstinate : blows are the proper remedies for those : but blows laid on in a way different from the ordinary. He that wilfully neglects his book, and stubbornly refuses any thing he can do, required of him by his father expressing himself in a positive serious command, should not be corrected with two or three angry lashes, for not performing his task, and the same punishment repeated again and again, upon every the like default. But, when it is brought to that pass, that wilfulness evidently shows itself, and makes blows necessary, I think the chastisement should be a little more sedate, and a little more severe, and the

whipping (mingled with admonitions between) so continued, till the impressions of it on the mind were found legible in the face, voice, and submission of the child, not so sensible of the smart as of the fault he has been guilty of, and melting in true sorrow under it. If such a correction as this, tried some few times at fit distances, and carried to the utmost severity, with the visible displeasure of the father all the while, will not work the effect, turn the mind, and produce a future compliance, what can be hoped from blows, and to what purpose should they be any more used ?   Beating, when you can expect no good from it, will look more like the fury of an enraged enemy, than the good-will of a compassionate friend; and such chastisement carries with it only provocation without any prospect of amendment.   If it be any father's misfortune to have a son thus perverse and untractable, I know not what more he can do but pray for him.   But I imagine, if a right course be taken with children from the beginning, very few will be found to be such; and when there are any such instances, they are not to be the rule for the education of those who are better natured, and may be managed with better usage.

88. *Tutor*.—If a tutor can be got, that, thinking himself in the father's place, charged with his care, and relishing these things, will at the beginning apply himself to put them in practice, he will afterwards find his work very easy : and you will, I guess, have your son in a little time, a greater proficient in both learning and breeding, than perhaps you imagine.   But let him by no means beat him, at any time, without your consent and direction.

89. He must be sure also to shew him the example of the things he would have the child practise, and carefully preserve him from the influence of ill precedents, especially the most dangerous of all, that of the servants, from whose company he is to be kept, not by prohibitions, for that will but give him an itch, but by other ways I have mentioned.[1]

[1] See secs. 59, 68, 69.

90. *Governor.*—In all the whole business of education, there is nothing like to be less hearkened to, or harder to be well observed, than what I am now going to say ; and that is, That I would, from their first beginning to talk, have some discreet, sober, nay wise person about children, whose care it should be to fashion them aright, and keep them from all ill, especially the infection of bad company. I think this province requires great sobriety, temperance, tenderness, diligence, and discretion, qualities hardly to be found united in persons that are to be had for ordinary salaries, nor easily to be found any where. As to the charge of it, I think it will be the money best laid out that can be about our children ; and therefore, though it may be expensive more than is ordinary, yet it cannot be thought dear. He that at any rate procures his child a good mind, well-principled, tempered to virtue and usefulness, and adorned with civility and good breeding, makes a better purchase for him, than if he laid out the money for an addition of more earth to his former acres. Spare it in toys and play-games, in silk and ribbons, laces and other useless expenses, as much as you please ; but be not sparing in so necessary a part as this. 'Tis not good husbandry to make his fortune rich, and his mind poor. I have often, with great admiration, seen people lavish it profusely in tricking up their children in fine clothes, lodging and feeding them sumptuously, allowing them more than enough of useless servants, and yet at the same time starve their minds, and not take sufficient care to cover that, which is the most shameful nakedness, *viz.*, their natural wrong inclinations and ignorance. This I can look on as no other than a sacrificing to their own vanity ; it showing more their pride, than true care of the good of their children. Whatsoever you employ to the advantage of your son's mind, will show your true kindness, though it be to the lessening of his estate. A wise and good man can hardly want either the opinion or reality of being great and happy. But he that is foolish or vicious, can be neither great nor happy, what estate soever you leave

him : and I ask you, whether there be not men in the world, whom you had rather have your son be, with £500 per annum, than some other you know, with £5,000 ?

91. The consideration of charge ought not, therefore, to deter those who are able : the great difficulty will be, where to find a proper person. For those of small age, parts, and virtue, are unfit for this employment : and those that have greater, will hardly be got to undertake such a charge. You must therefore look out early, and enquire everywhere; for the world has people of all sorts : and I remember, Montaigne says in one of his essays, that the learned Castalio was fain to make trenchers at Basle, to keep himself from starving, when his father would have given any money for such a tutor for his son, and Castalio have willingly embraced such an employment upon very reasonable terms : but this was for want of intelligence.[1]

92. If you find it difficult to meet with such a tutor as we desire, you are not to wonder. I only can say, Spare no care nor cost to get such an one. All things are to be had that way : and I dare assure you, that, if you can get a good one, you will never repent the charge; but will always have the satisfaction to think it the money of all other the best laid out. But be sure take no body upon friends, or charitable, no, nor bare great commendations. Nor will the reputation of a sober man, with learning enough (which is all usually required in a tutor), serve the turn. In this choice be as curious, as you would in that of a wife for him : for you must not think of trial, or changing afterwards ; that will cause great inconvenience to you, and greater to your son. When I consider the scruples and cautions I here lay in your way, methinks it looks as if I advised you to some

[1] *Essais*, i., chap. xxxiv., "D'un defaut de nos polices." But Locke has constructed an anecdote out of a bare reference to the death of the French humanist Sébastien Castalion (1515-1563), and the elder Montaigne's suggestion of a Public Inquiry Office, which would keep buyers and sellers reciprocally informed. On Castalion, or Castellion, see Foster Watson, *The English Grammar Schools*, p. 338 *ff*.

thing, which I would have offered at, but in effect not done. But he that shall consider, how much the business of a tutor, rightly employed, lies out of the road, and how remote it is from the thoughts of many, even of those who propose to themselves this employment, will perhaps be of my mind, that one fit to educate and form the mind of a young gentleman, is not every where to be found ; and that more than ordinary care is to be taken in the choice of him, or else you may fail of your end.

93. *The tutor must be well-bred and of a graceful carriage ; these qualities he should seek to form in the young gentleman.*[1]

94. *The tutor must know the world and must exhibit the world to his pupil as it really is.*

[Thus, by safe and insensible degrees, he will pass from a boy to a man ; which is the most hazardous step in all the whole course of life. This therefore should be carefully watched, and a young man with great diligence handed over it ; and not, as now usually is done, be taken from a governor's conduct, and all at once thrown into the world under his own, not without manifest dangers of immediate spoiling ; there being nothing more frequent, than instances of the great looseness, extravagancy and debauchery, which young men have run into, as soon as they have been let loose from a severe and strict education : which, I think, may be chiefly imputed to their wrong way of breeding, especially in this part ; for having been bred up in a great ignorance of what the world truly is, and finding it quite another thing, when they come into it, than what they were taught it should be, and so imagined it was, are easily persuaded, by other kind of tutors, which they are sure to meet with, that the discipline they were kept under, and the lectures that were read to them, were but the formalities of education, and the restraints of childhood ; that the freedom belonging to men, is to take their swing in a full enjoyment of what was before forbidden them. . . . The only fence against the world is a thorough knowledge of it. . . .

[1] Italic type is used to indicate a summary of a passage inserted in editions later than the first.

This, I confess, containing one great part of wisdom, is not the product of some superficial thoughts, or much reading; but the effect of experience and observation in a man, who has lived in the world with his eyes open, and conversed with men of all sorts. And therefore I think it of most value to be instilled into a young man, upon all occasions which offer themselves, that, when he comes to launch into the deep himself, he may not be like one at sea without a line, compass, or sea-chart; but may have some notice beforehand of the rocks and shoals, the currents and quicksands, and know a little how to steer, that he sink not, before he get experience. He that thinks not this of more moment to his son, and for which he more needs a governor, than the languages and learned sciences, forgets of how much more use it is to judge right of men, and manage his affairs wisely with them, than to speak Greek and Latin, or argue in mood and figure;[1] or to have his head filled with the abstruse speculations of natural philosophy, and metaphysics; nay, than to be well versed in Greek and Roman writers, though that be much better for a gentleman, than to be a good Peripatetic or Cartesian:[2] because those ancient authors observed and painted mankind well, and give the best light into that kind of knowledge. He that goes into the eastern parts of Asia, will find able and acceptable men, without any of these: But without virtue, knowledge of the world, and civility, an accomplished and valuable man can be found nowhere.

A great part of the learning now in fashion in the schools of Europe, and that goes ordinarily into the round of education, a gentleman may, in a good measure, be unfurnished with, without any great disparagement to himself, or prejudice to his affairs.[3] But prudence and good breeding are, in all the stations and occurrences of life, necessary; and most young men suffer in the want

[1] *I.e.*, to be expert in formal logic, "hog-shearing," as Locke liked to term it.

[2] *I.e.*, an adherent of Aristotle or of Descartes, of the ancient or of the modern philosophy.   [3] See Introduction, p. 3.

of them; and come rawer, and more awkward, into the
world, than they should, for this very reason; because
these qualities, which are, of all other, the most necessary
to be taught, and stand most in need of the assistance
and help of a teacher, are generally neglected, and
thought but a slight, or no part of a tutor's business.
Latin and learning make all the noise: and the main
stress is laid upon his proficiency in things, a great part
whereof belongs not to a gentleman's calling; which is,
to have the knowledge of a man of business, a carriage[1]
suitable to his rank, and to be eminent and useful in his
country, according to his station. Whenever either spare
hours from that, or an inclination to perfect himself in
some parts of knowledge, which his tutor did but just
enter him in, set him upon any study; the first rudiments of it, which he learned before, will open the way
enough for his own industry to carry him as far as his
fancy will prompt, or his parts enable him to go: or, if
he thinks it may save his time and pains, to be helped
over some difficulties by the hand of a master, he may
then take a man that is perfectly well skilled in it, or
choose such an one as he thinks fittest for his purpose.
But to initiate his pupil in any part of learning, as far
as is necessary for a young man in the ordinary course
of his studies, an ordinary skill in the governor is enough.
Nor is it requisite that he should be a thorough scholar,
or possess in perfection all those sciences, which it is
convenient a young gentleman should have a taste of,
in some general view, or short system. A gentleman,
that would penetrate deeper, must do it by his own
genius and industry afterwards; for nobody ever went
far in knowledge, or became eminent in any of the
sciences, by the discipline and constraint of a master.[2]

The great work of a governor is to fashion the carriage,
and form the mind; to settle in his pupil good habits,
and the principles of virtue and wisdom; to give him,
by little and little, a view of mankind; and work him

[1] Deportment, bearing.
[2] This is the keynote of the "Conduct of the Understanding."

into a love and imitation of what is excellent and praise-
worthy; and in the prosecution of it, to give him vigour,
activity, and industry. The studies which he sets him
upon, are but, as it were, the exercises of his faculties,
and employment of his time, to keep him from sauntering
and idleness, to teach him application, and accustom him
to take pains, and to give him some little taste of what
his own industry must perfect. For who expects, that
under a tutor a young gentleman should be an accomplished critic, orator, or logician; go to the bottom of
metaphysics, natural philosophy, or mathematics; or be
a master in history or chronology? Though something
of each of these is to be taught him: but it is only to
open the door, that he may look in, and, as it were, begin
an acquaintance, but not to dwell there: and a governor
would be much blamed, that should keep his pupil too
long, and lead him too far in most of them. But of good
breeding, knowledge of the world, virtue, industry, and
a love of reputation, he cannot have too much: and if
he have these, he will not long want what he needs or
desires of the other.

And since it cannot be hoped, he should have time
and strength to learn all things, most pains should be
taken about that which is most necessary; and that
principally looked after, which will be of most and
frequentest use to him in the world.

Seneca complains of the contrary practice in his time;
and yet the Burgersdiciuses and the Scheiblers[1] did not
swarm in those days, as they do now in these. What
would he have thought, if he had lived now, when the

[1] Franco Burgersdijck (1590-1635) was the author of a long-
celebrated and widely-read textbook of logic (*Institutiones Logi-
carum libri duo*, Leyden, 1626) which was read by undergraduates
in their first year at Cambridge so late as 1710. Waterland (*Advice
to a Student*, 1706) recommends it as a first book on its subject.
Christoph Scheibler was the author of a "philosophic com-
pendium" which, in less than 200 small pages of Latin, set forth
the principles of logic, metaphysics, physics, geometry, astronomy,
optics, ethics, politics, and economics. The sixth edition of
Scheibler's *Philosophia Compendiosa* is dated 1639 (Oxford).

tutors think it their great business to fill the studies and heads of their pupils with such authors as these? He would have had much more reason to say, as he does, " Non vitæ, sed scholæ discimus," we learn not to live, but to dispute, and our education fits us rather for the university than the world. But it is no wonder, if those who make the fashion suit it to what they have, and not to what their pupils want. The fashion being once established, who can think it strange, that in this, as well as in all other things, it should prevail; and that the greatest part of those, who find their account in an easy submission to it, should be ready to cry out heresy, when anyone departs from it? It is nevertheless matter of astonishment, that men of quality and parts should suffer themselves to be so far misled by custom and implicit faith. Reason, if consulted with, would advise that their children's time should be spent in acquiring what might be useful to them, when they come to be men, rather than to have their heads stuffed with a deal of trash, a great part whereof they usually never do (it is certain they never need to) think on again as long as they live; and so much of it, as does stick by them, they are only the worse for. This is so well known that I appeal to parents themselves, who have been at cost to have their young heirs taught it, whether it be not ridiculous for their sons to have any tincture of that sort of learning, when they come abroad into the world : whether any appearance of it would not lessen and disgrace them in company. And that certainly must be an admirable acquisition, and deserves well to make a part in education, which men are ashamed of, where they are most concerned to show their parts and breeding.

There is yet another reason why politeness of manners and knowledge of the world should principally be looked after in a tutor : and that is, because a man of parts and years may enter a lad far enough in any of those sciences which he has no deep insight into himself. Books in these will be able to furnish him, and give him light and precedency enough, to go before a young follower; but

he will never be able to set another right in the knowledge of the world, and above all, in breeding, who is a
novice in them himself.

This is a knowledge he must have about him, worn
into him by use and conversation, and a long forming
himself by what he has observed to be practised and
allowed in the best company. This, if he has it not of
his own, is no where to be borrowed, for the use of his
pupil; or if he could find pertinent treatises of it in
books, that would reach all the particulars of an English
gentleman's behaviour, his own ill-fashioned example, if
he be not well-bred himself, would spoil all his lectures;
it being impossible, that any one should come forth well-
fashioned out of unpolished, ill-bred company.

I say this, not that I think such a tutor is every day
to be met with, or to be had at the ordinary rates: but
that those, who are able, may not be sparing of inquiry
or cost, in what is of so great moment; and that other
parents, whose estates will not reach to greater salaries,
may yet remember what they should principally have an
eye to in the choice of one to whom they would commit
the education of their children; and what part they
should chiefly look after themselves, whilst they are
under their care, and as often as they come within their
observation; and not think that all lies in Latin and
French, or some dry systems of logic and philosophy.]

95.[1] *Familiarity.*—But to return to our method again.
Though I have mentioned the severity of the father's
brow, and the awe settled thereby in the mind of
children when young, as one main foundation whereby
their education is to be managed; yet I am far from
being of an opinion that it should be continued all along
to them, whilst they are under the discipline and
government of pupilage. I think it should be relaxed,
as fast as their age, discretion, and good behaviour could
allow it; even to that degree, that a father will do well,
as his son grows up and is capable of it, to talk
familiarly with him; nay, ask his advice and consult

[1] Sec. 91 in first edition.

with him about those things wherein he has any knowledge or understanding. By this the father will gain two things, both of great moment. The one is, that it will put serious considerations into his son's thoughts, better than any rules or advices he can give him. The sooner you treat him as a man, the sooner he will begin to be one : and if you admit him into serious discourses sometimes with you, you will insensibly raise his mind above the usual amusements of youth, and those trifling occupations which it is commonly wasted in. For it is easy to observe, that many young men continue longer in the thought and conversation of school-boys, than otherwise they would, because their parents keep them at that distance, and in that low rank, by all their carriage to them.

96. Another thing of greater consequence, which you will obtain by such a way of treating him, will be his friendship. Many fathers, though they proportion to their sons liberal allowances, according to their age and condition; yet they keep them as much unacquainted with their estates and all other concernments as if they were strangers. This if it looks not like jealousy, yet it wants those marks of kindness and intimacy, which a father should show to his son ; and, no doubt, often hinders or abates that cheerfulness and satisfaction, wherewith a son should address himself to, and rely upon, his father. And I cannot but often wonder to see fathers, who love their sons very well, yet so order the matter, by a constant stiffness, and a mien of authority and distance to them all their lives, as if they were never to enjoy or have any comfort from those they love best in the world, till they had lost them by being removed into another. Nothing cements and establishes friendship and good-will, so much as confident communication of concernments and affairs. Other kindnesses without this, leave still some doubts ; but when your son sees you open your mind to him, that you interest him in your affairs, as things you are willing should in their turn come into his hands, he will be concerned for them as for

his own; wait his season with patience, and love you in
the meantime, who keep him not at the distance of a
stranger. This will also make him see, that the enjoyment you have is not without care; which the more he is
sensible of, the less will he envy you the possession, and
the more think himself happy under the management
of so favourable a friend, and so careful a father. There
is scarce any young man of so little thought, or so void
of sense, that would not be glad of a sure friend, that he
might have recourse to, and freely consult on occasion.
The reservedness and distance that fathers keep, often
deprives their sons of that refuge, which would be of
more advantage to them than an hundred rebukes and
chidings. Would your son engage in some frolic, or take
a vagary,[1] were it not much better he should do it with,
than without your knowledge? For since allowances
for such things must be made to young men, the more
you know of his intrigues and designs, the better will
you be able to prevent great mischiefs; and, by letting
him see what is like to follow, take the right way of
prevailing with him to avoid less inconveniences.[2] Would
you have him open his heart to you, and ask your advice?
You must begin to do so with him first, and by your
carriage beget that confidence.

97. But whatever he consults you about, unless it lead
to some fatal and irremediable mischief, be sure you
advise only as a friend of more experience; but with
your advice mingle nothing of command or authority, no
more than you would to your equal, or a stranger. That
would be to drive him for ever from any farther demanding, or receiving advantage from your counsel. You
must consider, that he is a young man, and has pleasures
and fancies, which you are past. You must not expect
his inclinations should be just as yours, nor that at twenty

---

[1] A departure from the ordinary routine, "a day off," an "out-
leap" (sec. 97). This section should be compared with Montaigne's
Essay already mentioned, ii., chap. viii., "On the Affection of
Fathers for their Children."

[2] *I.e.*, inconveniences which are less than "great mischiefs."

he should have the same thoughts you have at fifty. All that you can wish is, that since youth must have some liberty, some out-leaps, they might be with the ingenuity[1] of a son, and under the eye of a father, and then no very great harm can come of it. The way to obtain this, as I said before, is (according as you find him capable) to talk with him about your affairs, propose matters to him familiarly, and ask his advice; and when he ever lights on the right, follow it as his, and if it succeeds well, let him have the commendation. This will not at all lessen your authority, but increase his love and esteem of you. Whilst you keep your estate, the staff will still be in your own hands; and your authority the surer, the more it is strengthened with confidence and kindness. For you have not that power you ought to have over him, till he comes to be more afraid of offending so good a friend, than of losing some part of his future expectation.

98. *Familiar discourse is a mode of discipline which should also be used by the tutor.*

99. *Reverence.*—When, by making your son sensible that he depends on you, and is in your power, you have established your authority; and by being inflexibly severe in your carriage to him, when obstinately persisting in any ill-natured trick which you have forbidden, especially lying, you have imprinted on his mind that awe which is necessary; and on the other side, when (by permitting him the full liberty due to his age, and laying no restraint in your presence to those childish actions, and gaiety of carriage, which, whilst he is very young, is as necessary to him as meat or sleep) you have reconciled him to your company, and made him sensible of your care and love of him by indulgence and tenderness, especially caressing him on all occasions wherein he does any thing well, and being kind to him after a thousand fashions, suitable to his age, which nature teaches parents better than I can: when, I say, by these ways of tenderness and affection, which parents never want for their children, you have also planted in him a particular affec-

---

[1] *I.e.*, ingenuousness.

tion for you, he is then in the state you could desire, and
you have formed in his mind that true reverence, which is
always afterwards carefully to be increased and maintained in both parts of it, love and fear, as the great
principles whereby you will always have hold upon him
to turn his mind to the ways of virtue and honour.

100. *Temper.*—When this foundation is once well laid,
and you find this reverence begin to work in him, the
next thing to be done, is carefully to consider his temper,[1]
and the particular constitution of his mind.   Stubbornness, lying, and ill-natured actions, are not (as has been
said) to be permitted in him from the beginning, whatever his temper be : those seeds of vices are not to be
suffered to take any root, but must be suppressed in
their appearance ; and your authority is to be established
from the very dawning of any knowledge in him, that it
may operate as a natural principle, whereof he never
perceived the beginning, never knew what it was, or
could be otherwise.   By this, if the reverence he owes
you be established early, it will always be sacred to him,
and it will be as hard for him to resist it as the principles
of his nature.

101. Having thus very early established your authority,
and, by the gentler applications of it, shamed him out of
what leads towards any immoral habit ; as soon as you
have observed it in him (for I would by no means have
chiding used, much less blows, till obstinacy and in-
corrigibleness make it absolutely necessary), it will be
fit to consider which way the natural make of his mind
inclines him.   Some men, by the unalterable frame of
their constitutions, are stout, others timorous ; some confident, others modest, tractable or obstinate, curious or
careless.   There are not more differences in men's faces,
and the outward lineaments of their bodies, than there
are in the makes and tempers of their minds[2] ; only there
is this difference, that the distinguishing characters of
the face, and the lineaments of the body, grow more

[1] Temperament.
[2] *Cf.* secs. 139, 176, 216, and see *Conduct*, sec. 2.

plain and visible with time and age, but the peculiar physiognomy of the mind is most discernible in children, before art and cunning have taught them to hide their deformities, and conceal their ill inclinations under a dissembled outside.

102.[1] Begin therefore betimes nicely to observe your son's temper, and that, when he is under least restraint. See what are his predominant passions and prevailing inclinations; whether he be fierce or mild, bold or bashful, compassionate or cruel, open or reserved, etc. For as these are different in him, so are your methods to be different, and your authority must hence take measures to apply it self [in] different ways to him. These native propensities,[2] these prevalences of constitution, are not to be cured by rules, or a direct contest, especially those of them that are the humbler and meaner sort, which proceed from fear and lowness of spirit; though with art they may be much mended, and turned to good purposes. But of this be sure, after all is done, the bias will always hang on that side that nature first placed it : and, if you carefully observe the characters of his mind now in the first scenes of his life, you will ever after be able to judge which way his thoughts lean, and what he aims at even hereafter, when, as he grows up, the plot thickens, and he puts on several shapes to act it.

103. *Dominion.*—I told you before, that children love liberty,[3] and therefore they should be brought to do the things that are fit for them, without feeling any restraint laid upon them. I now tell you, they love something more ; and that is dominion : and this is the first original of most vicious habits, that are ordinary and natural. This love of power and dominion shews itself very early, and that in these two things.

104. We see children (as soon almost as they are born, I am sure long before they can speak) cry, grow peevish, sullen, and out of humour, for nothing but to have their wills. They would have their desires submitted to by

[1] Sec. 97 in first edition.   [2] "Propensions" in text.
[3] Secs. 73-76, 103, 128-9, 148-154, 167, 202.

others; they contend for a ready compliance from all about them, especially from those that stand near or beneath them in age or degree, as soon as they come to consider others with those distinctions.

105.[1] Another thing, wherein they show their love of dominion, is their desire to have things to be theirs; they would have propriety and possession, pleasing themselves with the power [which] that seems to give, and the right they thereby have to dispose of them as they please. He that has not observed these two humours working very betimes in children, has taken little notice of their actions : and he that thinks that these two roots of almost all the injustice and contention that so disturb human life, are not early to be weeded out, and contrary habits introduced, neglects the proper season to lay the foundations of a good and worthy man. To do this, I imagine, these following things may somewhat conduce.

106. 1. *Craving.*—That a child should never be suffered to have what he craves, or so much as speaks for, much less if he cries for it. What then, would you not have them declare their wants ? Yes, that is very fit; and 'tis as fit that with all tenderness they should be hearkened to, and supplied, at least whilst they are very little. But 'tis one thing to say, I am hungry; another to say, I would have roast-meat. Having declared their wants, their natural wants, the pain they feel from hunger, thirst, cold, or any other necessity of nature, 'tis the duty of their parents, and those about them, to relieve them : but children must leave it to the choice and ordering of their parents what they think properest for them, and how much; and must not be permitted to choose for themselves, and say, I would have wine, or white-bread; the very naming of it should make them lose it.

107.[2] This is for natural wants which must be relieved; but for all wants of fancy and affectation, they should never, if once declared, be hearkened to, or complied with. By this means they will be brought to get a

<hr />

[1] Sec. 100 in first edition.   [2] Sec. 102 in first edition.

mastery over their inclinations, and learn the art of stifling their desires as soon as they rise up in them, and before they take vent, when they are easiest to be subdued, which will be of great use to them in the future course of their lives. By this I do not mean that they should not have the things that one perceives would delight them; 'twould be inhumanity and not prudence to treat them so. But they should not have the liberty to carve or crave anything to themselves; they should be exercised in keeping their desires under, till they have got the habit of it, and it be grown easy; they should accustom themselves to be content in the want of what they wished for; and the more they practised modesty and temperance in this, the more should those about them study to reward them with what is suited and acceptable to them; which should be bestowed on them, as if it were a natural consequence[1] of their good behaviour, and not a bargain about it. But you will lose your labour, and what is more, their love and reverence too, if they can receive from others what you deny them. This is to be kept very stanch,[2] and carefully to be watched. And here the servants come again in my way.

108. *Curiosity.*—If this be begun betimes, and they accustom themselves early to silence their desires, this useful habit will settle in them; and, as they come to grow up in age and discretion, they may be allowed greater liberty; when reason comes to speak in them, and not passion. For whenever reason would speak, it should be hearkened to. But, as they should never be heard, when they speak for any thing they would have, unless it be first proposed to them; so they should always be heard, and fairly and kindly answered, when they ask after anything they would know, and desire to be informed about. Curiosity should be as carefully cherished in children, as other appetites suppressed.[3]

[1] See secs. 43-61, 72, 84, 124.
[2] *I.e.*, to be very stiffly adhered to.
[3] See sec. 118.

109. 2. *Complaints.*—Children, who live together, often strive for mastery, whose wills shall carry it over the rest; whoever begins the contest, should be sure to be crossed in it. But not only that, but they should be taught to have all the deference, complaisance, and civility one for the other imaginable. This, when they see it procures them respect, and that they lose no superiority by it, but on the contrary, they grow into love and esteem with every body, they will take more pleasure in, than in insolent domineering; for so plainly is the other.

The complaints of children once against another, which is usually but the desiring the assistance of another to revenge them, should not be favourably received, nor hearkened to. It weakens and effeminates their minds to suffer them to complain: and if they endure sometimes crossing or pain from others, without being permitted to think it strange or intolerable, it will do them no harm to learn sufferance, and harden them early. But, though you give no countenance to the complaints of the querulous, yet take care to suppress all insolence and ill-nature. When you observe it yourself, reprove it before the injured party: but if the complaint be of something really worth your notice and prevention another time, then reprove the offender by himself alone, out of sight of him that complained, and make him go and ask pardon, and make reparation. Which coming thus, as it were, from himself, will be the more cheerfully performed, and more kindly received, the love strengthened between them, and a custom of civility grow familiar amongst your children.

110. 3. *Liberality.*—As to the having and possessing of things, teach them to part with what they have easily and freely to their friends; and let them find by experience, that the most liberal has always most plenty, with esteem and commendation to boot, and they will quickly learn to practise it. This, I imagine, will make brothers and sisters kinder and civiller to one another, and consequently to others, than twenty rules about good manners, with which children are ordinarily perplexed

and cumbered. Covetousness, and the desire of having in our possession, and under our dominion, more than we have need of, being the root of all evil, should be early and carefully weeded out; and the contrary quality, of a readiness to impart to others, implanted. This should be encouraged by great commendation and credit, and constantly taking care, that he loses nothing by his liberality. Let all the instances he gives of such freeness be always repaid, and with interest; and let him sensibly perceive, that the kindness he shows to others is no ill husbandry for himself;[1] but that it brings a return of kindness, both from those that receive it, and those who look on. Make this a contest among children, who shall out-do one another this way. And by this means, by a constant practice, children having made it easy to themselves to part with what they have, goodnature may be settled in them into an habit, and they may take pleasure, and pique themselves in being kind, liberal, and civil to others.

111. *Crying.*—Crying is a fault that should not be tolerated in children; not only for the unpleasant and unbecoming noise it fills the house with, but for more considerable reasons, in reference to the children themselves, which is to be our aim in education.

Their crying is of two sorts; either stubborn and domineering, or querulous and whining.

1. Their crying is very often a contention for mastery, and an open declaration of their insolence or obstinacy; when they have not the power to obtain their desire, they will, by their clamour and sobbing, maintain their title and right to it. This is open justifying themselves, and a sort of remonstrance of the unjustness of the oppression which denies them what they have a mind to.

112. 2. Sometimes their crying is the effect of pain or true sorrow, and a bemoaning themselves under it.

These two, if carefully observed, may, by the mien, looks, and actions, and particularly by the tone of their

---

[1] *Cf.* sec. 119.

crying, be easily distinguished; but neither of them must be suffered, much less encouraged.

1. The obstinate or stomachful crying should by no means be permitted; because it is but another way of flattering their desires, and encouraging those passions, which 'tis our main business to subdue : and if it be, as often it is, upon the receiving any correction, it quite defeats all the good effects of it; for any chastisement, which leaves them in this declared opposition, only serves to make them worse. The restraints and punishments laid on children are all misapplied and lost, as far as they do not prevail over their wills, teach them to submit their passions, and make their minds supple and pliant to what their parents' reason advises them now, and so prepare them to obey what their own reason shall advise hereafter. But if, in anything wherein they are crossed, they may be suffered to go away crying, they confirm themselves in their desires, and cherish the ill humour, with a declaration of their right, and a resolution to satisfy their inclination the first opportunity. This therefore is another reason why you should seldom chastise your children : for, whenever you come to that extremity, 'tis not enough to whip or beat them; you must do it till you find you have subdued their minds; till with submission and patience they yield to the correction; which you shall best discover by their crying, and their ceasing from it upon your bidding. Without this, the beating of children is but a passionate tyranny over them : and it is mere cruelty, and not correction, to put their bodies in pain, without doing their minds any good. As this gives us a reason why children should seldom be corrected, so it also prevents their being so. For if, whenever they are chastised, it were done thus without passion, soberly and yet effectually too, laying on the blows and smart, not all at once, but slowly, with reasoning between, and with observation how it wrought, stopping when it had made them pliant, penitent and yielding; they would seldom need the like punishment again, being made careful to avoid the fault that deserved it. Besides, by

this means, as the punishment would not be lost, for
being too little, and not effectual, so it would be kept
from being too much, if we gave off as soon as we perceived that it reached the mind, and that was bettered.
For since the chiding or beating of children should be
always the least that possibly may be, that which is laid
on in the heat of anger, seldom observes that measure,
but is commonly more than it should be, though it prove
less than enough.

113. 2. Many children are apt to cry, upon any little
pain they suffer; and the least harm that befalls them,
puts them into complaints and bawling. This few
children avoid : for it being the first and natural way to
declare their sufferings or wants, before they can speak,
the compassion that is thought due to that tender age,
foolishly encourages, and continues it in them long
after they can speak. 'Tis the duty, I confess, of those
about children, to compassionate them, whenever they
suffer any hurt; but not to show it in pitying them.
Help and ease them the best you can, but by no means
bemoan them. This softens their minds, and makes the
little harms that happen to them sink deep into that
part which alone feels, and make larger wounds there,
than otherwise they would. They should be hardened
against all sufferings, especially of the body, and have a
tenderness only of shame and for reputation. The many
inconveniences this life is exposed to, require we should
not be too sensible of every little hurt. What our minds
yield not to, makes but a slight impression, and does us
but very little harm; 'tis the suffering of our spirits that
gives and continues the pain. This brawniness and
insensibility of mind, is the best armour we can have
against the common evils and accidents of life; and
being a temper that is to be got by exercise and custom,
more than any other way, the practice of it should be
begun betimes, and happy is he that is taught it early.
That effeminacy of spirit, which is to be prevented or
cured, as nothing, that I know, so much increases in
children as crying; so nothing, on the other side, so

much checks and restrains, as their being hindered from that sort of complaining.   In the little harms they suffer, from knocks and falls, they should not be pitied for falling, but bid do so again ; which is a better way to cure their falling than either chiding or bemoaning them.   But, let the hurts they receive be what they will, stop their crying, and that will give them more quiet and ease at present, and harden them for the future.

114. The former sort of crying requires severity to silence it ; and where a look, or a positive command, will not do it, blows must.   For it proceeding from pride, obstinacy and wilfulness, the will, where the fault lies, must be bent, and made to comply, by a rigour sufficient to subdue it : but this latter, being ordinarily from soft- ness of mind, a quite contrary cause, ought to be treated with a gentler hand.   Persuasion, or diverting the thoughts another way, or laughing at their whining, may perhaps be at first the proper method.   But for this, the circumstances of the thing, and the particular temper of the child, must be considered : no certain unvariable rules can be given about it; but it must be left to the prudence of the parents or tutor.   But this I think I may say in general, that there should be a constant discountenancing of this sort of crying also ; and that the father, by his looks, words, and authority, should always stop it, mixing a greater degree of rough- ness in his looks or words, proportionably as the child is of a greater age, or a sturdier temper ; but always let it be enough to master the disorder.

[115. *Children should be trained to be courageous.* Keep children from frights of all kinds when they are young. . . .   By gentle degrees accustom them to things they are too much afraid of. . . .   Inuring children gently to suffer some degrees of pain without shrinking is a way to gain firmness to their minds.]

116.[1] *Cruelty.*—One thing I have frequently observed in children, that when they have got possession of any

---

[1] Sec. 110 in first edition.

poor creature, they are apt to use it ill; they often torment and treat very roughly young birds, butterflies, and such other poor animals which fall into their hands, and that with a seeming kind of pleasure. This, I think, should be watched in them; and if they incline to any such cruelty, they should be taught the contrary usage; for the custom of tormenting and killing of beasts will, by degrees, harden their minds even towards men; and they who delight in the suffering and destruction of inferior creatures, will not be apt to be very compassionate or benign to those of their own kind. Our practice takes notice of this, in the exclusion of butchers from juries of life and death. Children should from the beginning be bred up in an abhorrence of killing or tormenting any living creature, and be taught not to spoil or destroy anything, unless it be for the preservation or advantage of some other that is nobler. And truly, if the preservation of all mankind, as much as in him lies, were every one's persuasion, as indeed it is every one's duty, and the true principle to regulate our religion, politics, and morality by, the world would be much quieter and better natured than it is. But to return to our present business; I cannot but commend both the kindness and prudence of a mother I knew, who was wont always to indulge her daughters, when any of them desired dogs, squirrels, birds, or any such things, as young girls use[1] to be delighted with: but then, when they had them, they must be sure to keep them well, and look diligently after them, that they wanted nothing, or were not ill used; for, if they were negligent in their care of them, it was counted a great fault, which often forfeited their possession; or at least they failed not to be rebuked for it, whereby they were early taught diligence and good-nature. And, indeed, I think people should be accustomed from their cradles to be tender to all sensible creatures, and to spoil or waste nothing at all. This delight they take in doing of mischief, whereby I mean spoiling of any thing to no

_____
[1] *I.e.*, are accustomed.

purpose, but more especially the pleasure they take to put any thing in pain that is capable of it, I cannot persuade myself to be any other than a foreign and introduced disposition, a habit borrowed from custom and conversation.[1] People teach children to strike, and laugh when they hurt, or see harm come to others; and they have the examples of most about them to confirm them in it. All the entertainments of talk and history is of nothing almost but fighting and killing; and the honour and renown that is bestowed on conquerors (who for the most part are but the great butchers of mankind), farther mislead growing youths, who by this means come to think slaughter the laudable business of mankind, and the most heroic of virtues. This custom plants unnatural appetites and reconciles us to that which it has laid in the way to honour. Thus, by fashion and opinion, that comes to be a pleasure, which in itself neither is, nor can be any. This ought carefully to be watched, and early remedied, so as to settle and cherish the contrary and more natural temper of benignity and compassion in the room of it; but still by the same gentle methods, which are to be applied to the other two faults before mentioned. But pray remember that the mischiefs or harms that come by play, inadvertency, or ignorance, and were not known to be harms, or designed for mischief's sake, though they may perhaps be sometimes of considerable damage, yet are not at all, or but very gently, to be taken notice of. For this, I think, I cannot too often inculcate, that whatever miscarriage a child is guilty of, and whatever be the consequence of it, the thing to be regarded in taking notice of it, is only what root it springs from, and what habit it is like to establish; and to that the correction ought to be directed, and the child not to suffer any punishment for any harm which may have come by his play or inadvertency. The faults to be amended lie in the mind; and if they are such as either age will cure, or no ill habits will follow from, the present action, whatever displeasing

[1] *I.e.*, intercourse.

circumstances it may have, is to be passed by without any animadversion.

[117. *Children must treat servants with civility.* Children should not be suffered to lose the consideration of human nature in the shufflings of outward conditions.]

118.[1] *Curiosity.*—Curiosity in children (which I had occasion just to mention, section 108) is but an appetite after knowledge, and therefore ought to be encouraged in them, not only as a good sign, but as the great instrument nature has provided to remove that ignorance they were born with, and which, without this busy inquisitiveness, will make them dull and useless creatures. The ways to encourage it, and keep it active and vigorous, are, I suppose, these following:

1. Not to check or discountenance any inquiries he shall make, nor suffer them to be laughed at; but to answer all his questions, and explain the matters he desires to know, so as to make them as much intelligible to him as suits the capacity of his age and knowledge. But confound not his understanding with explications or notions that are above it, or with the variety or number of things that are not to his present purpose. Mark what 'tis his mind aims at in the question, and not what words he expresses it in: and, when you have informed and satisfied him in that, you shall see how his thoughts will proceed on to other things, and how by fit answers to his inquiries he may be led on farther than perhaps you could imagine. For knowledge to the understanding is acceptable as light to the eyes:[2] and children are pleased and delighted with it exceedingly, especially if they see that their inquiries are regarded, and that their desire of knowing is encouraged and commended. And I doubt not, but one great reason why many children abandon themselves wholly to silly sports, and trifle away all their time in trifling, is, because they have

---

[1] Sec. 111 in first edition.
[2] " For knowledge is grateful to the understanding as light to the eyes "—in later editions.

found their curiosity balked, and their inquiries neglected. But had they been treated with more kindness and respect, and their questions answered, as they should, to their satisfaction, I doubt not but they would have taken more pleasure in learning, and improving their knowledge, wherein there would be still newness and variety, which is what they are delighted with, than in returning over and over to the same play and playthings.

119. 2. To this serious answering their questions, and informing their understandings in what they desire, as if it were a matter that needed it, should be added some peculiar ways of commendation.   Let others, whom they esteem, be told before their faces of the knowledge they have in such and such things; and since we are all, even from our cradles, vain and proud creatures, let their vanity be flattered with things that will do them good,[1] and let their pride set them on work on something which may turn to their advantage.   Upon this ground you shall find, that there cannot be a greater spur to the attaining what you would have the eldest learn and know himself, than to set him upon teaching it his younger brothers and sisters.

120. 3. As children's inquiries are not to be slighted, so also great care is to be taken that they never receive deceitful and eluding answers.   They easily perceive when they are slighted or deceived, and quickly learn the trick of neglect, dissimulation and falsehood, which they observe others to make use of.   We are not to entrench upon truth in any conversation, but least of all with children; since, if we play false with them, we not only deceive their expectation, and hinder their knowledge, but corrupt their innocence, and teach them the worst of vices.   They are travellers newly arrived in a strange country, of which they know nothing : we should therefore make conscience not to mislead them.   And though their questions seem sometimes not very material, yet they should be seriously answered; for however they

[1] This advice, like that in section 110 on teaching liberality, has very naturally made Locke many enemies.

may appear to us (to whom they are long since known)
inquiries not worth the making, they are of moment to
those who are wholly ignorant. Children are strangers
to all we are acquainted with; and all the things they
meet with, are at first unknown to them, as they once
were to us : and happy are they who meet with civil
people, that will comply with their ignorance, and help
them to get out of it. If you or I now should be set
down in Japan, with all our prudence and knowledge
about us, a conceit whereof makes us perhaps so apt to
slight the thoughts and inquiries of children; should we,
I say, be set down in Japan, we should, no doubt (if we
would inform ourselves of what is there to be known),
ask a thousand questions, which, to a supercilious or
inconsiderate Japaner, would seem very idle and impertinent; and yet to us would be natural; and we
should be glad to find a man so kind and humane as to
answer them and instruct our ignorance. When any
new thing comes in their way, children usually ask the
common question of a stranger, What is it? whereby
they ordinarily mean nothing but the name; and therefore to tell them how it is called, is usually the proper
answer to that demand. The next question usually is,
What is it for?[1] And to this it should be answered
truly and directly : the use of the thing should be told,
and the way explained, how it serves to such a purpose,
as far as their capacities can comprehend it; and so of
any other circumstances they shall ask about it; not
turning them going till you have given them all the
satisfaction they are capable of, and so leading them by
your answers into farther questions. And perhaps, to a
grown man, such conversation will not be altogether so
idle and insignificant as we are apt to imagine. The
native and untaught suggestions of inquisitive children
do often offer things that may set a considering man's
thoughts on work. And I think there is frequently
more to be learned from the unexpected questions of a
child, than the discourses of men, who talk in a road,

[1] Usually asked at a later stage in the child's development.

according to the notions they have borrowed, and the prejudices of their education.

121.[1] 4. Perhaps it may not sometimes be amiss to excite their curiosity, by bringing strange and new things in their way, on purpose to engage their inquiry, and give them occasion to inform themselves about them; and if by chance their curiosity leads them to ask what they should not know, it is a great deal better to tell them plainly that it is a thing that belongs not to them to know, than to pop them off with a falsehood or a frivolous answer.

122. *Pertness.*—Pertness, that appears sometimes so early, proceeds from a principle that seldom accompanies a strong constitution of body, or ripens into a strong judgment of mind. If it were desirable to have a child a more brisk talker, I believe there might be ways found to make him so; but, I suppose, a wise father had rather that this son should be able and useful, when a man, than pretty company and a diversion to others whilst a child; though, if that too were to be considered, I think I may say, there is not so much pleasure to have a child prattle agreeably as to reason well. Encourage, therefore, his inquisitiveness all you can, by satisfying his demands and informing his judgment as far as it is capable. When his reasons are any way tolerable, let him find the credit and commendation of them; and when they are quite out of the way, let him, without being laughed at for his mistake, be gently put into the right; and, take care, as much as you can, that in this inclination he shews to reasoning about every thing no body balk or impose upon him. For, when all is done, this, as the highest and most important faculty of our minds, deserves the greatest care and attention in cultivating it; the right improvement and exercise of our reason being the highest perfection that a man can attain to in this life.

123. *Sauntering.*—Contrary to this busy inquisitive temper, there is sometimes observable in children a list-

---

[1] Sec. 114 in first edition.

less carelessness, a want of regard to any thing, ang
a sort of trifling, even at their business.   This saunterind
humour I look on as one of the worst qualities that can
appear in a child, as well as one of the hardest to be
cured, where it is natural.   But, it being liable to be
mistaken in some cases, care must be taken to make
a right judgment concerning that trifling at their books
or business, which may sometimes be complained of in a
child.   Upon the first suspicion a father has that his son
is of a sauntering temper, he must carefully observe him,
whether he be listless and indifferent in all his actions,
or whether in some things alone he be slow and sluggish,
but in others vigorous and eager : for though he find
that he does loiter at his book, and let a good deal of
the time he spends in his chamber or study run idly
away, he must not presently conclude that this is from a
sauntering humour in his temper ; it may be childishness, and a preferring something to his study which his
thoughts run on ; and he dislikes his book, as is natural,
because it is forced upon him as a task.[1]   To know this
perfectly, you must watch him at play, when he is out of
his place and time of study, following his own inclinations ; and see there, whether he be vigorous and active ;
whether he designs anything, and with labour and
eagerness pursues it, till he has accomplished what he
aimed at ; or whether he lazily and listlessly dreams
away his time.   If this sloth be only when he is about
his book, I think it may be easily cured ; if it be in his
temper, it will require a little more pains and attention
to remedy it.

124. If you are satisfied, by his earnestness at play, or
any thing else he sets his mind on, in the intervals
between his hours of business, that he is not of himself
inclined to laziness, but that only want of relish of his
book makes him negligent and sluggish in his application to it, the first step is to try, by talking to him
kindly of the folly and inconvenience of it, whereby he
loses a good part of his time, which he might have for

[1] See Introduction, p. 15.

7

his diversion : but be sure to talk calmly and kindly, and not much at first, but only these plain reasons in short.   If this prevails, you have gained the point in the most desirable way, which is reason and kindness.   If it prevails not, try to shame him out of it, by laughing at him for it, asking every day, when he comes to table, if there be no strangers there, " how long he was that day about his business ?"   And if he has not done it, in the time he might be well supposed to have despatched it, expose and turn him into ridicule for it; but mix no chiding, only put on a pretty cold brow towards him, and keep it till he reform; and let his mother, tutor, and all about him, do so too.[1]   If this work not the effect you desire, then tell him he shall be no longer troubled with a tutor to take care of his education : you will not be at the charge to have him spend his time idly with him; but since he prefers this or that (whatever play he delights in) to his book, that only he shall do; and so in earnest set him to work on his beloved play, and keep him steadily and in earnest to it morning and afternoon, till he be fully surfeited, and would, at any rate, change it for some hours at his book again : but when you thus set him a task of his play, you must be sure to look after him yourself, or set somebody else to do it, that may constantly see him employed in it, and that he be not permitted to be idle at that too.   I say, your self look after him; for it is worth the father's while, whatever business he has, to bestow two or three days upon his son, to cure so great a mischief as is sauntering at his business.

125. This is what I propose, if it be idleness not from his general temper, but a peculiar or acquired aversion to learning, which you must be careful to examine and distinguish, which you shall certainly know by the way above proposed.   But though you have your eyes upon him to watch what he does with the time he has at his own disposal, yet you must not let him perceive that you or any body else do so.   For that may restrain him from

<hr>

[1] See sec. 53, *note.*

following his own inclination, and that being the thing his head or heart is upon, and not daring to prosecute it for fear of you, he may forbear doing other things, and so seem to be idle and negligent, when in truth it is nothing but being intent on that which the fear of your eye or knowledge keeps him from executing. You must therefore, when you would try him, give him full liberty; but let some body whom you can trust observe what he does. And it will be best he should have his play-day of liberty, when you and all that he may suspect to have an eye upon him are abroad, that so he may without check follow his natural inclination. Thus by his employing of such times of liberty, you will easily discern whether it be listlessness in his temper, or aversion to his book that makes him saunter away his time of study.

126. If listlessness and dreaming be his natural disposition, this unpromising temper is one of the hardest to be dealt with, because it generally carrying with it an indifferency for future things, may be attributed to want of foresight and want of desire; and how to plant or increase either of these, where Nature has given a cold or contrary temper, is not I think very easy. As soon as it is perceived, the first thing to be done is to find out his most predominate passion, and carefully examine what it is to which the greatest bent of his mind has the most steady and earnest tendency. And when you have found that, you must set that on work to excite his industry to any thing else. If he loves praise, or play, or fine clothes, etc., or, on the other side, dreads shame and disgrace, your displeasure, etc., whatever it be that he loves most, except it be sloth (for that will never set him on work), let that be made use of to excite him to activity. For in this listless temper you are not to fear an excess of appetite (as in all other cases) by cherishing it. 'Tis that which you want, and therefore must labour to stir up and increase. For where there is no desire, there will be no industry.

127. If you have not hold enough upon him this way

to stir up vigour and activity in him, you must employ
him in some constant bodily labour, whereby he may get
a habit of doing something.   The keeping him hard to
some study, were the better way to get him an habit of
exercising and applying his mind.   But, because this is
an invisible attention, and nobody can tell when he is or
is not idle at it, you must find bodily employments for
him, which he must be constantly busied in and kept to ;
and if they have some little hardship and shame in them,
it may not be the worse, to make them the sooner weary
him, and desire to return to his book.   But be sure, when
you exchange his book for his other labour, set him such
a task, to be done in such a time, as may allow him no
opportunity to be idle.   Only, after you have by this
way brought him to be attentive and industrious at his
book, you may, upon his despatching his study within
the time set him, give him as a reward some respite from
his other labour ; which you may diminish, as you find
him grow more and more steady in his application ; and,
at last, wholly take off, when his sauntering at his book
is cured.

128. *Compulsion.*—We formerly observed, that variety
and freedom was that that delighted children, and recommended their plays to them ; and that therefore their
book, or anything we would have them learn, should not
be enjoined them as business.[1]   This their parents, tutors,
and teachers are apt to forget ; and their impatience to
have them busied in what is fit for them to do suffers
them not to deceive them into it : but, by the repeated
injunctions they meet with, children quickly distinguish
between what is required of them and what not.   When
this mistake has once made his book uneasy to him, the
cure is to be applied at the other end.   And since it will be
then too late to endeavour to make it a play to him, you
must take the contrary course ; observe what play he is
most delighted with ; enjoin that, and make him play so
many hours every day, not as a punishment for playing,

[1] Secs. 72-74, 84, 123, 148, 149, 167, 202.   *Cf.* secs. 126, 127, and
see Introduction, p. 15.

but as if it were the business required of him.   This, if
I mistake not, will, in a few days, make him so weary of
his most beloved sport, that he will prefer his book, or
any thing to it, especially if it may redeem him from any
part of the task of play that is set him; and he may be
suffered to employ some part of the time destined to his
task of play in his book, or such other exercise as is
really useful to him.   This I at least think a better cure
than that forbidding (which usually increases the desire)
or any other punishment that should be made use of to
remedy it.   For when you have once glutted his appetite
(which may safely be done in all things but eating and
drinking), and made him surfeit of what you would have
him avoid, you have put into him a principle of aversion,
and you need not so much fear afterwards his longing
for the same thing again.

129. This, I think, is sufficiently evident, that children
generally hate to be idle.   All the care then is, that their
busy humour should be constantly employed in something
of use to them; which if you will attain, you must make
what you would have them do a recreation to them, and
not a business.   The way to do this, so that they may
not perceive you have any hand in it, is this proposed
here, viz. to make them weary of that which you would
not have them do, by enjoining and making them, under
some pretence or other, do it till they are surfeited.   For
example: Does your son play at top and scourge too
much?   Enjoin him to play so many hours every day,
and look that he do it; and you shall see he will quickly
be sick of it, and willing to leave it.   By this means,
making the recreations you dislike a business to him, he
will of himself with delight betake himself to those things
you would have him do, especially if they be proposed as
rewards for having performed his task in that play which
is commanded him.   For, if he be ordered every day to
whip his top so long as to make him sufficiently weary,
do you not think he will apply himself with eagerness to
his book, and wish for it, if you promise it him as a reward
of having whipped his top lustily, quite out all the time

that is set him?[1] Children, in the things they do, if they comport with their age, find little difference, so they may be doing: the esteem they have for one thing above another, they borrow from others; so that what those about them make to be a reward to them, will really be so. By this art, it is in their governor's choice, whether scotch-hoppers shall reward their dancing, or dancing their scotch-hoppers; whether peg-top, or reading, playing at trap, or studying the globes, shall be more acceptable and pleasing to them; all that they desire being to be busy, and busy, as they imagine, in things of their own choice, and which they receive as favours from their parents, or others for whom they have respect, and with whom they would be in credit. A set of children thus ordered, and kept from the ill example of others, would all of them, I suppose, with as much earnestness and delight, learn to read, write, and what else one would have them, as others do their ordinary plays: and the eldest being thus entered, and this made the fashion of the place, it would be as impossible to hinder them from learning the one, as it is ordinarily to keep them from the other.

130. *Play-games.*—Playthings, I think, children should have, and of all sorts, but still to be in the keeping of their tutors, or somebody else, whereof the child should have in his power but one at once, and should not be suffered to have another, but when he restored that. This teaches them betimes to be careful of not losing or spoiling the things they have; whereas plenty and variety in their own keeping, makes them wanton and careless, and teaches them from the beginning to be squanderers and wasters.[2] These, I confess, are little things, and such as will seem beneath the care of a governor; but nothing that may form children's minds is to be overlooked and neglected: and whatsoever introduces habits, and settles customs in them, deserves the care and attention of their governors, and is not a small thing in its consequences.

---

[1] *I.e.*, throughout the stipulated time.   [2] Secs. 150-154.

[*Except things like battle-dores, which are above their skill, playthings should not be bought, but contrived by children themselves.* "If they sit gaping to have such things drop into their mouths, they should go without them."]

131. *Lying.*—Lying is so ready and cheap a cover for any miscarriage, and so much in fashion amongst all sorts of people, that a child can hardly avoid observing the use is made of it on all occasions, and so can scarce be kept, without great care, from getting into it. But it is so ill a quality, and the mother of so many ill ones that spawn from it and take shelter under it, that a child should be brought up in the greatest abhorrence of it imaginable : it should be always (when occasionally it comes to be mentioned) spoke of before him with the utmost detestation, as a quality so wholly incompetent with a gentleman, that nobody of any credit can bear the imputation of a lie ; that is proper only to beggars'-boys and the abhorred rascality, and not tolerable in any one, who would converse with people of condition, or have any esteem or reputation in the world. And the first time he is found in a lie, it should rather be wondered at, as a monstrous thing in him, than reproved as an ordinary fault. If that keeps him not from relapsing, the next time he must be sharply rebuked, and fall into the state of great displeasure of his father and mother, and all about him, who take notice of it. And if this way work not the cure, you must come to blows ; for, after he has been thus warned, a premeditated lie must always be looked upon as obstinacy, and never be permitted to 'scape unpunished.

132. *Excuses.*—Children, afraid to have their faults seen in their naked colours, will, like the rest of the sons of Adam, be apt to make excuses. This is a fault usually bordering upon, and leading to untruth, and is not to be indulged in them ; but yet, it ought to be cured rather with shame than roughness. If therefore, when a child is questioned for anything, his first answer be an excuse, warn him soberly to tell the truth ; and

then, if he persists to shuffle it off with a falsehood, he must be chastised.   But if he directly confess, you must commend his ingenuity,[1] and pardon the fault, be it what it will; and pardon it so, that you never so much as reproach him with it, or mention it to him again.   For if you would have him in love with ingenuity, and by a constant practice make it habitual to him, you must take care that it never procure him the least inconvenience ; but, on the contrary, his own confession bringing always with it perfect impunity, should be, besides, encouraged by some marks of approbation.   If his excuse be such at any time that you cannot prove it to have any falsehood in it, let it pass for true, and be sure not to show any suspicion of it.   Let him keep up his reputation with you as high as is possible; for, when once he finds he has lost that, you have lost a great and your best hold upon him.   Therefore let him not think he has the character of a liar with you, as long as you can avoid it without flattering him in it.   Thus some slips in truth may be overlooked.   But, after he has once been corrected for a lie, you must be sure never after to pardon it in him, whenever you find, and take notice to him, that he is guilty of it : for it being a fault, which he has been forbid, and may, unless he be wilful, avoid, the repeating of it is perfect perverseness, and must have the chastisement due to that offence.

133. This is what I have thought, concerning the general method of educating a young gentleman ; which, though I am apt to suppose may have some influence on the whole course of his education, yet I am far from imagining it contains all those particulars which his growing years or peculiar temper may require.   But this being premised in general, we shall, in the next place, descend to a more particular consideration of the several parts of his education.

134. That which every gentleman (that takes any care of his education) desires for his son, besides the estate he leaves him, is contained I suppose in these four things,

---

[1] *I.e.*, ingenuousness, candour.

Virtue, Wisdom, Breeding, and Learning. I will not trouble myself whether these names do not some of them sometimes stand for the same thing, or really include one another. It serves my turn here to follow the popular use of these words, which, I presume, is clear enough to make me be understood, and I hope there will be no difficulty to comprehend my meaning.

135. *Virtue.*—I place Virtue as the first and most necessary of those endowments that belong to a man or a gentleman, as absolutely requisite to make him valued and beloved by others, acceptable or tolerable to himself ; without that, I think, he will be happy neither in this nor the other world.

136. *God.*—As the foundation of this, there ought very early to be imprinted on his mind a true notion of God, as of the independent Supreme Being, Author and Maker of all things, from whom we receive all our good, who loves us, and gives us all things ; and, consequent to it, a love and reverence of this Supreme Being. This is enough to begin with, without going to explain this matter any farther, for fear, lest by talking too early to him of spirits, and being unseasonably forward to make him understand the incomprehensible nature of that infinite being, his head be either filled with false, or perplexed with unintelligible notions of him. Let him only be told upon occasion, of God, that made and governs all things, hears and sees everything, and does all manner of good to those that love and obey him. You will find, that being told of such a God, other thoughts will be apt to rise up fast enough in his mind about him ; which, as you observe them to have any mistakes, you must set right. And I think it would be better, if men generally rested in such an idea of God, without being too curious in their notions about a being, which all must acknowledge incomprehensible ; whereby many, who have not strength and clearness of thought to distinguish between what they can, and what they cannot know, run themselves into superstition or atheism, making God like themselves, or (because they cannot comprehend any thing else) none

at all.[1] [And I am apt to think, the keeping children constantly morning and evening to acts of devotion to God, as to their Maker, Preserver, and Benefactor, in some plain and short form of prayer, suitable to their age and capacity, will be of much more use to them in religion, knowledge, and virtue, than to distract their thoughts with curious inquiries into his inscrutable essence and being.]

137. *Spirits.*—Having by gentle degrees, as you find him capable of it, settled such an idea of God in his mind, and taught him to pray to him, forbear any discourse of other spirits, till the mention of them coming in his way, upon occasion hereafter to be set down, and his reading the Scripture history, put him upon that inquiry.[2]

138. *Goblins.*—But even then, and always whilst he is young, be sure to preserve his tender mind from all impressions and notions of sprites and goblins, or any fearful apprehensions in the dark. It being the usual method of servants to awe children, and keep them in subjection, by telling them of Raw-Head and Bloody-Bones, and such other names, as carry with them the ideas of some hurtful, terrible things inhabiting darkness, this must be carefully prevented. For though by this foolish way they may keep them from little faults, yet the remedy is much worse than the disease, and there are stamped upon their minds ideas that follow them with terror and affrightment. For such bugbear thoughts, once got into the tender minds of children, sink deep there, and fasten themselves so, as not easily, if ever, to be got out again ; and whilst they are there, frequently haunt them with strange visions, making children dastards when alone, and afraid of their shadows and darkness all their lives after. For it is to be taken notice, that the first impressions sink deepest into the minds of children, and the notions they are possessed with when young are scarce by any industry or art ever after quite wiped out.

[1] With this deistic creed contrast the recommendations for religious instruction in secs. 157-159 below.
[2] See secs. 191, 192.

I have had those complain to me, when men, who had been thus used when young, that, though their reason corrected the wrong ideas they had taken in, and though they were satisfied that there was no cause to fear invisible beings more in the dark than in the light, yet that these notions were apt still, upon any occasion, to start up first in their prepossessed fancies, and not to be removed without some pains. And, to let you see how lasting frightful images are, that take place in the mind early, I here tell you a pretty remarkable, but true story. There was in a town in the West[1] a man of a disturbed brain, whom the boys used to tease, when he came in their way : this fellow one day, seeing in the street one of those lads that used to vex him, stepped into a cutler's shop he was near, and, there seizing on a naked sword, made after the boy, who seeing him coming so armed, betook himself to his feet, and ran for his life, and by good luck, had strength and heels enough to reach his father's house before the madman could get up to him. The door was only latched ; and when he had the latch in his hand, he turned about his head to see how near his pursuer was, who was at the entrance of the porch, with his sword up ready to strike ; and he had just time to get in and clap-to the door, to avoid the blow, which, though his body escaped, his mind did not. This frightening idea made so deep an impression there, that it lasted many years, if not all his life after ; for telling this story when he was a man, he said, that after that time till then, he never went in at that door (that he could remember) at any time, without looking back, whatever business he had in his head, or how little soever, before he came thither, he thought of this madman.

If children were let alone, they would be no more afraid in the dark than of broad sunshine;[2] they would

[1] The draft of 1684 says, "Gloucester."

[2] It is characteristic of Locke's psychology to explain fear of darkness as a result of personal experience. But many children spontaneously, and quite apart from experience, exhibit fear of darkness and of strangers, two forms of that emotion which were wholesome at a remote period of human history, though they have now outlived their usefulness in normal civilized life.

in their turns as much welcome the one for sleep, as the other to play in ; there should be no distinction made to them, by any discourse, of more danger or terrible things in the one than the other. But, if the folly of any one about them should do them this harm, to make them think there is any difference between being in the dark and winking, you must get it out of their minds as soon as you can ; and let them know that God, who made all things good for them, made the night, that they might sleep the better and the quieter ; and that they being under his protection, there is nothing in the dark to hurt them. What is to be known more of God and good spirits is to be deferred till the time we shall hereafter mention ; and of evil spirits, it will be well if you can keep him from wrong fancies about them, till he is ripe for that sort of knowledge.

139. *Truth.*—Having laid the foundations of virtue in a true notion of a God, such as the creed wisely teaches, as far as his age is capable, and by accustoming him to pray to him, the next thing to be taken care of, is to keep him exactly to speaking of truth, and by all the ways imaginable inclining him to be good-natured. Let him know, that twenty faults are sooner to be forgiven, than the straining of truth to cover any one by an excuse. And to teach him betimes to love and be good-natured to others, is to lay early the true foundation of an honest man ; all injustice generally springing from too great love of ourselves and too little of others.

This is all I shall say of this matter in general, and is enough for laying the first foundations of virtue in a child. As he grows up, the tendency of his natural inclination[1] must be observed ; which, as it inclines him, more than is convenient, on one or t'other side, from the right path of virtue, ought to have proper remedies applied. For few of Adam's children are so happy as not to be born with some bias in their natural temper, which it is the business of education either to take off, or counterbalance : but to enter into particulars of this

[1] See sec. 101, *note.*

would be beyond the design of this short treatise of education. I intend not a discourse of all the virtues and vices, and how each virtue is to be attained, and every particular vice by its peculiar remedies cured ; though I have mentioned some of the most ordinary faults, and the ways to be used in correcting them.

140. *Wisdom.*—Wisdom I take, in the popular acceptation, for a man's managing his business ably and with foresight in this world. This is the product of a good natural temper, application of mind and experience together, and not to be taught children. The greatest thing that in them can be done towards it, is to hinder them, as much as may be, from being cunning ; which, being the ape of wisdom, is the most distant from it that can be : and as[1] an ape, for[2] the likeness it has to a man, wanting what really should make him so, is by so much the uglier. Cunning is only the want of understanding ; which, because it cannot compass its ends by direct ways, would do it by a trick and circumvention ; and the mischief of it is, a cunning trick helps but once, but hinders ever after. No cover was ever made either so big or so fine as to hide itself. Nobody was ever so cunning, as to conceal their being so : and when they are once discovered, every body is shy, every body distrustful of crafty men ; and all the world forwardly join to oppose and defeat them : whilst the open, fair, wise man has every body to make way for him, and goes directly to his business. To accustom a child to have true notions of things, and not to be satisfied till he has them ; to raise his mind to great and worthy thoughts ; and to keep him at a distance from falsehood and cunning, which has always a broad mixture of falsehood in it, is the fittest preparation of a child for wisdom, which being learned from time, experience, and observation, and an acquaintance with men, their tempers and designs [is] not to be expected in the ignorance and inadvertency of childhood, or the inconsiderate heat and unwariness of youth : all that can be done towards it, during this unripe age, is,

[1] *I.e.*, like. [2] *I.e.*, because of.

as I have said, to accustom them to truth and submission
to reason ; and, as much as may be, to reflection on their
own actions.

141. *Breeding.*—The next good quality belonging to a
gentleman is good breeding. There are two sorts of ill
breeding ; the one, a sheepish bashfulness ; and the other,
a misbecoming negligence and disrespect in our carriage ;
both which are avoided by duly observing this one rule,
*Not to think meanly of ourselves, and not to think meanly
of others.*[1]

142. The first part of this rule must not be understood
in opposition to humility, but to assurance. We ought
not to think so well of ourselves as to stand upon our
own value ; or assume a preference to others, because of
any advantage we may imagine we have over them ; but
modestly to take what is offered, when it is our due.
But yet we ought to think so well of ourselves, as to
perform those actions which are incumbent on and expected of us, without discomposure or disorder, in whose
presence soever we are, keeping that respect and distance
which is due to every one's rank and quality. There is
often in people, especially children, a clownish shame-
facedness before strangers, or those above them ; they are
confounded in their thoughts, words, and looks, and so
lose themselves in that confusion, as not to be able to
do any thing, or at least not to do it with that freedom
and gracefulness which pleases and makes them acceptable. The only cure for this, as for any miscarriage, is
by use to introduce the contrary habit. But since we
cannot accustom ourselves to converse with strangers
and persons of quality without being in their company,
nothing can cure this part of ill breeding but change
and variety of company, and that of persons above us.

143. As the before-mentioned consists in too great a
concern how to behave ourselves towards others, so the
other part of ill breeding lies in the appearance of too
little care of pleasing or showing respect to those we have

[1] With secs. 141-146 *cf.* Montaigne, i., chap. xxv., " En cette
eschole du commerce des hommes," etc., and i., chap. xxiii.

to do with. To avoid these, two things are requisite: first, a disposition of the mind not to offend others : and, secondly, the most acceptable and agreeable way of expressing that disposition. From the one, men are called civil : from the other, well-fashioned. The latter of these is that decency and gracefulness of looks, voice, words, motions, gestures, and of all the whole outward demeanour which pleases in company, and makes those easy and delighted whom we converse with. This is, as it were, the language whereby that internal civility of the mind is expressed ; and being very much governed by the fashion and custom of every country, as other languages are, must, in the rules and practice of it, be learned chiefly from observation, and the carriage of those who are allowed to be exactly well-bred. The other part, which lies in the mind, is that general good-will and regard for all people, which makes any one have a care not to show, in his carriage, any contempt, dis-respect, or neglect of them ; but to express, according to the fashion and way of that country, a respect and value for them, according to their rank and condition.

144. There is another fault in good manners, and that is, excess of ceremony, and an obstinate persisting to force upon another what is not his due, and what he cannot take without folly or shame. This seems rather a design to expose than oblige, or at least looks like a contest for mastery ; and at best is but troublesome, and so can be no part of good breeding, which has no other use nor end but to make people easy and satisfied in their conversation with us. This is a fault few young people are apt to fall into ; but yet, if they are ever guilty of it, or are suspected to incline that way, they should be told of it, and warned of this mistaken civility. The thing they should endeavour and aim at in conversa-tion, should be to show respect, esteem, and good-will, by paying to every one that common ceremony and regard which is in civility due to them. To do this, without a suspicion of flattery, dissimulation, or meanness, is a great skill, which good sense, reason and good company

can only teach ; but is of so much use in civil life, that it
is well worth the studying.

145. Though the managing ourselves well in this part
of our behaviour has the name of good breeding, as if
peculiarly the effect of education ; yet, as I have said,
young children should not be much perplexed about it ;
I mean, about putting off their hats and making legs
modishly.[1]   Teach them humility and to be good-
natured if you can, and this sort of manners will not be
wanting : civility being, in truth, nothing but a care not
to show any slighting or contempt of any one in conversation.   What are the most allowed and esteemed
ways of expressing this, we have above observed.   It is
as peculiar and different, in several countries of the world,
as their languages : and therefore, if it be rightly considered, rules and discourses, made to children about it,
are as useless and impertinent as it would be now and then
to give a rule or two of the Spanish tongue to one that
converses only with Englishmen.   Be as busy as you
please with discourses of civility to your son ; such as is
his company, such will be his manners.   A ploughman
of your neighbourhood, that has never been out of his
parish, read what lectures you please to him, will be as
soon in his language, as his carriage, a courtier ; that is,
in neither will be more polite than those he uses to
converse with : and therefore of this no other care can
be taken.   And, in good earnest, if I were to speak my
mind freely, so children do nothing out of obstinacy,
pride, and ill-nature, it is no great matter how they put
off their hats or make legs.   If you can teach them to
love and respect other people, they will, as their age
requires it, find ways to express it acceptably to every
one, according to the fashions they have been used to :
and, as to their motions, and carriage of their bodies, a
dancing-master, as has been said, when it is fit, will teach
them what is most becoming.   In the meantime, when
they are young, people expect not that children should
be over-mindful of these ceremonies ; carelessness is

---

[1] *I.e.,* bowing in the accustomed fashion.

allowed to that age, and becomes them as well as compliments do grown people : or, at least, if some very nice[1] people will think it a fault, I am sure it is a fault that should be over-looked, and left to time and conversation only to cure : and therefore I think it not worth your while to have your son (as I often see children are) molested or chid about it. But where there is pride or ill-nature appearing in his carriage, there he must be persuaded or shamed out of it.

[Forwardness to talk, frequent interruptions in arguing, and loud wrangling, are too often observable amongst grown people even of rank amongst us. . . . Was it not, think you, an entertaining spectacle, to see two ladies of quality accidentally seated on the opposite sides of a room, set round with company, fall into a dispute, and grow so eager in it, that in the heat of their controversy, edging by degrees their chairs forwards, they were in a little time got up close to one another in the middle of the room ; where they for a good while managed the dispute as fiercely as two game-cocks in the pit, without minding or taking any notice of the circle, which could not all the while forbear smiling ? This I was told by a person of quality, who was present at the combat, and did not omit to reflect upon the indecencies that warmth in dispute often runs people into ; which, since custom makes too frequent, education should take the more care of.]

146. *Company.*—This that I have said here, if it were reflected on, would perhaps lead us a little farther, and let us see of what influence company is. 'Tis not the modes of civility alone that are imprinted by conversation ;[2] the tincture of company sinks deeper than the outside ; and possibly, if a true estimate were made of the morality and religions of the world, we should find that the far greater part of mankind received even those opinions and ceremonies they would die for, rather from the fashions of their countries, and the constant practice of those about them, than from any conviction of their

---

[1] *I.e.*, exacting.   [2] Intercourse.

reasons. I mention this only to let you see of what moment I think company is to your son in all the parts of his life, and therefore how much that one part is to be weighed and provided for, it being of greater force to work upon him than all you can do besides.[1]

147. *Learning.*—You will wonder, perhaps, that I put learning last, especially if I tell you I think it the least part. This will seem strange in the mouth of a bookish man : and this making usually the chief, if not only bustle and stir about children, this being almost that alone, which is thought on, when people talk of education, makes it the greater paradox. When I consider what a-do is made about a little Latin and Greek, how many years are spent in it, and what a noise and business it makes to no purpose, I can hardly forbear thinking that the parents of children still live in fear of the school-master's rod, which they look on as the only instrument of education ; as a language or two to be its whole business. How else is it possible, that a child should be chained to the oar seven, eight, or ten of the best years of his life, to get a language or two, which I think might be had at a great deal cheaper rate of pains and time, and be learned almost in playing ?[2]

Forgive me therefore, if I say, I cannot with patience think, that a young gentleman should be put into the herd, and be driven with a whip and scourge, as if he were to run the gauntlet through the several classes, " *ad capiendum ingenii cultum.*"[3] " What then," say you, " would you not have him write and read ? Shall he be more ignorant than the clerk of our parish, who takes Hopkins and Sternhold[4] for the best poets in the world, whom yet he makes worse than they are by his ill reading?"

[1] See secs. 67, 68.
[2] " We do amiss to spend seven or eight years merely in scraping together so much miserable Latin and Greek as might be learnt otherwise easily and delightfully in one year."—MILTON, *Of Education* (1644).
[3] " In order to acquire an education of his natural ability."
[4] The metrical version of the Psalms, by Thos. Sternhold and John Hopkins, first published *temp.* Ed. VI.

Not so, not so fast, I beseech you. Reading, and writing, and learning, I allow to be necessary, but yet not the chief business. I imagine you would think him a very foolish fellow, that should not value a virtuous or a wise man infinitely before a great scholar. Not but that I think learning a great help to both, in well-disposed minds ; but yet it must be confessed also, that in others not so disposed, it helps them only to be the more foolish or worse men. I say this, that, when you consider of the breeding of your son, and are looking out for a school-master, or a tutor, you would not have (as is usual) Latin and logic only in your thoughts. Learning must be had, but in the second place, as subservient only to greater qualities. Seek out somebody that may know how discreetly to frame his manners ; place him in hands where you may, as much as possible, secure his innocence, cherish and nurse up the good, and gently correct and weed out any bad inclinations, and settle in him good habits. This is the main point ; and this being provided for, learning may be had into the bargain, and that, as I think, at a very easy rate, by methods that may be thought on.

148. *Reading.*—When he can talk, 'tis time he should begin to learn to read. But as to this, give me leave here to inculcate again what is very apt to be forgotten, *viz.* that a great care is to be taken that it be never made as a business to him, nor he look on it as a task.[1] We naturally, as I said, even from our cradles, love liberty, and have therefore an aversion to many things for no other reason but because they are enjoined us. I have always had a fancy that learning might be made a play and recreation to children ; and that they might be brought to desire to be taught, if it were proposed to them as a thing of honour, credit, delight, and recreation, or as a reward for doing something else, and if they were never chid or corrected for the neglect of it. That which confirms me in this opinion, is, that amongst the Portu-

---

[1] See secs. 73-76, 103, 128-129, 167, 202. The opinion is most emphatically stated in sec. 49.

gueses, 'tis so much a fashion and emulation amongst their children to learn to read and write, that they cannot hinder them from it : they will learn it one from another and are as intent on it as if it were forbid them. I remember, that being at a friend's house, whose younger son, a child in coats, was not easily brought to his book (being taught to read at home by his mother) I advised to try another way than requiring it of him as his duty. We therefore, in a discourse on purpose amongst ourselves in his hearing, but without taking any notice of him, declared, that it was the privilege and advantage of heirs and elder brothers to be scholars ;[1] that this made them fine gentlemen and beloved by everybody : and that for younger brothers, it was a favour to admit them to breeding ; to be taught to read and write was more than came to their share ; they might be ignorant bumpkins and clowns, if they pleased.   This so wrought upon the child, that afterwards he desired to be taught ; would come himself to his mother to learn : and would not let his maid be quiet, till she heard him his lesson. I doubt not but some way like this might be taken with other children ; and, when their tempers are found, some thoughts be instilled into them, that might set them upon desiring of learning themselves, and make them seek it, as another sort of play or recreation.   But then, as I said before, it must never be imposed as a task, nor made a trouble to them.   There may be dice and play-things, with the letters on them, to teach children the alphabet by playing ; and twenty other ways may be found, suitable to their particular tempers, to make this kind of learning a sport to them.[2]

149. Thus children may be cozened into a knowledge of the letters ; be taught to read, without perceiving it to be anything but a sport, and play themselves into that others are whipped for.   Children should not have anything like work, or serious, laid on them ; neither their

[1] A deliberate perversion of an opinion which was current in Locke's day, when " heirs and elder brothers " were often thought to be above the necessity of learning.
[2] See note, p. 180.

minds nor bodies will bear it. It injures their healths ; and their being forced and tied down to their books, in an age at enmity with all such restraint, has, I doubt not, been the reason why a great many have hated books and learning all their lives after : it is like a surfeit, that leaves an aversion behind, not to be removed.

150.[1] I have therefore thought, that if playthings[2] were fitted to this purpose, as they are usually to none, contrivances might be made to teach children to read, whilst they thought they were only playing. For example ; What if an ivory-ball were made like that of the Royal-Oak lottery,[3] with thirty-two sides, or one rather of twenty-four or twenty-five sides ; and upon several of those sides pasted on an A, upon several others B, on others C, and on others D ? I would have you begin with but these four letters, or perhaps only two at first ; and when he is perfect in them, then add another ; and so on, till each side having one letter, there be on it the whole alphabet. This I would have others play with before him, it being as good a sort of play to lay a stake who shall first throw an A or B, as who upon dice shall throw six or seven. This being a play amongst you, tempt him not to it, lest you make it business ; for I would not have him understand it is anything but a play of older people, and I doubt not but he will take to it of himself. And that he may have the more reason to think it is a play, that he is sometimes in favour admitted to, when the play is done, the ball should be laid up safe out of his reach, that so it may not, by his having it in his keeping at any time, grow stale to him.

151.[4] To keep up his eagerness to it, let him think it a game belonging to those above him ; and when by this means he knows the letters, by changing them into

---

[1] Sec. 143 in first edition.   [2] See sec. 130.

[3] Possibly, a kind of round game at cards, prizes or stakes going to the holders of cards indicated by the " throw " of the " lottery-ball," a polyhedron with numbers marked on its faces, and used as dice.

[4] Sec. 143 in first edition.

syllables, he may learn to read, without knowing how he did so, and never have any chiding or trouble about it, nor fall out with books, because of the hard usage and vexation they have caused him.   Children, if you observe them, take abundance of pains to learn several games, which, if they should be enjoined them, they would abhor as a task and business.   I know a person of great quality (more yet to be honoured for his learning and virtue than for his rank and high place) who, by pasting on the six vowels (for in our language Y is one) on the six sides of a die, and the remaining eighteen consonants on the sides of three other dice, has made this a play for his children, that he shall win, who, at one cast, throws most words on these four dice ; whereby his eldest son, yet in coats,[1] has played himself into spelling, with great eagerness, and without once having been chid for it, or forced to it.

152.[2] I have seen little girls exercise whole hours together, and take abundance of pains to be expert at dibstones,[3] as they call it.   Whilst I have been looking on, I have thought it wanted only some good contrivance to make them employ all that industry about something that might be more useful to them ; and methinks it is only the fault and negligence of elder people that it is not so.   Children are much less apt to be idle than men ; and men are to be blamed, if some part of that busy humour be not turned to useful things ; which might be made usually as delightful to them as those they are employed in, if men would be but half so forward to lead the way as these little apes would be to follow.   I imagine some wise Portuguese heretofore began this fashion amongst the children of his country, where I have been told, as I said,[4] it is impossible to hinder the children from learning to

---

[1] Not old enough to be breeched.

[2] Sec. 144 in first edition.

[3] " Tossing pebbles.   A child's game " (T. Wright, *Dictionary of Obsolete and Provincial English*).   London children still play the game in the streets, using a ball and four pebbles, and keeping one of the five objects in the air while moving one of the others on the ground.

[4] Sec. 148.

read and write : and in some parts of France they teach one another to sing and dance from the cradle.

153. The letters pasted upon the sides of the dice, or polygon, were best to be of the size of those of the folio Bible to begin with, and none of them capital letters ; when once he can read what is printed in such letters, he will not long be ignorant of the great ones : and in the beginning he should not be perplexed with variety.   With this die also, you might have a play just like the Royal-Oak, which would be another variety ; and play for cherries, or apples, etc.

154. Besides these, twenty other plays might be invented, depending on letters, which those, who like this way, may easily contrive, and get made to this use, if they will.   But the four dice above-mentioned I think so easy and useful, that it will be hard to find any better, and there will be scarce need of any other.

155. Thus much for learning to read, which let him never be driven to, nor chid for ; cheat him into it if you can, but make it not a business for him.   'Tis better it be a year later before he can read, than that he should this way get an aversion to learning.   If you have any contests with him, let it be in matters of moment, of truth, and good-nature ; but lay no task on him about A B C. Use your skill to make his will supple and pliant to reason : teach him to love credit and commendation ; to abhor being thought ill or meanly of, especially by you and his mother ; and then the rest will come all easily.   But, I think, if you will do that, you must not shackle and tie him up with rules about indifferent matters, nor rebuke him for every little fault, or perhaps some that to others would seem great ones.   But of this I have said enough already.

156. When by these gentle ways he begins to be able to read, some easy, pleasant book, suited to his capacity, should be put into his hands, wherein the entertainment that he finds might draw him on, and reward his pains in reading ; and yet not such as should fill his head with perfectly useless trumpery, or lay the principles of vice and folly.   To this purpose I think Æsop's Fables the

best, which being stories apt to delight and entertain a
child, may yet afford useful reflections to a grown man ;
and if his memory retain them all his life after, he will not
repent to find them there, amongst his manly thoughts
and serious business. If his Æsop has pictures in it, it
will entertain him much the better, and encourage him to
read when it carries the increase of knowledge with it :
for such visible objects children hear talked of in vain,
and without any satisfaction, whilst they have no ideas
of them ; those ideas being not to be had from sounds,
but from the things themselves,[1] or their pictures. And
therefore, I think, as soon as he begins to spell, as many
pictures of animals should be got him as can be found,
with the printed names to them, which at the same time
will invite him to read, and afford him matter of inquiry
and knowledge. Reynard the Fox is another book, I
think, that may be made use of to the same purpose.
And if those about him will talk to him often about the
stories he has read, and hear him tell them, it will, besides
other advantages, add encouragement and delight to his
reading, when he finds there is some use and pleasure in it,
which in the ordinary method, I think, learners do not
till late ; and so take books only for fashionable amusements, or impertinent troubles, good for nothing.

157. The Lord's Prayer, the Creeds, and Ten Commandments, 'tis necessary he should learn perfectly by
heart ; but, I think, not by reading them himself in his
primer, but by somebody's repeating them to him, even
before he can read. But learning by heart, and learning
to read, should not, I think, be mixed, and so one made
to clog the other. But his learning to read should be made
as little trouble or business to him as might be.

---

[1] Derived directly from Locke's experiential psychology, the
principle here implied assumed the highest importance in the
theories of Rousseau and of Pestalozzi. The ninth letter of Pestalozzi's *How Gertrude teaches her Children* (1801) begins thus : " If
I look back and ask myself what have I personally accomplished
for human instruction, I discover this : In recognizing Intuition
(*Anschauung*) as the absolute basis of all knowledge, I have established the highest principle of instruction." *Cf*. sec. 166.

What other books there are in English of the kind of those above-mentioned, fit to engage the liking of children, and tempt them to read, I do not know ; but am apt to think that children, being generally delivered over to the method of schools, where the fear of the rod is to enforce, and not any pleasure of the employment to invite, them to learn ; this sort of useful books, amongst the number of silly ones that are of all sorts, have yet had the fate to be neglected ; and nothing that I know has been considered of this kind out of the ordinary road of the horn-book, primer, psalter, Testament, and Bible.[1]

158. As for the Bible, which children are usually employed in to exercise and improve their talent in reading, I think, the promiscuous reading of it through by chapters as they lie in order, is so far from being of any advantage to children, either for the perfecting their reading or principling their religion, that perhaps a worse could not be found.   For what pleasure or encouragement can it be to a child, to exercise himself in reading those parts of a book where he understands nothing ?   And how little are the law of Moses, the Song of Solomon, the prophecies in the Old, and the Epistles and Apocalypse in the New Testament, suited to a child's capacity ?   And though the history of the Evangelists and the Acts have something easier ; yet, taken all together, it is very disproportionate to the understanding of childhood.   I grant, that the principles of religion are to be drawn from thence, and in the words of the Scripture ; yet none should be proposed to a child but such as are suited to a child's capacity and notions.   But it is far from this to read through the whole Bible, and that for reading's sake.   And what an odd jumble of thoughts must a child have in his head, if he have any at all, such as he should have concerning religion,

[1] The books from which children usually learned to read the vernacular at home, following ancient tradition; within living memory, the Bible was used for this purpose in certain elementary schools.   The hornbook and primer contained the alphabet, syllables, the Lord's Prayer and Creed ; the former got its name from the thin horn plate used to protect the printed page from the reader's finger.   See A. E. Tuer's *History of the Horn Book*, 1897.

who in his tender age reads all the parts of the Bible indifferently, as the word of God, without any other distinction. I am apt to think that this, in some men, has been the very reason why they never had clear and distinct thoughts of it all their lifetime.

159. And now I am by chance fallen on this subject, give me leave to say, that there are some parts of the Scripture which may be proper to be put into the hands of a child to engage him to read ; such as are the story of Joseph and his brethren, of David and Goliath, of David and Jonathan, etc., and others, that he should be made to read for his instruction ; as that, " What you would have others do unto you, do you the same unto them ;" and such other easy and plain moral rules, which, being fitly chosen, might often be made use of, both for reading and instruction together. But the reading of the whole Scripture indifferently is what I think very inconvenient for children, till, after having been made acquainted with the plainest fundamental parts of it, they have got some kind of general view of what they ought principally to believe and practice, which yet, I think, they ought to receive in the very words of the Scripture, and not in such, as men prepossessed by systems and analogies, are apt in this case to make use of, and force upon them. Dr. Worthington,[1] to avoid this, has made a catechism which has all its answers in the precise words of the Scripture, a thing of good example and such a sound form of words, as no Christian can except against as not fit for his child to learn. Of this, as soon as he can say the Lord's Prayer, Creed, and Ten Commandments by heart, it may be fit for him to learn a question every day, or every week, as his understanding is able to receive and his memory to retain them. And when he has this catechism perfectly

[1] John Worthington (1618-1671), Master of Jesus College, Cambridge, one of Hartlib's correspondents. His book, *A form of sound words, or a scripture catechism, shewing what a Christian is to believe and practise in order to salvation : very useful to persons of all ages and capacities as well as children*, was published posthumously in 1673, and was still appearing in 1755. It is a primer of theology, very unsuitable to children in form and matter.

by heart, so as readily and roundly to answer to any question in the whole book, it may be convenient to lodge in his mind the moral rules, scattered up and down in the Bible, as the best exercise of his memory, and that which may be always a rule to him, ready at hand, in the whole conduct of his life.[1]

160. *Writing.*—When he can read English well, it will be seasonable to enter him in writing. And here the first thing should be taught him is, to hold his pen right ; and this he should be perfect in, before he should be suffered to put it to paper : for not only children, but anybody else, that would do anything well, should never be put upon too much of it at once, or be set to perfect themselves in two parts of an action at the same time, if they can possibly be separated. When he has learned to hold his pen right, (to hold it betwixt the thumb and forefinger alone, I think best ; but on this you should consult some good writing-master, or any other person who writes well and quick) then next he should learn how to lay his paper, and place his arm and body to it. These practices being got over, the way to teach him to write without much trouble, is to get a plate graved with the characters of such a hand as you like best : but you must remember to have them a pretty deal bigger than he should ordinarily write ; for every one naturally comes by degrees to write a less hand than he at first was taught, but never a bigger. Such a plate being graved, let several sheets of good writing-paper be printed off with red ink, which he has nothing to do but to go over with a good pen filled with black ink, which will quickly bring his hand to the formation of those characters, being at first showed where to begin, and how to form every letter. And when he can do that well, he must then exercise on fair paper ; and so may easily be brought to write the hand you desire.[2]

---

[1] These concrete directions for religious instruction do not follow the principles enunciated in section 136 ; yet in both places religion is presented rather as a philosophy than as a life to be lived. During childhood at least the latter is the more necessary standpoint for the educator.

[2] See note, p. 180.

161. *Drawing.*—When he can write well, and quick, I think it may be convenient, not only to continue the exercise of his hand in writing, but also to improve the use of it farther in drawing, a thing very useful to a gentleman on several occasions, but especially if he travel, as that which helps a man often to express, in a few lines well put together, what a whole sheet of paper in writing would not be able to represent and make intelligible.   How many buildings may a man see, how many machines and habits meet with, the ideas whereof would be easily retained and communicated by a little skill in drawing; which being committed to words, are in danger to be lost, or at best but ill retained in the most exact descriptions ?   I do not mean that I would have your son a perfect painter ; to be that to any tolerable degree, will require more time than a young gentleman can spare from his other improvements of greater importance ; but so much insight into perspective, and skill in drawing, as will enable him to represent tolerably on paper any thing he sees, except faces, may, I think, be got in a little time, especially if he have a genius to it : but where that is wanting, unless it be in the things absolutely necessary, it is better to let him pass them by quietly, than to vex him about them to no purpose : and therefore in this, as in all other things not absolutely necessary, the rule holds, " *Nihil invitâ Minervâ.*"[1]

[¶ 1. Short-hand, an art, as I have been told, known only in England, may perhaps be thought worth the learning, both for despatch in what men write for their own memory, and concealment of what they would not have lie open to every eye. . . . Mr. Rich's,[2] the best contrived of any I have seen, may, as I think, by one who knows and considers grammar well, be made much easier and shorter.]

162. *French.*—As soon as he can speak English, it is time for him to learn some other language : this nobody doubts of, when French is proposed.   And the reason is,

---

[1] Nothing contrary to inborn capacity.
[2] Jeremiah Rich, fl. *temp.* Commonwealth.

because people are accustomed to the right way of teaching that language, which is by talking it into children in constant conversation, and not by grammatical rules. The Latin tongue would easily be taught the same way, if his tutor, being constantly with him, would talk nothing else to him, and make him answer still in the same language.[1] But because French is a living language, and to be used more in speaking, that should be first learned, that the yet pliant organs of speech might be accustomed to a due formation of these sounds, and he get the habit of pronouncing French well, which is the harder to be done the longer it is delayed.

163. *Latin.*—When he can speak and read French well, which in this method is usually in a year or two, he should proceed to Latin, which 'tis a wonder parents, when they have had the experiment in French, should not think ought to be learned the same way by talking and reading. Only care is to be taken, whilst he is learning these foreign languages, by speaking and reading nothing else to his tutor, that he do not forget to read English, which may be preserved by his mother, or somebody else, hearing him read some chosen parts of the Scripture, or other English book, every day.

164. Latin I look upon as absolutely necessary to a gentleman ; and indeed custom, which prevails over every thing, has made it so much a part of education, that even those children are whipped to it, and made spend many hours of their precious time uneasily in Latin, who, after they are once gone from school, are never to have more to do with it as long as they live. Can there be anything more ridiculous than that a father should waste his own money, and his son's time, in setting him to learn the Roman language, when, at the same time, he designs him for a trade, wherein he, having no use of Latin, fails

[1] Montaigne (*Essais* i., chap. xxv.) tells us that he was taught to speak by a German, ignorant of French, but very well versed in Latin, that he learned little French till he was six years old, by which time, " without art, book, grammar, rule or scourge," he had learned a Latinity as pure as his schoolmaster's.

not to forget that little which he brought from school, and
which it is ten to one he abhors for the ill usage it pro-
cured him ?[1] Could it be believed, unless we had everywhere amongst us examples of it, that a child should be
forced to learn the rudiments of a language which he is
never to use in the course of life he is designed to, and
neglect all the while the writing a good hand, and casting
account[s], which are of great advantage in all conditions
of life, and to most trades indispensably necessary ?
But though these qualifications, requisite to trade and
commerce, and the business of the world, are seldom or
never to be had at grammar-schools, yet thither not only
gentlemen send their younger sons, intended for trades,
but even tradesmen and farmers fail not to send their
children, though they have neither intention nor ability
to make them scholars. If you ask them, why they do
this, they think it as strange a question, as if you should
ask them, why they go to church. Custom serves for
reason, and has, to those that take it for reason, so con-
secrated this method, that it is almost religiously observed
by them ; and they stick to it, as if their children had
scarce an orthodox education unless they learned Lily's
grammar.[2]

165.[3] But how necessary soever Latin be to some, and
is thought to be to others, to whom it is of no manner of
use or service, yet the ordinary way of learning it in a
grammar-school, is that, which having had thoughts
about, I cannot be forward to encourage. The reasons
against it are so evident and cogent, that they have prevailed with some intelligent persons to quit the ordinary
road, not without success, though the method made use
of was not exactly that which I imagine the easiest, and in

[1] Locke's objection is not that Latin is useless (*cf.* sec. 186), but
that the pupils in question get a merely truncated instruction.
[2] William Lily, first High Master of St. Paul's School (1512-1522).
For some three centuries and a half, the Latin grammar associated
with his name was regarded as the standard school-book. For its
history see Foster Watson, *The English Grammar Schools*, chaps.
xv., xvi.
[3] Sec. 157 in first edition.

short is this : to trouble the child with no grammar at all, but to have Latin, as English has been, without the perplexity of rules, talked into him ; for, if you will consider it, Latin is no more unknown to a child, when he comes into the world, than English : and yet he learns English without master, rule, or grammar ; and so might he Latin too, as Tully did, if he had somebody always to talk to him in this language. And when we so often see a French woman teach an English girl to speak and read French perfectly in a year or two, without any rule of grammar, or anything else, but prattling to her, I cannot but wonder, how gentlemen have overseen[1] this way for their sons, and thought them more dull or incapable than their daughters.

166.[2] If therefore a man could be got who himself speaks good Latin, who would be always about your son and talk constantly to him and make him read Latin,[3] that would be the true, genuine and easy way of teaching him Latin, and that I could wish ; since besides teaching him a language without pains or chiding (which children are wont to be whipped for at school six or seven years together) he might at the same time not only form his mind and manners, but instruct him also in several sciences such as are a good part of geography, astronomy, chronology, anatomy, besides some parts of history and all other parts of knowledge of things that fall under the senses, and require little more than memory. For there, if we would take the true way, our knowledge should begin and in those things be laid the foundation,[4] and not in the abstract notions of logic and metaphysics, which are fitter to amuse than inform the understanding in its first setting out towards knowledge. In which abstract speculations when young men have had their heads employed a while,[5] without finding the success and improvement or use of it which they expected, they are

---

[1] *I.e.*, overlooked.   [2] Sec. 157 in first edition.
[3] " And suffer him to speak or read nothing else " in later editions.
[4] See note on sec. 156.   [5] See sec. 188.

apt to have mean thoughts either of learning or themselves, to quit their studies and throw away their books,
as containing nothing but hard words and empty sounds ;
or else concluding that if there be any real knowledge
in them, they themselves have not understandings
capable of it ; and that that is so, perhaps I could assure
you upon my own experience. Amongst other things
to be learned by a young man in this method, whilst
others of his age are wholly taken up with Latin and
languages, I may also set down geometry for one, having
known a young gentleman, bred something after this
way, able to demonstrate several propositions in Euclid
before he was thirteen.[1]

167. But if such a man cannot be got, who speaks
good Latin, and being able to instruct your son in all
these parts of knowledge, will undertake it by this
method ; the next best is to have him taught as near
this way as may be, which is by taking some easy and
pleasant book, such as Æsop's Fables, and writing the
English translation (made as literal as it can be) in one
line, and the Latin words, which answer each of them,
just over it in another. These let him read every day
over and over again, till he perfectly understands the
Latin. (But have a care still, whatever you are teaching
him, of clogging him with too much at once, or making
anything his business but down-right virtue, or reproving
him for anything but vice.) And then go on to another
fable, till he be also perfect in that, not omitting what
he is already perfect in, but sometimes reviewing that,
to keep it in his memory. And when he comes to write,
let these be set him for copies, which, with the exercise
of his hand, will also advance him in Latin. This being
a more imperfect way than by talking Latin unto him ;
the formation of the verbs first, and afterwards the declensions of the nouns and pronouns perfectly learned by
heart, may facilitate his acquaintance with the genius
and manner of the Latin tongue, which varies the signification of verbs and nouns, not as the modern languages
do, by particles prefixed, but by changing the last

[1] The original draft of 1684 does not go beyond this section.

syllables. More than this of grammar I think he need not have, till he can read himself Sanctii Minerva,[1] with Scioppius [and Perizonius's] notes.[2]

[In teaching of children this too, I think, it is to be observed, that in most cases, where they stick, they are not to be farther puzzled, by putting them upon finding it out themselves ; as by asking such questions as these, *viz.*, Which is the nominative case ? in the sentence they are to construe, or demanding what " ausero " signifies, to lead them to the knowledge what " abstulere " signifies, etc., when they cannot readily tell. This wastes time only in disturbing them ; for whilst they are learning, and applying themselves with attention, they are to be kept in good humour, and everything made easy to them, and as pleasant as possible. Therefore, wherever they are at a stand, and are willing to go forward, help them presently over the difficulty, without any rebuke or chiding ; remembering, that where harsher ways are taken, they are the effect only of pride and peevishness in the teacher, who expects children should instantly be masters of as much as he knows : whereas he should rather consider that his business is to settle in them habits, not angrily to inculcate rules, which serve for little in the conduct of our lives ; at least are of no use to children, who forget them as soon as given. In sciences, where their reason is to be exercised, I will not deny but this method may sometimes be varied, and difficulties proposed on purpose to excite industry and accustom the mind to employ its own strength and sagacity in reasoning. But yet, I guess, this is not to

[1] *Minerva, seu de causis linguæ Latinæ Commentarius,* published first in 1587, was a celebrated textbook which long retained its popularity. Its author was Francesco Sanchez, or Sanctius (1523-1601), professor of Greek at Salamanca. Amended or annotated editions were produced by the German, Scioppius (Caspar Schoppe, 1576-1649), and the Dutchman, Perizonius (Jacob Voorbroek, 1651-1715). The fourth edition by the last named appeared in 1714; it was a volume of about one thousand pages.

[2] The remainder of the section is later than the first edition ; its pedagogical importance will be appreciated.

be done to children whilst very young; nor at their entrance upon any sort of knowledge : then everything of itself is difficult, and the great use and skill of a teacher is to make all as easy as he can. But particularly in learning of languages there is least occasion for posing of children. For languages being to be learnt by rote, custom, and memory, are then spoken in greatest perfection, when all rules of grammar are utterly forgotten. I grant the grammar of a language is sometimes very carefully to be studied : but it is only to be studied by a grown man, when he applies himself to the understanding of any language critically, which is seldom the business of any but professed scholars. This, I think, will be agreed to, that if a gentleman be to study any language, it ought to be that of his own country, that he may understand the language, which he has constant use of, with the utmost accuracy.

There is yet a farther reason why masters and teachers should raise no difficulties to their scholars ; but, on the contrary, should smooth their way and readily help them forwards where they find them stop. Children's minds are narrow and weak, and usually susceptible but of one thought at once. Whatever is in a child's head, fills it for the time, especially if set on with any passion. It should therefore be the skill and art of the teacher, to clear their heads of all other thoughts, whilst they are learning of any thing, the better to make room for what he would instil into them, that it may be received with attention and application, without which it leaves no impression. The natural temper of children disposes their minds to wander.[1] Novelty alone takes them ; whatever that presents, they are presently eager to have a taste of, and are as soon satiated with it. They quickly grow weary of the same thing, and so have almost their whole delight in change and variety. It is a contradiction to the natural state of childhood for them to fix their fleeting thoughts. Whether this be owing to the temper of their brains, or the quickness or instability of their

[1] *Cf. Conduct*, sec. 30.

animal spirits, over which the mind has not yet got a full command ; this is visible, that it is a pain to children to keep their thoughts steady to any thing. A lasting, continued attention is one of the hardest tasks that can be imposed on them : and therefore, he that requires their application, should endeavour to make what he proposes as grateful and agreeable as possible ; at least, he ought to take care not to join any displeasing or frightful idea with it. If they come not to their books with some kind of liking and relish, it is no wonder their thoughts should be perpetually shifting from what disgusts them, and seek better entertainment in more pleasing objects, after which they will unavoidably be gadding.

It is, I know, the usual method of tutors to endeavour to procure attention in their scholars, and to fix their minds to the business in hand by rebukes and corrections, if they find them ever so little wandering. But such treatment is sure to produce the quite contrary effect. Passionate words or blows from the tutor, fill the child's mind with terror and affrightment, which immediately takes it wholly up, and leaves no room for other impressions. I believe there is nobody that reads this, but may recollect what disorder hasty or imperious words from his parents or teachers have caused in his thoughts ; how for the time it has turned his brains so that he scarce knew what was said by or to him : he presently lost the sight of what he was upon ; his mind was filled with disorder and confusion, and in that state was no longer capable of attention to any thing else.

It is true, parents and governors ought to settle and establish their authority, by an awe over the minds of those under their tuition ; and to rule them by that : but when they have got an ascendant over them, they should use it with great moderation, and not make themselves such scarecrows, that their scholars should always tremble in their sight. Such an austerity may make their government easy to themselves, but of very little use to their pupils. It is impossible children should learn any thing

whilst their thoughts are possessed and disturbed with
any passion, especially fear, which makes the strongest
impression on their yet tender and weak spirits. Keep
the mind in an easy, calm temper, when you would have
it receive your instructions, or any increase of knowledge. It is as impossible to draw fair and regular
characters on a trembling mind as on a shaking paper.

The great skill of a teacher is to get and keep the attention of his scholar: whilst he has that, he is sure to advance as fast as the learner's abilities will carry him;
and without that, all his bustle and pother will be to
little or no purpose. To attain this, he should make the
child comprehend (as much as may be) the usefulness of
what he teaches him; and let him see, by what he has
learned, that he can do something which he could not do
before, something which gives him some power and real
advantage above others who are ignorant of it[1]. To this he
should add sweetness in all his instructions; and by a certain tenderness in his whole carriage, make the child sensible
that he loves him, and designs nothing but his good; the
only way to beget love in the child, which will make him
hearken to his lessons, and relish what he teaches him.

Nothing but obstinacy should meet with any imperiousness or rough usage. All other faults should be corrected
with a gentle hand; and kind, encouraging words will
work better and more effectually upon a willing mind,
and even prevent a good deal of that perverseness which
rough and imperious usage often produces in well-disposed and generous minds. It is true, obstinacy and
wilful neglects must be mastered, even though it cost
blows to do it: but I am apt to think perverseness in
the pupils is often the effect of frowardness in the tutor;
and that most children would seldom have deserved
blows, if needless and misapplied roughness had not
taught them ill-nature, and given them an aversion to
their teacher, and all that comes from him.

Inadvertency, forgetfulness, unsteadiness, and wandering of thought, are the natural faults of childhood; and

[1] Cf. "Let her have companions in learning, whose success she
may envy, praise of whom may incite her to imitate them." St
Jerome *ad Laetam*. See p. 180 below.

therefore, when they are not observed to be wilful, are to be mentioned softly, and gained upon by time. If every slip of this kind produces anger and rating, the occasions of rebuke and corrections will return so often, that the tutor will be a constant terror and uneasiness to his pupils ; which one thing is enough to hinder their profiting by his lessons, and to defeat all his methods of instructions.

Let the awe he has got upon their minds be so tempered with the constant marks of tenderness and good-will, that affection may spur them to their duty, and make them find a pleasure in complying with his dictates. This will bring them with satisfaction to their tutor ; make them hearken to him, as to one who is their friend, that cherishes them, and takes pains for their good ; this will keep their thoughts easy and free, whilst they are with him, the only temper wherein the mind is capable of receiving new informations, and of admitting into itself those impressions, which if not taken and retained, all that they and their teacher do together, is lost labour ; there is much uneasiness, and little learning.]

168.[1] When, by this way of interlining Latin and English one with another, he has got a moderate knowledge of the Latin tongue, he may then be advanced a little farther to the reading of some other easy Latin book, such as Justin, or Eutropius ;[2] and to make the reading and understanding of it the less tedious and difficult to him, let him help himself, if he please, with the English translation. Nor let the objection, that he will then know it only by rote (which is when well considered not of any moment against, but plainly for this way of learning a language), fright any one. For languages are only to be learned by rote ; and a man, who does not

---

[1] Sec. 159 in first edition.
[2] Justin wrote (probably in the third century of the Christian era) an abridgement of a much earlier Universal History ; he was regarded in the Middle Ages as the model historian. See Sandys' *A History of Classical Scholarship*, vols. i., ii. Flavius Eutropius, another historical compiler, belongs to the fourth century.

speak English or Latin perfectly by rote, so that having thought of the thing he would speak of, his tongue of course, without thought of rule of grammar, falls into the proper expressions and idiom of that language, does not speak it well, nor is master of it. And I would fain have any one name to me that tongue, that any one can learn or speak as he should do, by the rules of grammar. Languages were made not by rules or art, but by accident, and the common use of the people. And he that will speak them well, has no other rule but that; nor any thing to trust to but his memory, and the habit of speaking after the fashion learned from those that are allowed to speak properly, which, in other words, is only to speak by rote.

Grammar.—It will possibly be asked here, Is grammar then of no use? And have those who have taken so much pains in reducing several languages to rules and observations, who have written so much about declensions and conjugations, about concords and syntaxis, lost their labour, and been learned to no purpose? I say not so; grammar has its place, too. But this I think I may say, There is more stir a great deal made with it than there needs, and those are tormented about it, to whom it does not at all belong; I mean children, at the age wherein they are usually perplexed with it in grammar schools.[1]

[There is nothing more evident, than that languages learned by rote serve well enough for the common affairs of life, and ordinary commerce. Nay, persons of quality of the softer sex, and such of them as have spent their time in well-bred company, show us, that this plain, natural way, without the least study or knowledge of grammar, can carry them to a great degree of elegance and politeness in their language: and there are ladies who, without knowing what tenses and participles, adverbs and prepositions are, speak as properly, and as correctly (they might take it for an ill compliment, if I said as any country school-master) as most gentlemen who have been bred up in the ordinary methods of grammar-

---

[1] The relevance of the remainder of this section to the "Direct Method" of teaching languages will be noticed.

schools. Grammar therefore we see may be spared in
some cases. The question then will be, To whom should
it be taught, and when ? To this I answer,

1. Men learn languages for the ordinary intercourse of
society, and communication of thoughts in common life,
without any farther design in their use of them. And
for this purpose the original way of learning a language
by conversation, not only serves well enough, but is to
be preferred, as the most expedite, proper, and natural.
Therefore to this use of language one may answer, That
grammar is not necessary. This so many of my readers
must be forced to allow, as understand what I here say,
and who, conversing with others, understand them without having ever been taught the grammar of the English
tongue : which I suppose is the case of incomparably the
greatest part of Englishmen ; of whom I have never yet
known any one who learned his mother-tongue by rules.

2. Others there are, the greatest part of whose business
in this world is to be done with their tongues, and with
their pens ; and to those it is convenient, if not necessary,
that they should speak properly and correctly, whereby
they may let their thoughts into other men's minds the
more easily and with the greater impression. Upon this
account it is, that any sort of speaking, so as will make
him be understood, is not thought enough for a gentleman. He ought to study grammar, amongst the other
helps of speaking well : but it must be the grammar of
his own tongue, of the language he uses, that he may
understand his own country speech nicely,[1] and speak it
properly, without shocking the ears of those it is addressed
to, with solecisms, and offensive irregularities. And to
this purpose grammar is necessary : but it is the grammar
only of their own proper tongues, and to those only who
would take pains in cultivating their language, and in
perfecting their styles. Whether all gentlemen should
not do this, I leave to be considered, since the want of
propriety and grammatical exactness is thought very
misbecoming one of that rank, and usually draws on one

[1] Precisely.

guilty of such faults the censure of having had a lower breeding and worse company than suits with his quality. If this be so (as I suppose it is), it will be matter of wonder, why young gentlemen are forced to learn the grammars of foreign and dead languages, and are never once told of the grammar of their own tongues : they do not so much as know there is any such thing, much less is it made their business to be instructed in it. Nor is their own language ever proposed to them as worthy their care and cultivating, though they have daily use of it, and are not seldom in the future course of their lives judged of, by their handsome or awkward way of expressing themselves in it. Whereas the languages, whose grammars they have been so much employed in, are such as probably they shall scarce ever speak or write ; or, if upon occasion this should happen, they shall be excused for the mistakes and faults they make in it. Would not a Chinese, who took notice of this way of breeding, be apt to imagine that all our young gentlemen were designed to be teachers and professors of the dead languages of foreign countries, and not to be men of business in their own ?

3. There is a third sort of men who apply themselves to two or three foreign dead (and which amongst us are called the learned) languages, make them their study, and pique themselves upon their skill in them. No doubt those who propose to themselves the learning of any language with this view, and would be critically exact in it, ought carefully to study the grammar of it. I would not be mistaken here, as if this were to undervalue Greek and Latin : I grant these are languages of great use and excellency ; and a man can have no place amongst the learned, in this part of the world, who is a stranger to them. But the knowledge a gentleman would ordinarily draw for his use, out of the Roman and Greek writers, I think he may attain without studying the grammars of those tongues, and, by bare reading, may come to understand them sufficiently for all his purposes. How much farther he shall at any time be concerned to look into the

grammar and critical niceties of either of these tongues, he himself will be able to determine, when he comes to propose to himself the study of anything that shall require it. Which brings me to the other part of the inquiry, *viz.*—

" When grammar should be taught ?"

To which, upon the premised grounds, the answer is obvious, *viz.*—

That if grammar ought to be taught at any time, it must be to one that can speak the language already : how else can he be taught the grammar of it ? This, at least, is evident from the practice of the wise and learned nations amongst the ancients. They made it a part of education to cultivate their own, not foreign tongues. The Greeks counted all other nations barbarous, and had a contempt for their languages. And, though the Greek learning grew in credit amongst the Romans, towards the end of their commonwealth, yet it was the Roman tongue that was made the study of their youth : their own language they were to make use of, and therefore it was their own language they were instructed and exercised in.

But more particularly to determine the proper season for grammar, I do not see how it can reasonably be made any one's study, but as an introduction to rhetoric : when it is thought time to put any one upon the care of polishing his tongue, and of speaking better than the illiterate, then is the time for him to be instructed in the rules of grammar, and not before. For grammar being to teach men not to speak, but to speak correctly, and according to the exact rules of the tongue, which is one part of elegancy, there is little use of the one to him that has no need of the other : where rhetoric is not necessary, grammar may be spared.[1] I know not why any one should waste his time, and beat his head about the Latin grammar, who does not intend to be a critic, or make speeches, and write dispatches in it. When any one finds in himself a neces-

[1] In the mother-tongue, as much rhetoric as goes to making " composition " is necessary, and to that extent grammar cannot be spared. See secs. 171, 172, 189.

sity or disposition to study any foreign language to the bottom, and to be nicely exact in the knowledge of it, it will be time enough to take a grammatical survey of it. If his use of it be only to understand some books written in it, without a critical knowledge of the tongue itself, reading alone, as I have said, will attain this end, without charging the mind with the multiplied rules and intricacies of grammar.]

169. For the exercise of his writing, let him sometimes translate Latin into English; but the learning of Latin being nothing but the learning of words, a very unpleasant business both to young and old, join as much other real knowledge[1] with it as you can, beginning still with that which lies most obvious to the senses; such as is the knowledge of minerals, plants, and animals, and particularly timber and fruit-trees, their parts and ways of propagation, where a great deal may be taught a child, which will not be useless to the man.   But more especially geography, astronomy, and anatomy.

170. But if, after all, his fate be to go to school to get the Latin tongue, 'tis in vain to talk to you concerning the method I think best to be observed in schools.   You must submit to that you find there, not expect to have it changed for your son; but yet by all means obtain, if you can, that he be not employed in making Latin themes and declamations, and, least of all, verses of any kind. You may insist on it, if it will do any good, that you have no design to make him either a Latin orator or poet, but barely would have him understand perfectly a Latin author; and that you observe those who teach any of the modern languages, and that with success, never amuse their scholars to make speeches or verses either in French or Italian, their business being language barely, and not invention.

[1] " Real " in the sense of " positive," and opposed to both " verbal " and " rational " or " demonstrative."   *Cf.* the use of the German term, *Realien,* to include such studies as history, geography, and the observational and experimental stages of science.   See sec. 178.   Either the advice given is contradictory of sec. 173 below, or Locke does not regard this " real knowledge " as a strain on the mind.

171. *Themes.*—But to tell you, a little more fully, why I would not have him exercised in making of themes and verses. 1. As to themes, they have, I confess, the pretence of something useful, which is to teach people to speak handsomely and well on any subject ; which, if it could be attained this way, I own would be a great advantage ; there being nothing more becoming a gentleman, nor more useful in all the occurrences of life, than to be able, on any occasion, to speak well, and to the purpose. But this I say, that the making of themes, as is usual in schools, helps not one jot towards it. For do but consider what 'tis in making a theme, that a young lad is employed about ; 'tis to make a speech on some Latin saying, as, " *Omnia vincit amor,*" or " *Non licet in bello bis peccare,*"[1] etc. And here the poor lad, who wants knowledge of these things he is to speak of, which is to be had only from time and observation, must set his invention on the rack, to say something where he knows nothing, which is a sort of Egyptian tyranny, to bid them make bricks who have not yet any of the materials. And therefore it is usual, in such cases, for the poor children to go to those of higher forms with this petition, " Pray give me a little sense ;" which, whether it be more reasonable or more ridiculous, is not easy to determine. Before a man can be in any capacity to speak on any subject, it is necessary he be acquainted with it ; or else it is as foolish to set him to discourse of it, as to set a blind man to talk of colours, or a deaf man of music. And would you not think him a little cracked who would require another to make an argument on a moot-point,[2] who understands nothing of our laws ? And what, I pray, do school-boys understand concerning those matters, which are used to be proposed to them in their themes, as subjects to discourse on, to whet and exercise their fancies ?

[1] " Love conquers all things."   " In warfare, one is not allowed to blunder twice."
[2] A legal point, as to which lawyers themselves might differ. The term belongs to the history of legal education, a " moot-point " being a topic for argument by law-students before the seniors of their Inn.

172. In the next place consider the language that their themes are made in. 'Tis Latin, a language foreign in their country, and long since dead everywhere;[1] a language which your son, 'tis a thousand to one, shall never have an occasion once to make a speech in as long as he lives, after he comes to be a man ; and a language, wherein the manner of expressing oneself is so far different from ours, that to be perfect in that, would very little improve the purity and facility of his English style.   Besides that, there is now so little room or use for set speeches in our own language in any part of our English business, that I can see no pretence for this sort of exercise in our schools ; unless it can be supposed, that the making of set Latin speeches should be the way to teach men to speak well in English extempore.   The way to that I should think rather to be this : that there should be proposed some rational and material question to young gentlemen, when they are of a fit age for such exercise, which they should extempore or after a little meditation in the place, speak to, without penning of anything.   For I ask, if we will examine the effects of this way of learning to speak well, who speak best in any business, when occasion calls them to it upon any debate ; either those who have accustomed themselves to compose and write down before-hand what they would say ; or those, who thinking only of the matter, to understand that as well as they can, use themselves only to speak extempore ?   And he that shall judge by this, will be little apt to think, that the accustoming him to studied speeches, and set compositions, is the way to fit a young gentleman for business.

173. But perhaps we shall be told, It is to improve and perfect them in the Latin tongue.   It is true, that is their proper business at school ; but the making of themes is not the way to it : that perplexes their brains, about invention of things to be said, not about the signification of words to be learnt : and when they are making a theme, it is thoughts they search and sweat for, and not lan-

---

[1] A statement to be accepted with some reservations. Locke himself wrote Latin letters to his foreign correspondents down to the month in which he died.

guage. But the learning and mastery of a tongue being uneasy and unpleasant enough in itself, should not be cumbered with any other difficulties, as is done in this way of proceeding.[1] In fine, if boys' invention be to be quickened by such exercise, let them make themes in English, where they have facility and a command of words, and will better see what kind of thoughts they have, when put into their own language. And if the Latin tongue is to be learned, let it be done the easiest way, without toiling and disgusting the mind by so uneasy an employment as that of making speeches joined to it.

174. *Verses.*—If these may be any reasons against children's making Latin themes at school, I have much more to say, and of more weight, against their making verses, verses of any sort ; for if he has no genius to poetry, it is the most unreasonable thing in the world to torment a child, and waste his time about that which can never succeed ; and if he have a poetic vein,[2] it is to me the strangest thing in the world, that the father should desire or suffer it to be cherished or improved. Methinks the parents should labour to have it stifled and suppressed as much as may be ; and I know not what reason a father can have to wish his son a poet, who does not desire to have him bid defiance to all other callings and business : which is not yet the worst of the case ; for if he proves a successful rhymer, and gets once the reputation of a wit, I desire it may be considered what company and places he is like to spend his time in, nay, and estate too. For it is very seldom seen that any one discovers mines of gold or silver in Parnassus. 'Tis a pleasant air, but a barren soil ; and there are very few instances of those who have added to their patrimony by anything they have reaped from thence. Poetry and gaming, which usually go together, are alike in this too, that they seldom bring any advantage, but to those who have nothing else to live on. Men of estates almost constantly go away losers ; and 'tis well if they escape at a cheaper rate than their

---

[1] Compare sec. 169, above.
[2] *Conduct*, sec. 4, "Many a good poetic vein is buried under a trade."

whole estates, or the greatest part of them. If therefore you would not have your son the fiddle to every jovial company, without whom the sparks could not relish their wine, nor know how to pass an afternoon idly ; if you would not have him waste his time and estate to divert others, and contemn the dirty acres left him by his ancestors, I do not think you will much care he should be a poet, or that his school-master should enter him in versifying. But yet, if any one will think poetry a desirable quality in his son, and that the study of it would raise his fancy and parts, he must needs yet confess, that, to that end, reading the excellent Greek and Roman poets is of more use than making bad verses of his own, in a language that is not his own. And he, whose design it is to excel in English poetry, would not, I guess, think the way to it were to make his first essays in Latin verses.[1]

175. Another thing, very ordinary in the vulgar method of grammar-schools, there is, of which I see no use at all, unless it be to balk young lads in the way of learning languages, which, in my opinion, should be made as easy and pleasant as may be ; and that which was painful in it as much as possible quite removed. That which I mean, and here complain of, is, their being forced to learn by heart great parcels of the authors which are taught them ; wherein I can discover no advantage at all, especially to the business they are upon. Languages are to be learnt only by reading and talking, and not by scraps of authors got by heart ; which, when a man's head is stuffed with, he has got the just furniture of a pedant, and it is the ready way to make him one, than which there is nothing less becoming a gentleman. For what can be more ridiculous, than to mix the rich and handsome thoughts and sayings of others with a deal of poor stuff of his own ; which is thereby the more exposed, and has no other grace in it, nor will otherwise recommend the speaker, than a thread-bare russet-coat would,

---

[1] This section is beyond apology ; but it is characteristic of the author's grave æsthetic limitations, and *may* be reminiscent of verse-making at Westminster under Busby.

that was set off with large patches of scarlet and glittering brocard ? Indeed, where a passage comes in the way, whose matter is worth remembrance, and the expression of it very close and excellent (as there are many such in the ancient authors), it may not be amiss to lodge it in the minds of young scholars, and with such admirable strokes of those great masters sometimes exercise the memories of school-boys. But their learning of their lessons by heart, as they happen to fall out in their books without choice or distinction, I know not what it serves for, but to mispend their time and pains, and give them a disgust and aversion to their books, wherein they find nothing but useless trouble.

[176.[1] I hear it is said, That children should be employed in getting things by heart, to exercise and improve their memories. I could wish this were said with as much authority of reason, as it is with forwardness of assurance ; and that this practice were established upon good observation, more than old custom ; for it is evident, that strength of memory is owing to a happy constitution, and not to any habitual improvement got by exercise. It is true, what the mind is intent upon, and for fear of letting it slip, often imprints afresh on itself by frequent reflection, that it is apt to retain, but still according to its own natural strength of retention. An impression made on bees-wax or lead will not last so long as on brass or steel.[2] Indeed, if it be renewed often, it may last the longer ; but every new reflecting on it is a new impression, and it is from thence one is to reckon, if one would know how long the mind retains it. But the learning pages of Latin by heart, no more fits the memory for retention of anything else, than the graving of one sentence in lead, makes it[3] the more capable of retaining firmly any other

[1] Especially valuable in connection with the doctrines of "formal training" and "memory training." The section cannot be reconciled with the opinion that Locke invented the "disciplinary conception of education."

[2] "All improvement of the memory lies in the line of *elaborating the associates* of each of the several things to be remembered. No amount of culture would seem capable of modifying a man's *general* retentiveness." (Wm. James, *Psychology*, Briefer Course, p. 296.)

[3] *Sc.* the lead. Compare *Conduct*, sec. 28, *note*.

characters. If such a sort of exercise of the memory were able to give it strength, and improve our parts, players of all other people must needs have the best memories, and be the best company : but whether the scraps they have got into their heads this way, make them remember other things the better ; and whether their parts be improved proportionably to the pains they have taken in getting by heart other sayings, experience will show. Memory is so necessary to all parts and conditions of life, and so little is to be done without it, that we are not to fear it should grow dull and useless for want of exercise, if exercise would make it grow stronger. But I fear this faculty of the mind is not capable of much help and amendment in general, by any exercise or endeavour of ours, at least not by that used upon this pretence in grammar-schools. And if Xerxes was able to call every common soldier by his name, in his army, that consisted of no less than a hundred thousand men, I think it may be guessed he got not this wonderful ability by learning his lessons by heart, when he was a boy. This method of exercising and improving the memory by toilsome repetitions, without book, of what they read, is, I think, little used in the education of princes ; which, if it had that advantage that is talked of, should be as little neglected in them, as in the meanest school-boys : princes having as much need of good memories as any men living, and have generally an equal share in this faculty with other men : though it has never been taken care of this way. What the mind is intent upon, and careful of, that it remembers best, and for the reason above-mentioned : to which if method and order be joined, all is done, I think, that can be, for the help of a weak memory ; and he that will take any other way to do it, especially that of charging it with a train of other people's words, which he that learns cares not for, will, I guess, scarce find the profit answer half the time and pains employed in it.

I do not mean hereby, that there should be no exercise given to children's memories. I think their memories should be employed, but not in learning by rote whole pages out of books, which, the lesson being once said, and that task over, are delivered up again to oblivion, and neglected for ever. This mends neither the memory nor the mind. What they should learn by heart out of authors, I have above mentioned : and such wise and useful sentences being once given in charge to their memories, they should never be suffered to forget again, but be often called to account for them : whereby, besides the use those sayings may be to them in their future life, as so many good rules and observations, they will be taught to reflect often, and bethink themselves what they have to remember, which is the only way to make the memory quick and useful. The custom of frequent reflection will keep their minds from running adrift, and call their thoughts home from useless, inattentive roving : and therefore, I think, it may do well, to give them something every day to remember ; but something still, that is in itself worth the remembering, and what you would never have out of mind, whenever you call, or they themselves search for it. This will oblige them often to turn their thoughts inwards, than which you cannot wish them a better intellectual habit.]

177.[1] But under whose care soever a child is put to be taught, during the tender and flexible years of his life, this is certain, it should be one who thinks Latin and language the least part of education ; one, who knowing how much virtue, and a well-tempered soul, is to be preferred to any sort of learning or language, makes it his chief business to form the mind of his scholars, and give that a right disposition : which, if once got, though all the rest should be neglected, would, in due time, produce all the rest ; and which, if it be not got, and settled, so as to keep out ill and vicious habits, languages and sciences, and all the other accomplishments of education, will be to no purpose, but to make the worse or more dangerous man. And indeed, whatever stir there is made about getting of Latin, as the great and difficult business, his mother may teach it him herself, if she will but spend two or three hours in a

[1] Sec. 167 in first edition.

day with him, and make him read the evangelists in Latin to her: for she need but buy a Latin Testament, and having got somebody to mark the last syllable but one, where it is long, in words above two syllables (which is enough to regulate her pronunciation, and accenting the words), read daily in the gospels,[1] and then let her avoid understanding them in Latin, if she can. And when she understands the evangelists in Latin, let her, in the same manner, read Æsop's Fables, and so proceed on to Eutropius, Justin, and other such books. I do not mention this, as an imagination of what I fancy may do, but as of a thing I have known done, and the Latin tongue, with ease, got this way.

But to return to what I was saying: he that takes on him the charge of bringing up young men, especially young gentlemen, should have something more in him than Latin, more than even a knowledge in the liberal sciences; he should be a person of eminent virtue and prudence, and with good sense have good humour, and the skill to carry himself with gravity, ease, and kindness, in a constant conversation with his pupils.

178. At the same time that he is learning French and Latin, a child, as has been said, may also be entered in arithmetic, geography, chronology, history, and geometry, too. For if these be taught him in French or Latin, when he begins once to understand either of these tongues, he will get a knowledge in these sciences, and the language to boot.[2]

Geography.—Geography, I think, should be begun with; for the learning of the figure of the globe, the situation and boundaries of the four parts of the world, and that of particular kingdoms and countries, being only an

---

[1] "When the whim takes you to learn English, you have only to follow my method of reading every day a chapter of the New Testament, and in a month you will become master of it." So, in French of doubtful idiom, Locke wrote to Thoynard in September, 1679, perhaps describing his own mode of studying French. The letter is given in H. Ollion's *Notes sur la correspondance de John Locke—1678-1681* (Paris, 1908).

[2] See secs. 169, 173.

exercise of the eyes and memory, a child with pleasure will learn and retain them : and this is so certain, that I now live in the house with a child[1] whom his mother has so well instructed this way in geography, that he knew the limits of the four parts of the world, could readily point, being asked, to any country upon the globe, or any county in the map of England ; knew all the great rivers, promontories, straits, and bays in the world, and could find the longitude and latitude of any place, before he was six years old.[2] These things that he will thus learn by sight, and have by rote in his memory, are not all, I confess, that he is to learn upon the globes. But yet it is a good step and preparation to it, and will make the remainder much easier, when his judgment is grown ripe enough for it : besides that, it gets so much time now ; and by the pleasure of knowing things, leads him on insensibly to the gaining of languages.

179. *Arithmetic.*—When he has the natural parts of the globe well fixed in his memory, it may then be time to begin arithmetic. By the natural parts of the globe, I mean the several positions of the parts of the earth and sea, under different names and distinctions of countries ; not coming yet to those artificial and imaginary lines, which have been invented, and are only supposed, for the better improvement of that science.

180. Arithmetic is the easiest, and consequently the first sort of abstract reasoning, which the mind commonly bears, or accustoms itself to : and is of so general use in all parts of life and business, that scarce any thing is to be done without it. This is certain, a man cannot have too much of it, nor too perfectly ; he should therefore begin to be exercised in counting, as soon, and as far, as he is capable of it ; and do something in it every day, till he is master of the art of numbers. When he under-stands addition and subtraction, he may then be advanced

---

[1] Francis Cudworth Masham. See the Dedication to Edward Clarke, above.

[2] Locke is here untrue to his own principles in accepting words for ideas. See, too, sec. 181.

farther in geography, and after he is acquainted with
the poles, zones, parallel circles, and meridians, be taught
longitude and latitude, and the use of maps.[1] [Which
when he can readily do, he may then be entered in the
celestial ; and there going over all the circles again, with
a more particular observation of the ecliptic or zodiac,
to fix them all very clearly and distinctly in his mind,
he may be taught the figure and position of the several
constellations which may be showed him first upon the
globe, and then in the heavens.

Astronomy.—When that is done, and he knows pretty
well the constellations of this our hemisphere, it may be
time to give him some notions of this our planetary
world, and to that purpose it may not be amiss to make
him a draught of the Copernican system ; and therein
explain to him the situation of the planets, their respective distances from the sun, the centre of their revolu-
tions. This will prepare him to understand the motion
and theory of the planets, the most easy and natural
way. For since astronomers no longer doubt of the
motion of the planets about the sun, it is fit he should
proceed upon that hypothesis, which is not only the
simplest and least perplexing for a learner, but also the
likeliest to be true in itself.] But in this, as in all other
parts of instruction, great care must be taken with
children, to begin with that which is plain and simple,[2]
and to teach them as little as can be at once, and settle
that well in their heads, before you proceed to the next,
or anything new in that science. Give them first one
simple idea, and see that they take it right, and perfectly
comprehend it, before you go any farther ; and then add
some other simple idea, which lies next in your way to
what you aim it ; and so proceeding by gentle and in-

---

[1] Seven lines in the first edition are here replaced by the longer
passage below, in square brackets, from a later edition. *Cf. Conduct*, sec. 39, third paragraph.

[2] A sound principle which Locke's recommendations have just
contravened. It will be noticed that the Ptolemaic system is not
dismissed as impossible.

sensible steps, children, without confusion and amazement, will have their understandings opened, and their
thoughts extended, farther than could have been expected.
And when any one has learned any thing himself, there
is no such way to fix it in his memory, and to encourage
him to go on as to set him to teach it others.

181. *Geometry.*—When he has once got such an
acquaintance with the globes, as is above-mentioned,
he may be fit to be tried a little in geometry ; wherein I
think the six first books of Euclid enough for him to be
taught.   For I am in some doubt, whether more to a
man of business[1] be necessary or useful; at least if he
have a genius and inclination to it, being entered so far
by his tutor, he will be able to go on of himself, without
a teacher.

The globes therefore must be studied, and that diligently, and, I think, may be begun betimes, if the tutor
will but be careful to distinguish, what the child is capable
of knowing, and what not ; for which this may be a rule,
that perhaps will go a pretty way, *viz.*, That children
may be taught any thing that falls under their
senses, especially their sight, as far as their memories
only are exercised : and thus a child very young may
learn, which is the equator, which the meridian, etc.,
which Europe, and which England upon the globes, as
soon almost as he knows the rooms of the house he lives
in ; if care be taken not to teach him too much at once,
nor to set him upon a new part till that, which he is
upon, be perfectly learned and fixed in his memory.[2]

182.[3] *Chronology.*—With geography, chronology ought
to go hand in hand ; I mean the general part of it, so that
he may have in his mind a view of the whole current of
time, and the several considerable epochs that are made
use of in history.   Without these two, history, which is
the great mistress of prudence, and civil knowledge ; and
ought to be the proper study of a gentleman, or man of
business in the world ; without geography and chronology,

---

[1] Man of affairs, public man.   [2] See note to sec. 178, p. 147.
[3] Sec. 172 in first edition.

I say, history, will be very ill retained, and very little useful ; but be only a jumble of matters of fact, confusedly heaped together without order or instruction. It is by these two, that the actions of mankind are ranked into their proper places of times and countries ; under which circumstances, they are not only much easier kept in the memory, but in that natural order, are only capable to afford those observations which make a man the better and the abler for reading them.[1]

183.[2] When I speak of chronology as a science he should be perfect in, I do not mean the little controversies that are in it. These are endless, and most of them of so little importance to a gentleman, as not to deserve to be inquired into, were they capable of an easy decision. And therefore all that learned noise and dust of the chronologist is wholly to be avoided. The most useful book I have seen in that part of learning, is a small treatise of Strauchius, which is printed in twelves, under the title of " Breviarium Chronologicum," out of which may be selected all that is necessary to be taught a young gentleman concerning chronology ; for all that is in that treatise, a learner need not be cumbered with. He has in him the most remarkable or usual epochs reduced all to that of the Julian period, which is the easiest and plainest and surest method that can be made use of in chronology. To this treatise of Strauchius, Helvicus's tables may be added, as a book to be turned to on all occasions.[3]

[1] These considerations are usually forgotten by those who deprecate the learning of " dates."
[2] Sec. 172 in first edition.
[3] Both authors are recommended for the reading of Cambridge men in their first year, by Robert Green (1707). Christopher Helwig (1581-1617), professor at Giessen and critic of Ratke, wrote *Theatrum Historicum sive Chronologiæ systema novum . . . a mundi origine ad . . . annum* 1609, a series of tables intended to give the kind of information to be found in Mr. Gooch's well-known *Annals of Politics and Culture.* There were many subsequent editions, brought down to date. An English folio edition appeared in 1687. Giles Strauch, professor at Wittenberg, wrote *Breviarium Chronologicum,* a treatise on chronology, which appeared in English, translated " from the third edition," in 1699, a volume of nearly 500 pages.

184. *History.*—As nothing teaches, so nothing delights, more than history. The first of these recommends it to the study of grown men, the latter makes me think it the fittest for a young lad, who, as soon as he is instructed in chronology, and acquainted with the several epochs in use in this part of the world, and can reduce them to the Julian period, should then have some Latin history put into his hand. The choice should be directed by the easiness of the style ; for wherever he begins, chronology will keep it from confusion ; and the pleasantness of the subject inviting him to read, the language will insensibly be got, without that terrible vexation and uneasiness, which children suffer where they are put into books beyond their capacity, such as are the Roman orators and poets, only to learn the Roman language. When he has by reading mastered the easier, such perhaps as Justin, Eutropius, Quintus Curtius,[1] etc., the next degree to these will give him no great trouble, and thus by a gradual progress from the plainest and easiest historians,·he may at last come to read the most difficult and sublime of the Latin authors, such as are Tully,[2] Virgil, and Horace.

185. *Ethics.*—The knowledge of virtue, all along from the beginning, in all the instances he is capable of, being taught him, more by practice than rules ; and the love of reputation, instead of satisfying his appetite, being made habitual in him ; I know not whether he should read any other discourses of morality but what he finds in the Bible ; or have any system of ethics put into his hand, till he can read Tully's Offices, not as a school-boy to learn Latin, but as one that would be informed in the principles and precepts of virtue for the conduct of his life.

186. *Civil Law.*—When he has pretty well digested Tully's Offices [and added to it " Puffendorf de officio hominis et civis,"] it may be seasonable to set him upon

[1] See note, sec. 168. All three are historical compilers ; the precise date of the last is disputed, but it falls within the Christian era.
[2] Marcus Tullius Cicero.

" Grotius de jure belli et pacis," or, which perhaps is
the better of the two, " Puffendorf de jure naturali et
gentium,"[1] wherein he will be instructed in the natural
rights of men, and the original and foundations of society,
and the duties resulting from thence.   This general part
of civil law and history, are studies which a gentleman
should not barely touch at, but constantly dwell upon
and never have done with.   A virtuous and well-behaved
young man, that is well versed in the general part
of the civil law (which concerns not the chicane of
private cases, but the affairs and intercourse of civilized nations in general, grounded upon principles of
reason), understands Latin well, and can write a good
hand, one may turn loose into the world, with great
assurance that he will find employment and esteem
every where.[2]

187. *Law.*—It would be strange to suppose an English
gentleman should be ignorant of the law of his country.
This, whatever station he is in, is so requisite that from
a justice of the peace to a minister of state, I know no
place he can well fill without it.   I do not mean the
chicane or wrangling and captious part of the law ; a
gentleman whose business it is to seek the true measures
of right and wrong, and not the arts how to avoid doing
the one and secure himself in doing the other, ought to
be as far from such a study of the law, as he is concerned
diligently to apply himself to that wherein he may be
serviceable to his country.   And to that purpose I think
the right way for a gentleman to study our law, which
he does not design for his calling, is to take a view of our
English constitution and government, in the ancient
books of the common law, and some more modern writers,

[1] Two early writers on International Law : Hugo Grotius (1583-
1645), *On the Law of War and Peace*, 1625 ; Samuel Puffendorf
(1632-1694), *On Natural Law and the Law of Nations*, 1672, and its
abridgement, *De Officio hominis et civis juxta legem naturalem* (1673)
—*On the Duty of a Man and Citizen in respect of the Law of
Nature.*

[2] In Locke's opinion, the education of the sixteenth century still
retained justification.

who out of them have given an account of this government. And having got a true idea of that, then to read
our history, and with it join in every king's reign the
laws then made. This will give an insight into the
reason of our statutes, and show the true ground upon
which they came to be made, and what weight they ought
to have.[1]

188.[2] *Rhetoric, Logic.*—Rhetoric and logic being the
arts, that in the ordinary method usually follow immediately after grammar, it may perhaps be wondered that
I have said so little of them. The reason is, because of
the little advantage young people receive by them ; for
I have seldom or never observed any one to get the skill
of reasoning well, or speaking handsomely by studying
those rules which pretend to teach it :[3] and therefore I
would have a young gentleman take a view of them in
the shortest systems that could be found without dwell-
ing long on the contemplation and study of those formalities. Right reasoning is founded on something else
than the predicaments and predicables, and does not
consist in talking in mode and figure itself. But it is
beside my present business to enlarge upon this specula-
tion. To come therefore to what we have in hand ; if
you would have your son reason well, let him read
Chillingworth ;[4] and if you would have him speak well,
let him be conversant in Tully, to give him the true idea
of eloquence, and let him read those things that are well
written in English, to perfect his style in the purity of
our language.

189.[5] If the use and end of right reasoning be to have
right notions, and a right judgment of things, to distin-

<hr>

[1] In Locke's day, and later, residence at one of the Inns of Court
was regarded as a suitable completion of general education.

[2] Sec. 177 in first edition.

[3] *Cf.* sec. 166 and *Conduct*, secs. 4, 6, 31, 43, 44. It had been
Locke's duty at Oxford to teach logic to junior under-graduates.

[4] Wm. Chillingworth (1602-1644) embraced and then abjured
Catholicism, against which he wrote in *The Religion of Protestants
a Safe Way of Salvation*, 1638

[5] Sec. 177 in first edition.

guish betwixt truth and falsehood, right and wrong, and
to act accordingly, be sure not to let your son be bred
up in the art and formality of disputing, either practising
it himself, or admiring it in others ; unless, instead of an
able man, you desire to have him an insignificant wrangler,
opiniator[1] in discourse, and priding himself in contra-
dicting others; or which is worse, questioning every thing,
and thinking there is no such thing as truth to be sought,
but only victory, in disputing. [For this, in short, is
the way and perfection of logical disputes, that the
opponent never takes any answer, nor the respondent
ever yields to any argument.   This neither of them must
do, whatever becomes of truth or knowledge, unless he
will pass for a poor baffled wretch, and lie under the
disgrace of not being able to maintain whatever he has
once affirmed, which is the great aim and glory in disputing.] Truth is to be found and supported by a
mature and due consideration of things themselves, and
not by artificial terms and ways of arguing : which lead
not men so much into the discovery of truth, as into a
captious and fallacious use of doubtful words, which is
the most useless and disingenuous way of talking, and
most unbecoming a gentleman or a lover of truth of
any thing in the world.[2]

[There can scarce be a greater defect in a gentleman
than not to express himself well, either in writing or
speaking. But yet, I think, I may ask my reader,
Whether he doth not know a great many, who live upon their
estates, and so, with the name, should have the qualities
of gentlemen, who cannot so much as tell a story as they
should, much less speak clearly and persuasively in any
business ? This I think not to be so much their fault,
as the fault of their education ; for I must, without
partiality, do my countrymen this right, that where they
apply themselves, I see none of their neighbours outgo

---

[1] One who stands stiffly by his own opinion.
[2] The remainder of the section is invaluable in reference to the
method of teaching the mother-tongue. See, also, secs. 168, 171,
172.

them. They have been taught rhetoric, but yet never
taught how to express themselves handsomely with their
tongues, or pens, in the language they are always to use ;
as if the names of the figures[1] that embellished the discourses of those who understood the art of speaking,
were the very art and skill of speaking well. This, as
all other things of practice, is to be learned not by a few
or a great many rules given, but by exercise and application, according to good rules, or rather patterns, till habits
are got, and a facility of doing it well.

Agreeable hereunto, perhaps it might not be amiss, to
make children, as soon as they are capable of it, often
to tell a story of any thing they know ; and to correct at
first the most remarkable fault they are guilty of, in their
way of putting it together. When that fault is cured,
then to show them the next, and so on, till one after
another, all, at least the gross ones, are mended. When
they can tell tales pretty well, then it may be time to
make them write them. The fables of Æsop, the only
book almost that I know fit for children, may afford
them matter for this exercise of writing English, as well
as for reading and translating, to enter them in the
Latin tongue. When they are got past the faults of
grammar, and can join in a continued, coherent discourse
the several parts of a story, without bald and unhand-
some forms of transition (as is usual) often repeated ; he
that desires to perfect them yet farther in this, which
is the first step to speaking well, and needs no invention,
may have recourse to Tully ; and by putting in practice
those rules, which that master of eloquence gives in his
first book " De Inventione," section 20, make them
know wherein the skill and graces of a handsome narrative,
according to the several subjects and designs of it, lie.
Of each of which rules fit examples may be found out,
and therein they may be shown how others have practised them. The ancient classic authors afford plenty
of such examples, which they should be made not only

[1] Such rhetorical terms as " hyperbole," " meiosis," " hysteron-
proteron," etc.

to translate, but have set before them as patterns for their daily imitation.

When they understand how to write English with due connection, propriety, and order, and are pretty well masters of a tolerable narrative style, they may be advanced to writing of letters; wherein they should not be put upon any strains of wit or compliment, but taught to express their own plain easy sense, without any incoherence, confusion, or roughness. And when they are perfect in this, they may, to raise their thoughts, have set before them the example of Voiture's,[1] for the entertainment of their friends at a distance, with letters of compliment, mirth, raillery, or diversion; and Tully's epistles, as the best pattern, whether for business or conversation. The writing of letters has so much to do in all the occurrences of human life, that no gentleman can avoid showing himself in this kind of writing; occasions will daily force him to make this use of his pen, which, besides the consequences, that, in his affairs, his well or ill managing of it often draws after it, always lays him open to a severer examination of his breeding, sense, and abilities, than oral discourses; whose transient faults, dying for the most part with the sound that gives them life, and so not subject to a strict review, more easily escape observation and censure.

Had the methods of education been directed to their right end, one would have thought this, so necessary a part, could not have been neglected, whilst themes and verses in Latin, of no use at all, were so constantly everywhere pressed, to the racking of children's inventions beyond their strength, and hindering their cheerful progress in learning the tongues, by unnatural difficulties. But custom has so ordained it, and who dares disobey? And would it not be very unreasonable to require of a learned country school-master (who has all the tropes

---

[1] Vincent Voiture (1598-1648), society letter-writer and versifier, whose letters were highly valued far beyond the Rambouillet circle for which they were penned. See G. Lanson, *Histoire de la Littera-ture Française*, p. 385.

and figures in Farnaby's[1] Rhetoric at his fingers' end) to teach his scholar to express himself handsomely in English, when it appears to be so little his business or thought, that the boy's mother (despised, it is like, as illiterate, for not having read a system of logic and rhetoric) outdoes him in it ?

To write and speak correctly, gives a grace, and gains a favourable attention to what one has to say : and since it is English that an English gentleman will have constant use of, that is the language he should chiefly cultivate, and wherein most care should be taken to polish and perfect his style. To speak or write better Latin than English, may make a man be talked of ; but he would find it more to his purpose to express himself well in his own tongue, that he uses every moment, than to have the vain commendation of others for a very insignificant quality. This I find universally neglected, and no care taken anywhere to improve young men in their own language, that they may thoroughly understand and be masters of it. If any one among us have a facility or purity more than ordinary in his mother-tongue, it is owing to chance or his genius, or any thing, rather than to his education, or any care of his teacher. To mind what English his pupil speaks or writes, is below the dignity of one bred up amongst Greek and Latin, though he have but little of them himself. These are the learned languages, fit only for learned men to meddle with and teach ; English is the language of the illiterate vulgar ; though yet we see the polity of some of our neighbours hath not thought it beneath the public care, to promote and reward the improvement of their own language.[2] Polish-

---

[1] The *Index Rhetoricus* (1625), a small Latin textbook by Thomas Farnaby (1575[?]-1647), gentleman adventurer with Drake and Hawkins, classical scholar and distinguished private schoolmaster in London. For the *Index Rhetoricus*, see Foster Watson, *The English Grammar Schools*, p. 443.

[2] Locke may be thinking more particularly of the Académie Française (founded, 1634-1637), which began to publish its great Dictionary in 1694. Academies, or societies to encourage the literary development of vernaculars, steadily increased after the

ing and enriching their tongue, is no small business amongst them; it·hath colleges and stipends appointed it, and there is raised amongst them a great ambition and emulation of writing correctly: and we see what they are come to by it, and how far they have spread one of the worst languages possibly, in this part of the world, if we look upon it as it was in some few reigns backwards, whatever it be now. The great men amongst the Romans were daily exercising themselves in their own language; and we find yet upon record, the names of orators, who taught some of their emperors Latin, though it were their mother-tongue.

It is plain the Greeks were yet more nice in theirs; all other speech was barbarous to them but their own, and no foreign language appears to have been studied or valued amongst that learned and acute people; though it be past doubt, that they borrowed their learning and philosophy from abroad.

I am not here speaking against Greek and Latin: I think they ought to be studied, and the Latin, at least, understood well by every gentleman. But whatever foreign languages a young man meddles with (and the more he knows the better), that which he should critically study, and labour to get a facility, clearness, and elegancy to express himself in, should be his own, and to this purpose he should daily be exercised in it.]

190.[1] *Natural Philosophy.*—Natural philosophy, as a speculative science, I imagine we have none, and perhaps I may think I have reason to say we never shall. The works of nature are contrived by a wisdom, and operate by ways too far surpassing our faculties to discover, or capacities to conceive, for us ever to be able to reduce them into a science. Natural philosophy being the knowledge of the principles, properties, and operations of

---

foundation of the Florentine Accademia de la Crusca (1582). Outside Italy, the best-known are the Fruchtbringende Gesellschaft at Anhalt Köthen (1617) and the Académie Française.

[1] Sec. 177 in first edition.

things, as they are in themselves, I imagine there are two parts of it, one comprehending Spirits with their nature and qualities ; and the other Bodies.[1] The first of these is usually referred to metaphysics : but under what title soever the consideration of spirits comes, I think it ought to go before the study of matter and body, not as a science that can be methodized into a system, and treated of upon principles of knowledge ; but as an enlargement of our minds towards a truer and fuller comprehension of the intellectual world, to which we are led both by reason and revelation. And since the clearest and largest discoveries we have of other spirits, besides God and our own souls, is imparted to us from heaven by revelation, I think the information that at least young people should have of them, should be taken from that revelation. To this purpose, I conclude it would be well if there were made a good history of the Bible for young people to read ; wherein every thing that is fit to be put into it being laid down in its due order of time, and several things omitted which were suited only to riper age, that confusion which is usually produced by promiscuous reading of the Scripture, as it lies now bound up in our Bibles, would be avoided ; and also this other good obtained, that by reading of it constantly, there would be instilled into the minds of children a notion and belief of spirits, they having so much to do, in all the transactions of that history, which will be a good preparation to the study of bodies. For without the notion and allowance of spirit, our philosophy will be lame and defective in one main part of it, when it leaves out the contemplation of the most excellent and powerful part of the creation.

191.[2] Of this history of the Bible, I think, too, it would be well if there were a short and plain epitome

---

[1] A doctrine scarcely to be expected from one of the leaders in modern scientific thought. It is instructive to note that Locke refuses to conceive a *natural* philosophy apart from metaphysics ; yet his psychology shook itself free from metaphysic. See sec. 193.

[2] Sec. 179 in first edition, which has no section numbered 178.

made, containing the chief and most material heads for children to be conversant in, as soon as they can read. This, though it will lead them early in some notion of spirits, yet is not contrary to what I said above, that I would not have children troubled whilst young with notions of spirits ; whereby my meaning was that I think it inconvenient that their yet tender minds should receive early impressions of goblins, spectres, and apparitions, wherewith their maids and those about them are apt to fright them into a compliance with their orders, which often proves a great inconvenience to them all their lives after, by subjecting their minds to frights, fearful apprehensions, weakness, and superstition ; which, when coming abroad into the world and conversation, they grow weary and ashamed of, it not seldom happens, that to make, as they think, a thorough cure, and ease themselves of a load, [which] has sat so heavy on them, they throw away the thoughts of all spirits together, and so run into the other but worse extreme.[1]

192. The reason why I would have this premised to the study of bodies, and the doctrine of the Scriptures well imbibed, before young men be entered in natural philosophy, is, because matter being a thing that all our senses are constantly conversant with, it is so apt to possess the mind, and exclude all other beings but matter, that prejudice, grounded on such principles, often leaves no room for the admittance of spirits, or the allowing any such things as immaterial beings, " *in rerum natura ;*[2] when yet it is evident, that by mere matter and motion, none of the great phenomena of nature can be resolved : to instance but in that common one of gravity ;[3] which I think impossible to be explained by any natural operation of matter, or any other law of motion, but the positive will of a superior Being so ordering it. And therefore since the Deluge cannot be well explained, without admitting something out of the ordinary course of nature, I propose it to be considered, whether God's altering the

[1] See sec. 137.   [2] " In the nature of things."
[3] See sec. 194.

centre of gravity in the earth for a time (a thing as intelligible as gravity it self, which perhaps a little variation of causes, unknown to us, would produce) will not more easily account for Noah's flood, than any hypothesis yet made use of to solve it.[1] I hear the great objection to this is, that it would produce but a partial deluge. But this I mention by the by, to shew the necessity of having recourse to something beyond bare matter, and its motion, in the explication of nature ; to which the notions of spirits, and their power, as delivered in the Bible, where so much is attributed to their operation, may be a fit preparative ; reserving to a fitter opportunity a fuller explication of this hypothesis, and the application of it to all the parts of the Deluge, and any difficulties [that] can be supposed in the history of the Flood, as recorded in the Bible.

193. But to return to the study of natural philosophy : though the world be full of systems of it, yet I cannot say, I know any one which can be taught a young man as a science, wherein he may be sure to find truth and certainty, which is what all sciences give an expectation of.[2] I do not hence conclude, that none of them are to be read ; it is necessary for a gentleman, in this learned age, to look into some of them to fit himself for conversation : but whether that of Des Cartes be put into his hands, as that which is most in fashion, or it be thought fit to give him a short view of that and several others also ; I think the systems of natural philosophy, that have obtained in this part of the world, are to be read more to know the hypotheses, and to understand the terms and ways of talking of the several sects,[3] than with hopes to gain thereby a comprehensive, scientific, and satisfactory knowledge of the works of Nature ; only

[1] An oblique reference to Thomas Burnet's fantastic notions displayed in his *Theory of the Earth* (1684).

[2] See sec. 190, and *Essay*, iv., chap. iii., sec. 26. *Cf.* Introduction, p. 10.

[3] " Schools." *Cf. Conduct*, sec. 3 (at close). This fitting one's self " for conversation " is condemned in *Conduct*, sec. 19.

11

this may be said, that the modern Corpuscularians talk, in most things, more intelligibly than the Peripatetics, who possessed the schools immediately before them.[1] He that would look farther back, and acquaint himself with the several opinions of the ancients, may consult Dr. Cudworth's Intellectual System;[2] wherein that very learned author hath, with such accurateness and judgment, collected and explained the opinions of the Greek philosophers, that what principles they built on, and what were the chief hypotheses that divided them, is better to be seen in him than anywhere else that I know. But I would not deter any one from the study of nature, because all the knowledge we have, or possibly can have of it, cannot be brought into a science. There are very many things in it, that are convenient and necessary to be known to a gentleman; and a great many other, that will abundantly reward the pains of the curious with delight and advantage. But these, I think, are rather to be found amongst such writers as have employed themselves in making rational experiments and observations, than in starting barely speculative systems. Such writings, therefore, as many of Mr. Boyle's[3] are, with others that have writ of husbandry, planting, gardening, and the like, may be fit for a gentleman, when he has a little acquainted himself with some of the systems of the natural philosophy in fashion.

194. Though the systems of physic[s] that I have met with, afford little encouragement to look for certainty, or science, in any treatise, which shall pretend to give us a body of natural philosophy from the first principles

---

[1] *Cf.* sec. 94 and *Conduct*, sec. 29.   Corpuscularians like Descartes and Boyle, and Democritus and Epicurus in ancient times, taught that all phenomena are due to matter and its extension, divisibility, configuration and motion.

[2] Ralph Cudworth, Master of Christ's College, Cambridge, published *The True Intellectual System of the Universe* in 1678.

[3] Robert Boyle (1627-1691), a member of the private society (the " Invisible College "), which at Oxford and at Gresham College and elsewhere in London prosecuted experimental study. Boyle took a leading part in founding the Royal Society (1662).

of bodies in general ; yet the incomparable Mr. Newton [1] has shown how far mathematics, applied to some parts of nature, may, upon principles that matter of fact justify, carry us in the knowledge of some, as I may so call them, particular provinces of the incomprehensible universe. And if others could give us so good and clear an account of other parts of nature, as he has of this our planetary world, and the most considerable phenomena observable in it, in his admirable book " Philosophiæ naturalis Principia mathematica,"[1] we might in time hope to be furnished with more true and certain knowledge in several parts of this stupendous machine, than hitherto we could have expected. And though there are very few that have mathematics enough to understand his demonstrations ; yet the most accurate mathematicians, who have examined them, allowing them to be such, his book will deserve to be read, and give no small light and pleasure to those, who, willing to understand the motions, properties, and operations of the great masses of matter in this our solar system, will but carefully mind his conclusions, which may be depended on as propositions well proved.

195. *Greek.*—This is, in short, what I have thought concerning a young gentleman's studies ; wherein it will possibly be wondered that I should omit Greek, since amongst the Grecians is to be found the original, as it were, and foundation of all that learning which we have in this part of the world. I grant it so ; and will add, that no man can pass for a scholar, that is ignorant of the Greek tongue. But I am not here considering of the education of a professed scholar, but of a gentleman, to whom Latin and French, as the world now goes, is by every one acknowledged to be necessary. When he comes to be a man, if he has a mind to carry his studies farther, and look into the Greek learning, he will then easily get that tongue himself ; and if he has not that inclination, his learning of it under a tutor will be but lost labour,

[1] Isaac Newton (1642-1727) was not knighted till 1705. The *Principia* was published in 1687.

and much of his time and pains spent in that which will
be neglected and thrown away as soon as he is at liberty.
For how many are there of a hundred, even amongst
scholars themselves, who retain the Greek they carried
from school ; or ever improve it to a familiar reading,
and perfect understanding of Greek authors ?

[To conclude this part, which concerns a young gentleman's studies, his tutor should remember, that his business
is not so much to teach him all that is knowable, as to
raise in him a love and esteem of knowledge ; and to put
him in the right way of knowing and improving himself,
when he has a mind to it.]

*Later editions here insert quotations from La Bruyère
(" Moeurs de ce Siècle ")* " on the subject of languages."

Method.—[Order and constancy are said to make the
great difference between one man and another ; this I
am sure, nothing so much clears a learner's way, helps
him so much on in it, and makes him go so easy and
so far in any inquiry, as a good method. His governor
should take pains to make him sensible of this, accustom
him to order, and teach him method in all the applications of his thoughts ; show him wherein it lies, and the
advantages of it ; acquaint him with the several sorts
of it, either from general to particulars, or from particulars to what is more general ; exercise him in
both of them ; and make him see, in what cases each
different method is most proper, and to what ends it
best serves.

In history the order of time should govern ; in philosophical inquiries, that of nature, which in all progression
is to go from the place one is then in, to that which joins
and lies next to it ; and so it is in the mind, from the
knowledge it stands possessed of already, to that which
lies next, and is coherent to it, and so on to what it aims
at, by the simplest and most uncompounded parts it
can divide the matter into. To this purpose, it will be
of great use to his pupil to accustom him to distinguish
well, that is, to have distinct notions, wherever the mind
can find any real difference ; but as carefully to avoid

distinctions in terms, where he has not distinct and different clear ideas.[1]]

196. Besides what is to be had from study and books, there are other accomplishments necessary to a gentleman, to be got by exercise, and to which time is to be allowed, and for which masters must be had.

Dancing.—Dancing being that which gives graceful motions all the life, and, above all things, manliness and a becoming confidence to young children, I think it cannot be learned too early, after they are once of an age and strength capable of it. But you must be sure to have a good master, that knows, and can teach, what is graceful and becoming, and what gives a freedom and easiness to all the motions of the body. One that teaches not this is worse than none at all, natural unfashionableness being much better than apish, affected postures ; and I think it much more passable to put off the hat, and make a leg, like an honest country gentleman, than like an ill-fashioned dancing-master. For, as for the jigging part, and the figures of dances, I count that little or nothing farther than as it tends to perfect graceful carriage.

197. *Music.*—Music is thought to have some affinity with dancing, and a good hand, upon some instruments, is by many people mightily valued. But it wastes so much of a young man's time, to gain but a moderate skill in it, and engages often in such odd company, that many think it much better spared : and I have, amongst men of parts and business,[2] so seldom heard any one commended or esteemed for having an excellency in music, that amongst all those things, that ever came

---

[1] *Cf. Conduct*, sec. 39. " As a clear idea is that whereof the mind has such a full and evident perception as it does receive from an outward object operating duly on a well-disposed organ, so a distinct idea is that wherein the mind perceives a difference from all other ; and a confused idea is such an one as is not sufficiently distinguishable from another from which it ought to be distinguished " (*Essay concerning Human Understanding*, ii., chap. xxix.). See also the " Epistle to the Reader."

[2] Men of affairs, public men. *Cf.* note, sec. 210.

into the list of accomplishments, I think I may give it the last place. Our short lives will not serve us for the attainment of all things ; nor can our minds be always intent on something to be learned. The weakness of our constitutions, both of mind and body, requires that we should be often unbent : and he that will make a good use of any part of his life, must allow a large portion of it to recreation. At least this must not be denied to young people, unless, whilst you with too much haste make them old, you have the displeasure to set them in their graves, or a second childhood, sooner than you could wish. And therefore I think that the time and pains allotted to serious improvements should be employed about things of most use and consequence, and that too in the methods the most easy and short, that could be at any rate obtained ; and perhaps it would be none of the least secrets of education to make the exercises of the body and the mind, the recreation one to another. I doubt not but that something might be done in it, by a prudent man, that would well consider the temper and inclination of his pupil. For he that is wearied either with study or dancing, does not desire presently to go to sleep ; but to do something else which may divert and delight him. But this must be always remembered, that nothing can come into the account of recreation that is not done with delight.

198. Fencing, and riding the great horse,[1] are looked upon as so necessary parts of breeding, that it would be thought a great omission to neglect them : the latter of the two, being for the most part to be learned only in great towns, is one of the best exercises for health which is to be had in those places of ease and luxury ; and, upon that account, makes a fit part of a young gentleman's employment, during his abode there. And, as far as it conduces to give a man a firm and graceful seat on horseback, and to make him able to teach his horse to

---

[1] The management of the charger, especially in military parade; it was one of the chief aims of the French academies to teach this. See Introduction.

stop, and turn quick, and to rest on his haunches, is of use to a gentleman both in peace and war. But, whether it be of moment enough to be made a business of, and deserve to take up more of his time than should barely for his health be employed, at due intervals, in some such vigorous exercise, I shall leave to the discretion of parents and tutors ; who will do well to remember, in all the parts of education, that most time and application is to be bestowed on that which is like to be of greatest consequence and frequent use, in the ordinary course and occurrences of that life the young man is designed for.

199. *Fencing.*—As for fencing, it seems to me a good exercise for health, but dangerous to the life, the confidence of it being apt to engage in quarrels those that think they have some skill, and to make them often more touchy than needs, on points of honour, and slight provocations. Young men in their warm blood are forward to think they have in vain learned to fence if they never show their skill and courage in a duel ; and they seem to have reason. But how many sad tragedies that reason has been the occasion of, the tears of many a mother can witness.[1] A man that cannot fence will be more careful to keep out of bullies' and gamesters' company, and will not be half so apt to stand upon punctilios nor to give affronts, or fiercely justify them when given, which is that which usually makes the quarrel. And when a man is in the field, a moderate skill in fencing rather exposes him to the sword of his enemy, than secures him from it. And certainly a man of courage, who cannot fence at all, and therefore will put all upon one thrust, and not stand parrying, has the

[1] " Many bloody and notorious duels were fought about this time. The Duke of Grafton killed Mr. Stanley, brother to the Earl of Derby, indeed, upon an almost insufferable provocation. It is to be hoped his Majesty will at last severely remedy this unchristian custom " (Evelyn, *Diary*, Feb., 168⅚). This entry is not singular in its impatience with the foreign custom of the duel ; many similar passages occur in the literature of the time. Steele and Defoe notably opposed duelling a generation later.

odds against a moderate fencer, especially if he has skill
in wrestling. And therefore, if any provision be to be
made against such accidents, and a man be to prepare
his son for duels, I had much rather mine should be a
good wrestler, than an ordinary fencer ; which is the most
a gentleman can attain to in it, unless he will be constantly in the fencing school, and every day exercising.
But since fencing and riding the great horse are so
generally looked upon as necessary qualifications in the
breeding of a gentleman, it will be hard wholly to deny
any one of that rank these marks of distinction.   I shall
leave it therefore to the father, to consider, how far the
temper of his son, and the station he is like to be in, will
allow or encourage him to comply with fashions, which,
having very little to do with civil life, were yet formerly
unknown to the most warlike nations ; and seem to have
added little of force or courage to those who have received them ; unless we will think martial skill or prowess
have been improved by duelling, with which fencing
came into, and with which, I presume, it will go out of
the world.

200. These are my present thoughts concerning learning and accomplishments.   The great business of all is
virtue and wisdom.

" Nullum numen abest, si sit prudentia."[1]

Teach him to get a mastery over his inclinations, and
submit his appetite to reason. This being obtained,
and by constant practice settled into habit, the hardest
part of the task is over.   To bring a young man to this,
I know nothing which so much contributes as the love
of praise and commendation, which should therefore be
instilled into him by all arts imaginable.   Make his mind
as sensible of credit and shame as may be : and when
you have done that, you have put a principle into him
which will influence his actions, when you are not by,
to which the fear of a little smart of a rod is not com-

---

[1] " Where wisdom is, no heavenly power is wanting " (Juvenal,
Satires x. 365 and xiv. 315.)

parable, and which will be the proper stock, whereon
afterwards to graft the true principles of morality and
religion.[1]

201. *Trade.*—I have one more thing to add, which as
soon as I mention I shall run the danger to be suspected
to have forgot what I am about, and what I have above
written concerning education, which has all tended
towards a gentleman's calling, with which a trade seems
wholly to be inconsistent. And yet, I cannot forbear
to say, I would have him *learn a trade, a manual trade ;*
nay, two or three, but one more particularly.

202. The busy inclination of children being always to
be directed to something that may be useful to them,
the advantage may be considered of two kinds : 1. Where
the skill it self, that is got by exercise, is worth the having.
Thus skill not only in languages and learned sciences,
but in painting, turning, gardening, tempering and
working in iron, and all other useful arts, is worth the
having. 2. Where the exercise it self, without any consideration, is necessary or useful for health. Knowledge
in some things is so necessary to be got by children
whilst they are young, that some part of their time is to
be allotted to their improvement in them, though those
employments contribute nothing at all to their health :
such are reading and writing, and all other sedentary
studies, for the improvement of the mind, and are the
unavoidable business of gentlemen quite from their
cradles. Other manual arts, which are both got and
exercised by labour, do many of them by their exercise
contribute to our health too, especially such as employ
us in the open air. In these, then, health and improvement may be joined together, and of these should some
fit ones be chosen, to be made the recreations of one,
whose chief business is with books and study.[2] In this
choice, the age and inclination of the person is to be
considered, and constraint always to be avoided in bring-

[1] See secs. 53, 56-60.
[2] Rousseau requires Émile to learn hand-work, in order that he
may understand that " every idle citizen is a rogue."

ing him to it. For command and force may often create, but can never cure an aversion ; and whatever any one is brought to by compulsion he will leave as soon as he can, and be little profited, and less recreated by, whilst he is at it.[1]

203. *Painting.*—That which of all others would please me best would be a painter, were there not an argument or two against it not easy to be answered. First, ill painting is one of the worst things in the world ; and to attain a tolerable degree of skill in it, requires too much of a man's time. If he has a natural inclination to it, it will endanger the neglect of all other more useful studies, to give way to that ; and if he have no inclination to it, all the time, pains and money that shall be employed in it will be thrown away to no purpose. Another reason why I am not for painting in a gentleman is because it is a sedentary recreation, which more employs the mind than the body. A gentleman's more serious employment I look on to be study ; and when that demands relaxation and refreshment, it should be in some exercise of the body, which unbends the thought and confirms the health and strength. For these two reasons I am not for painting.

204. *Gardening—Joiner.*—In the next place, for a country gentleman, I should propose one, or rather both these—*viz.,* gardening and working in wood, as a carpenter, joiner, or turner, as being fit and healthy recreations for a man of study or business. For since the mind endures not to be constantly employed in the same thing or way ; and sedentary or studious men should have some exercise, that at the same time might divert their minds and employ their bodies ; I know none that could do better for a country gentleman than these two, the one of them affording him exercise, when the weather or season keeps him from the other. Besides, that, by being skilled in the one of them, he will be able to govern and teach his gardener ; by the other, contrive

[1] See secs. 72-74, 84, 103, 123, 128, 148, 149, 167, 202, and Introduction, p. 15.

and make a great many things both of delight and use : though these I propose not as the chief ends of his labour, but as temptations to it : diversion from his other more serious thoughts and employments by useful and healthy manual exercise being what I chiefly aim at in it.

[205. *The ancients reconciled manual labour with affairs of state, as in the instances of Gideon, Cincinnatus, Cato, and Cyrus.*]

206.[1] *Recreation.*—Nor let it be thought that I mistake when I call these or the like trades, diversions or recreations : for recreation is not being idle (as every one may observe), but easing the wearied part by change of business : and he that thinks diversion may not lie in hard and painful labour, forgets the early rising, hard riding, heat, cold and hunger of huntsmen, which is yet known to be the constant recreation of men of the greatest condition.   Delving, planting, inoculating,[2] or any the like profitable employments, would be no less a diversion than any of the idle sports in fashion, if men could but be brought to delight in them, which custom and skill in a trade will quickly bring any one to do.   And I doubt not, but there are to be found those, who, being frequently called to cards, or any other play, by those they could not refuse, have been more tired with these recreations, than with any the most serious employment of life ; though the play has been such as they have naturally had no aversion to, and with which they could willingly sometimes divert themselves.

207. Though when one reflects on these and other the like pastimes (as they are called) one finds they leave little satisfaction behind them, when they are over ; and most commonly give more vexation than delight to people, whilst they are actually engaged in them, and neither profit the mind nor the body.   They are plain instances to me that men cannot be perfectly idle ; they must be doing something.   The skill should be so to employ their time of recreation that it may relax and refresh the part that has been exercised, and is tired ;

[1] Sec. 193 in first edition.   [2] Grafting.

and yet do something, which, besides the present delight and ease, may produce what will afterwards be profitable. It has been nothing but the vanity and pride of greatness and riches, that has brought unprofitable and dangerous pastimes into fashion, and persuaded people into a belief, that the learning or putting their hands to any thing that was useful, could not be a diversion fit for a gentleman. This has been that which has given cards, dice, and drinking so much credit in the world ; and a great many throw away their spare hours in them, through the prevalency of custom, and want of some better employment to pass their time, more than from any real delight [that] is to be found in them, only because it being very irksome and uneasy to do nothing at all, they had never learned any laudable manual art wherewith to divert themselves ; and so they betake themselves to those foolish or ill ways in use, to help off their time, which a rational man, till corrupted by custom, could find very little pleasure in.

208. *Trade.*—I say not this, that I would never have a young gentleman accommodate himself to the innocent diversions in fashion amongst those of his age and condition. I am so far from having him austere and morose to that degree, that I would persuade him to more than ordinary complaisance for all the gaieties and diversions of those he converses with, and be averse or resty in nothing they should desire of him, that might become a gentleman and an honest man. But allowance being made for idle and jovial conversation, and all fashionable becoming recreations, I say, a young man will have time enough, from his serious and main business, to learn almost any trade. 'Tis want of application, and not of leisure, that men are not skilful in more arts than one ; and an hour in a day, constantly employed in such a way of diversion, will carry a man in a short time a great deal farther than he can imagine : which, if it were of no other use, but to drive the common, vicious, useless, and dangerous pastimes out of fashion, and to show there was no need of them, would deserve to be encouraged.

If men from their youth were weaned from that sauntering humour, wherein some, out of custom, let a good part
of their lives run uselessly away, without either business
or recreation, they would find time enough to acquire
dexterity and skill in hundreds of things,. which, though
remote from their proper callings, would not at all inter-
fere with them.   And therefore, I think, for this, as well
as other reasons before-mentioned, a lazy, listless humour,
that idly dreams away the days, is of all others the least
to be indulged, or permitted in young people.   It is the
proper state of one sick, and out of order in his health,
and is tolerable in nobody else, of what age or condition
soever.

209. To the arts above-mentioned may be added per-
fuming, varnishing, graving, and several sorts of working
in iron, brass, and silver : and if, as it happens to most
young gentlemen, that a considerable part of his time be
spent in a great town, he may learn to cut, polish, and
set precious stones, or employ himself in grinding and
polishing optical glasses.   Amongst the great variety
there is of ingenious manual arts, 'twill be impossible
that no one should be found to please and delight him,
unless he be either idle or debauched, which is not to be
supposed in a right way of education.   And since he
cannot be always employed in study, reading, and conversation, there will be many an hour, besides what his
exercises will take up, which, if not spent this way, will
be spent worse.   For, I conclude, a young man will
seldom desire to sit perfectly still and idle ; or if he does,
it is a fault that ought to be mended.

210. But if his mistaken parents, frightened with the
disgraceful names of mechanic and trade, shall have an
aversion to anything of this kind in their children ; yet
there is one thing relating to trade, which, when they consider, they will think absolutely necessary for their sons
to learn.

Merchants' Accounts.—Merchants' accounts, though a
science not likely to help a gentleman to get an estate, yet
possibly there is not any thing of more use and efficacy to

make him preserve the estate he has. 'Tis seldom observed that he who keeps an account of his income and expenses and thereby has constantly under view the course of his domestic affairs, lets them run to ruin ; and I doubt not but many a man gets behindhand before he is aware, or runs farther on, when he is once in, for want of this care, or the skill to do it. I would therefore advise all gentlemen to learn perfectly merchants' accounts, and not to think it is a skill that belongs not to them because it has received its name from, and has been chiefly practised by, men of traffic.[1]

211. When my young master has once got the skill of keeping accounts (which is a business of reason more than arithmetic), perhaps it will not be amiss, that his father from thenceforth require him to do it in all his concernments. Not that I would have him set down every pint of wine, or play, that costs him money ; the general name of expenses will serve for such things well enough : nor would I have his father look so narrowly into these accounts, as to take occasion from thence to criticize on his expenses. He must remember, that he himself was once a young man, and not forget the thoughts he had then, nor the right his son has to have the same, and to have allowance made for them. If therefore I would have the young gentleman obliged to keep an account, it is not at all to have that way a check upon his expenses (for what the father allows him, he ought to let him be fully master of), but only that he might be brought early into the custom of doing it, and that that might be made familiar and habitual to him betimes, which will be so useful and necessary to be constantly practised through the whole course of his life. A noble Venetian, whose son wallowed in the plenty of his father's riches, finding his son's expenses grow very high and extravagant, ordered his cashier to let him have for the future no more money than what he should count when he received it. This one would think no great restraint to a young gentleman's expenses, who could freely have as much money as

[1] In modern phrase, " business men." *Cf*. note, sec. 197.

he would tell.[1]   But yet this, to one who was used to nothing but the pursuit of his pleasures, proved a very great trouble, which at last ended in this sober and advantageous reflection : If it be so much pains to me barely to count the money I would spend, what labour and pains did it cost my ancestors, not only to count, but get it ?   This rational thought, suggested by this little pains imposed upon him, wrought so effectually upon his mind, that it made him take up, and from that time forwards prove a good husband.   This at least everybody must allow, that nothing is likelier to keep a man within compass than the having constantly before his eyes the state of his affairs in a regular course of accounts.

212. *Travel.*—The last part usually in education is travel, which is commonly thought to finish the work, and complete the gentleman.   I confess, travel into foreign countries has great advantages ; but the time usually chosen to send young men abroad, is, I think, of all other, that which renders them least capable of reaping those advantages.   Those which are proposed, as to the main of them, may be reduced to these two ; first, language ; secondly, an improvement in wisdom and prudence by seeing men, and conversing with people of tempers, customs, and ways of living, different from one another, and especially from those of his parish and neighbourhood. But from sixteen to one and twenty, which is the ordinary time of travel, men are, of all their lives, the least suited to these improvements.   The first season to get foreign languages, and form the tongue to their true accents, I should think, should be from seven to fourteen or sixteen ; and then too, a tutor with them is useful and necessary, who may, with those languages, teach them other things. But to put them out of their parents' view, at a great distance, under a governor, when they think themselves too much men to be governed by others, and yet have not prudence and experience enough to govern themselves : what is it, but to expose them to all the greatest

[1] *I.e.*, count.

dangers of their whole life, when they have the least fence and guard against them ?   Till that boiling, boisterous part of life comes in, it may be hoped, the tutor may have some authority ; neither the stubbornness of age, nor the temptation of examples of others can take him from his tutor's conduct, till fifteen or sixteen : but then, when he begins to consort himself with men, and think himself one ; when he comes to relish and pride himself in manly vices, and thinks it a shame to be any longer under the control and conduct of another : what can be hoped from even the most careful and discreet governor, when neither he has power to compel, nor his pupil a disposition to be persuaded ; but, on the contrary, has the advice of warm blood, and prevailing fashion, to hearken to the temptations of his companions, just as wise as himself, rather than to the persuasions of his tutor, who is now looked on as the enemy to his freedom ?   And when is a man so like to miscarry, as when at the same time he is both raw and unruly ?   This is the season of all his life that most requires the eye and authority of his parents and friends to govern it.   The flexibleness of the former part of a man's age, not yet grown up to be headstrong, makes it more governable and safe ; and, in the after-part, reason and foresight begin a little to take place, and mind a man of his safety and improvement.   The time therefore I should think the fittest for a young gentleman to be sent abroad would be either when he is younger, under a tutor, whom he might be the better for ; or when he was some years older, when he is of age to govern himself, and make observations of what he finds in other countries worthy his notice, and that might be of use to him after his return : and when too, being thoroughly acquainted with the laws and fashions, the natural and moral advantages and defects of his own country, he has something to exchange with those abroad, from whose conversation he hoped to reap any knowledge.

213. The ordering of travel otherwise is that, I imagine, which makes so many young gentlemen come back so little improved by it.   And if they do bring home with them any

knowledge of the places and people they have seen, it is
often an admiration of the worst and vainest practices
they met with abroad ; retaining a relish and memory of
those things wherein their liberty took its first swing,
rather than of what should make them better and wiser
after their return. And indeed, how can it be otherwise,
going abroad at the age they do, under a governor, who
is to provide their necessaries, and make their observations
for them ? Thus, under the shelter and pretence of a
governor, thinking themselves excused from standing upon
their own legs, or being accountable for their own conduct,
they very seldom trouble themselves with inquiries, or
making useful observations of their own. Their thoughts
run after play and pleasure, wherein they take it as a
lessening to be controlled ; but seldom trouble themselves
to examine the designs, observe the address, and consider
the arts, tempers, and inclinations of men they meet with ;
that so they may know how to comport themselves towards
them. Here he that travels with them, is to screen them,
get them out, when they have run themselves into the
briars ; and in all their miscarriages be answerable for
them.

214.[1] I confess, the knowledge of men is so great a skill,
that it is not to be expected a young man should presently[2]
be perfect in it. But yet his going abroad is to little
purpose, if travel does not somewhat open his eyes, make
him cautious and wary, and accustom him to look beyond
the outside, and, under the inoffensive guard of a civil and
obliging carriage, keep himself free and safe in his conversation with strangers, and all sorts of people, without
forfeiting their good opinion. He that is sent out to
travel at the age, and with the thoughts of a man designing
to improve himself, may get into the conversation and
acquaintance of persons of condition where he comes :
which, though a thing of most advantage to a gentleman
that travels, yet I ask, amongst our young men that go
abroad under tutors, What one is there of an hundred,
that ever visits any person of quality ? much less makes

[1] Sec. 202 in first edition. [2] Immediately, at once.

12

an acquaintance with such, from whose conversation he may learn what is good breeding in that country, and what is worth observation in it ; though from such persons it is, one may learn more in one day, than in a year's rambling from one June to another.   Nor indeed is it to be wondered ; for men of worth and parts will not easily admit the familiarity of boys who yet need the care of a tutor : though a young gentleman and stranger, appearing like a man, and showing a desire to inform himself in the customs, manners, laws, and government of the country he is in, will find welcome assistance and entertainment amongst the best and most knowing persons everywhere, who will be ready to receive, encourage, and countenance an ingenuous and inquisitive foreigner.

215.[1] This, how true soever it be, will not, I fear, alter the custom, which has cast the time of travel upon the worst part of a man's life ; but for reasons not taken from their improvement.   The young lad must not be ventured abroad at eight or ten, for fear of what may happen to the tender child, though he then runs ten times less risk than at sixteen or eighteen.   Nor must he stay at home till that dangerous heady age be over, because he must be back again by one and twenty, to marry and propagate.   The father cannot stay any longer for the portion, nor the mother for a new set of babies to play with ; and so my young master, whatever comes on't, must have a wife looked out for him, by that time he is of age ; though it would be no prejudice to his strength, his parts, nor his issue, if it were respited for some time, and he had leave to get, in years and knowledge, the start a little of his children, who are often found to tread too near upon the heels of their fathers, to the no great satisfaction either of son or father.   But the young gentleman being got within view of matrimony, 'tis time to leave him to his mistress.

216.[2] Though I am now come to a conclusion of what obvious remarks have suggested to me concerning educa-tion, I would not have it thought that I look on it as a

---

[1] Sec. 201 in first edition.   [2] Sec. 202 in first edition.

just treatise on this subject.   There are a thousand other things that may need consideration ; especially if one should take in the various tempers, different inclinations, and particular defaults, that are to be found in children ; and prescribe proper remedies.   The variety is so great, that it would require a volume ; nor would that reach it. Each man's mind has some peculiarity, as well as his face, that distinguishes him from all others ; and there are possibly scarce two children who can be conducted by exactly the same method.   Besides that, I think a prince, a nobleman, and an ordinary gentleman's son, should have different ways of breeding.   But having had here only some general views, in reference to the main end and aims in education, and those designed for a gentleman's son, who[m] being then very little, I considered only as white paper, or wax, to be moulded and fashioned as one pleases,[1] I have touched little more than those heads, which I judged necessary for the breeding of a young gentleman of his condition in general ; and have now published these my occasional thoughts, with this hope, that, though this be far from being a complete treatise on this subject, or such as that every one may find what will just fit his child in it ; yet it may give some small light to those, whose concern for their dear little ones makes them so irregularly[2] bold, that they dare venture to consult their own reason, in the education of their children, rather than wholly to rely upon old custom.

[1] See sec. 101, *note*.   [2] Unconventionally, unusually.

ADDITIONAL NOTES

p. 40, n. 1. "But children of gentyll nature take more profite by praise and lyghte rebuke than by stripes. For praises stere them to worshyp and rebuke doth withdrawe them from folye." *The Education or bringinge up of children translated oute of Plutarche* by Syr Thomas Eliot knyght, chap. ix. Elyot's translation of περὶ παίδων ἀγωγῆς c. 1535.

p. 116, n. 2. "Let boxwood or ivory letters be made for her, and let them be called by their names. Let her play with them, so that even her play may be learning. And let her not only learn the names in order and turn them into sing-song, but let the order itself be frequently changed, beginning, middle and end being confused, so that she not only recognizes them by sound but by sight also." St Jerome, *Epistle* cvii., to Laeta on the education of her daughter. Cp. also Quintilian, *Inst. Orat.*, bk i., chap. i., 26.

p. 123, n. 2. "When with trembling hand she moves the stylus across the wax tablet, either let her tender fingers be guided by another's hand placed over hers or let the characters be cut in the tablet, that her marks may be traced in those channels and not suffered to wander out of them." St Jerome to Laeta, *ut supra*. This is almost *verbatim* from Quintilian, bk i., chap. i., 27.

OF THE CONDUCT OF THE UNDERSTANDING

Apart from punctuation, the text here followed is that of vol. iii. in the ten-volume edition of Locke's " Works," 1812.

" Quid tam temerarium tamque indignum sapientis gravitate atque constantia, quam aut falsum sentire, aut quod non satis explorate perceptum sit, et cognitum, sine ulla dubitatione defendere ?"—Cicero, *De Natura Deorum*, i.[1]

1. *Introduction.*—The last resort a man has recourse to, in the conduct of himself, is his understanding : for though we distinguish the faculties of the mind, and give the supreme command to the will, as to an agent,[2] yet the truth is, the man, who is the agent, determines himself to this or that voluntary action, upon some precedent knowledge, or appearance of knowledge, in the understanding. No man ever sets himself about anything but upon some view or other, which serves him for a reason for what he does : and whatsoever faculties he employs, the understanding, with such light as it has, well or ill informed, constantly leads ; and by that light, true or false, all his operative powers are directed. The will itself, how absolute and uncontrollable soever it may be thought, never fails in its obedience to the dictates of the understanding. Temples have their sacred images, and we see what influence they have always had over a great

[1] What so rash and so unworthy of the earnestness and constancy of a philosopher, as unhesitatingly to maintain either what is felt to be false, or what has not been with sufficient certainty perceived and understood?

[2] One who *acts*. The discussion of the Will and its determination forms one of the longest chapters in the *Essay concerning Human Understanding*, ii., chap. xxi.

part of mankind. But in truth, the ideas and images in men's minds are the invisible powers that constantly govern them, and to these they all universally pay a ready submission.[1] It is therefore of the highest concernment that great care should be taken of the understanding, to conduct it right in the search of knowledge, and in the judgments it makes.

The logic now in use has so long possessed the chair, as the only art taught in the schools,[2] for the direction of the mind in the study of the arts and sciences, that it would perhaps be thought an affectation of novelty to suspect that rules that have served the learned world these two or three thousand years, and which, without any complaint of defects, the learned have rested in, are not sufficient to guide the understanding. And I should not doubt but this attempt would be censured as vanity or presumption, did not the great lord Verulam's authority justify it ; who, not servilely thinking learning could not be advanced beyond what it was, because for many ages it had not been, did not rest in the lazy approbation and applause of what was, because it was ; but enlarged his mind to what it might be. In his preface[3] to his Novum Organum, concerning logic, he pronounces thus : " Qui summas dialecticæ partes tribuerunt, atque inde fidissima scientiis præsidia comparari putarunt, verissime te optime viderunt intellectum humanum, sibi permissum, merito suspectum esse debere. Verum infirmior omnino est malo medicina ; nec ipsa mali expers. Siquidem dialectica, quæ recepta est, licet ad civilia et artes, quæ in sermone et opinione positæ sunt, rectissime adhibeatur ; naturæ tamen subtilitatem longo intervallo non attingit, et prensando quod non capit, ad errores potius stabiliendos et quasi figendos, quam ad viam veritati aperiendam valuit."

" They," says he, " who attributed so much to logic,

---

[1] *Cf.* Herbart: " Das Wollen wurzelt im Gedankenkreise," " The will takes root in the circle of thought "—that is in the complex of ideas. (*Umriss pädagogischer Vorlesungen*, § 58.)

[2] *I.e.*, of the University. See sec. 43, first paragraph.

[3] The passage does not occur there. See Fowler's edition of the *Novum Organon*, p. 165 (second edition).

perceived very well and truly that it was not safe to trust the understanding to itself without the guard of any rules. But the remedy reached not the evil, but became a part of it, for the logic which took [its] place, though it might do well enough in civil affairs and the arts, which consisted in talk and opinion, yet comes very far short of subtlety in the real performances of nature ; and, catching at what it cannot reach, has served to confirm and establish errors, rather than to open a way to truth." And therefore a little after he says, " That it is absolutely necessary that a better and perfecter use and employment of the mind and understanding should be introduced." " Necessario requiritur ut melior et perfectior mentis et intellectus humani usus et adoperatio introducatur."

2. *Parts.*—There is, it is visible, great variety in men's understandings, and their natural constitutions put so wide a difference between some men in this respect, that art and industry would never be able to master, and their very natures seem to want a foundation to raise on it that which other men easily attain unto.   Amongst men of equal education there is great inequality of parts.[1]   And the woods of America, as well as the schools of Athens, produce men of several abilities in the same kind.   Though this be so, yet I imagine most men come very short of what they might attain unto, in their several degrees, by a neglect of their understandings.   A few rules of logic are thought sufficient in this case for those who pretend to the highest improvement, whereas I think there are a great many natural defects in the understanding capable of amendment, which are overlooked and wholly neglected. And it is easy to perceive that men are guilty of a great many faults in the exercise and improvement of this faculty of the mind, which hinder them in their progress, and keep them in ignorance and error all their lives. Some of them I shall take notice of, and endeavour to point out proper remedies for, in the following discourse.

[1] *Cf. Thoughts*, secs. 101, 139, 176, 216, and sec. 32 below.   These passages are at variance with Locke's figures of the " white paper " and " wax."   See *Introduction*, p. 6.

3. *Reasoning.*—Besides the want of determined ideas,[1] and of sagacity and exercise in finding out and laying in order intermediate ideas, there are three miscarriages that men are guilty of, in reference to their reason, whereby this faculty is hindered in them from that service it might do and was designed for.   And he that reflects upon the actions and discourses of mankind will find their defects in this kind very frequent and very observable.

(1) The first is of those who seldom reason at all, but do and think according to the example of others, whether parents, neighbours, ministers, or who else they are pleased to make choice of to have an implicit faith in, for the saving of themselves the pains and trouble of thinking and examining for themselves.

(2) The second is of those who put passion in the place of reason, and being resolved that shall govern their actions and arguments, neither use their own, nor hearken to other people's reason, any farther than it suits their humour, interest, or party ; and these one may observe commonly content themselves with words which have no distinct ideas to them, though in other matters, that they come with an unbiassed indifferency[2] to, they want not abilities to talk and hear reason, where they have no secret inclination that hinders them from being tractable to it.

(3) The third sort is of those who readily and sincerely follow reason ; but for want of having that which one may call large, sound, roundabout sense, have not a full view of all that relates to the question, and may be of moment to decide it.   We are all shortsighted, and very often see but one side of a matter ; our views are not extended to all that has a connexion with it.   From this defect I think no man is free.   We see but in part, and we know but in part, and therefore it is no wonder we conclude not right from our partial views.   This might instruct the proudest esteemer of his own parts, how useful it is to talk and

[1] See *Essay*, Epistle to the Reader, and ii., chap. xxix., *Thoughts*, sec. 195.

[2] Impartiality.

consult with others, even such as come short of him in capacity, quickness, and penetration ; for since no one sees all, and we generally have different prospects of the same thing according to our different, as I may say, positions to it, it is not incongruous to think, nor beneath any man to try, whether another may not have notions of things which have escaped him, and which his reason would make use of if they came into his mind. The faculty of reasoning seldom or never deceives those who trust to it ; its consequences, from what it builds on, are evident and certain ; but that which it oftenest, if not only, mis- leads us in is, that the principles from which we conclude, the grounds upon which we bottom our reasoning, are but a part ; something is left out, which should go into the reckoning, to make it just and exact. Here we may imagine a vast and almost infinite advantage that angels and separate spirits[1] may have over us ; who in their several degrees of elevation above us may be endowed with more comprehensive faculties ; and some of them perhaps, having perfect and exact views of all finite beings that come under their consideration, can, as it were, in the twinkling of an eye, collect together all their scattered and almost boundless relations. A mind so furnished, what reason has it to acquiesce in the certainty of its conclusions ?

In this we may see the reason why some men of study and thought, that reason right and are lovers of truth, do make no great advances in their discoveries of it. Error and truth are uncertainly blended in their minds ; their decisions are lame and defective, and they are very often mistaken in their judgments : the reason whereof is, they converse but with one sort of men, they read but one sort of books, they will not come in the hearing but of one sort of notions ; the truth is, they canton out to them- selves a little Goshen[2] in the intellectual world, where light shines, and as they conclude, day blesses them ; but the rest of that vast expansum they give up to night

[1] *Cf. Essay*, iv., chap. iii., sec. 27.
[2] Genesis xlvii. 27.

and darkness, and so avoid coming near it. They have a pretty traffic with known correspondents, in some little creek ; within that they confine themselves, and are dexterous managers enough of the wares and products of that corner with which they content themselves, but will not venture out into the great ocean of knowledge, to survey the riches that nature hath stored other parts with, no less genuine, no less solid, no less useful than what has fallen to their lot, in the admired plenty and sufficiency of their own little spot, which to them contains whatsoever is good in the universe. Those who live thus mewed up within their own contracted territories, and will not look abroad beyond the boundaries that chance, conceit, or laziness has set to their inquiries, but live separate from the notions, discourses, and attainments of the rest of mankind, may not amiss be represented by the inhabitants of the Marian islands ;[1] who, being separated by a large tract of sea from all communion with the habitable parts of the earth, thought themselves the only people of the world. And though the straitness of the conveniences of life amongst them had never reached so far as to the use of fire, till the Spaniards, not many years since, in their voyages from Acapulco to Manilla, brought it amongst them ; yet, in the want and ignorance of almost all things, they looked upon themselves, even after that the Spaniards had brought amongst them the notice of variety of nations, abounding in sciences, arts, and conveniences of life, of which they knew nothing ; they looked upon themselves, I say, as the happiest and wisest people of the universe. But for all that, nobody, I think, will imagine them deep naturalists or solid metaphysicians ; nobody will deem the quickest-sighted amongst them to have very enlarged views in ethics or politics ;[2] nor can any one allow the most capable amongst them to be advanced so far in his understanding as to have any other knowledge but of the few little things of his and the

[1] The Ladrones, between New Guinea and Japan.
[2] A hint as to the limit to the usefulness of " sense training " in education. *Cf.* p. 203.

neighbouring islands within his commerce ;[1] but far enough from that comprehensive enlargement of mind which adorns a soul devoted to truth, assisted with letters, and a free generation[2] of the several views and sentiments of thinking men of all sides. Let not men, therefore, that would have a sight of what every one pretends to be desirous to have a sight of, truth in its full extent, narrow and blind their own prospect. Let not men think there is no truth but in the sciences that they study, or books that they read. To prejudice other men's notions, before we have looked into them, is not to show their darkness, but to put out our own eyes. " Try all things, hold fast that which is good,"[3] is a divine rule, coming from the Father of light and truth, and it is hard to know what other way men can come at truth, to lay hold of it, if they do not dig and search for it as for gold and hid treasure ; but he that does so must have much earth and rubbish before he gets the pure metal ; sand and pebbles and dross usually lie blended with it, but the gold is never the less gold, and will enrich the man that employs his pains to seek and separate it. Neither is there any danger he should be deceived by the mixture. Every man carries about him a touchstone, if he will make use of it, to distinguish substantial gold from superficial glitterings, truth from appearances. And indeed the use and benefit of this touchstone, which is natural reason, is spoiled and lost only by assuming prejudices, overweening presumption, and narrowing our minds. The want of exercising it in the full extent of things intelligible, is that which weakens and extinguishes this noble faculty in us. Trace it and see whether it be not so. The day-labourer in a country-village has commonly but a small pittance of knowledge, because his ideas and notions have been confined to the narrow bounds of a poor conversation and employment : the low mechanic of a country-town does somewhat out-do him : porters and cobblers of great cities surpass them. A country gentleman who, leaving Latin and learning in the university, removes thence to his

[1] Intercourse.   [2] Production.   [3] 1 Thess. v. 21.

mansion-house, and associates with neighbours of the same strain, who relish nothing but hunting and a bottle ; with those alone he spends his time, with those alone he converses, and can away with no company whose discourse goes beyond what claret and dissoluteness inspire. Such a patriot, formed in this happy way of improvement, cannot fail, as we see, to give notable decisions upon the bench at quarter-sessions, and eminent proofs of his skill in politics, when the strength of his purse and party have advanced him to a more conspicuous station.   To such a one, truly, an ordinary coffee-house gleaner of the city is an arrant[1] statesman, and as much superior to[2] as a man conversant about Whitehall and the court is to an ordinary shop-keeper.   To carry this a little farther : Here is one muffled up in the zeal and infallibility of his own sect, and will not touch a book or enter into debate with a person that will question any of those things which to him are sacred.   Another surveys our differences in religion with an equitable and fair indifference, and so finds, probably, that none of them are in everything unexceptionable. These divisions and systems were made by men, and carry the mark of fallible on them ; and in those whom he differs from, and till he opened his eyes had a general prejudice against, he meets with more to be said for a great many things than before he was aware of, or could have imagined. Which of these two now is most likely to judge right in our religious controversies, and to be most stored with truth, the mark all pretend to aim at ?   All these men that I have instanced in, thus unequally furnished with truth and advanced in knowledge, I suppose of equal natural parts ; all the odds between them has been the different scope that has been given to their understandings to range in, for the gathering up of information and furnishing their heads with ideas and notions and observations, whereon to employ their mind and form their understandings.

[1] Thorough.
[2] *I.e.*, the " coffee-house gleaner " is as much the superior of the gentleman described as the courtier is the superior of the shop-keeper.   The Court was at Whitehall at this date.

It will possibly be objected, "who is sufficient for all this?" I answer, more than can be imagined. Every one knows what his proper business is, and what, according to the character he makes of himself, the world may justly expect of him ; and to answer that, he will find he will have time and opportunity enough to furnish himself, if he will not deprive himself by a narrowness of spirit of those helps that are at hand. I do not say, to be a good geographer, that a man should visit every mountain, river, promontory, and creek upon the face of the earth, view the buildings and survey the land everywhere, as if he were going to make a purchase ; but yet every one must allow that he shall know a country better that makes often sallies into it and traverses up and down, than he that like a mill-horse goes still round in the same track, or keeps within the narrow bounds of a field or two that delight him. He that will inquire out the best books in every science, and inform himself of the most material authors of the several sects[1] of philosophy and religion, will not find it an infinite work to acquaint himself with the sentiments of mankind concerning the most weighty and comprehensive subjects. Let him exercise the freedom of his reason and understanding in such a latitude as this, and his mind will be strengthened, his capacity enlarged, his faculties improved ; and the light which the remote and scattered parts of truth will give to one another will so assist his judgment, that he will seldom be widely out, or miss giving proof of a clear head and a comprehensive knowledge. At least, this is the only way I know to give the understanding its due improvement to the full extent of its capacity, and to distinguish the two most different things I know in the world, a logical chicaner[2] from a man of reason. Only, he that would thus give the mind its flight, and send abroad his inquiries into all parts after truth, must be sure to settle in his head determined ideas[3] of all that he employs his thoughts about, and never fail to judge himself, and judge unbiassedly, of all that

[1] "Schools." *Cf. Thoughts*, sec. 193.   [2] Trickster.
[3] See p. 184, *note*.

he receives from others, either in their writings or discourses. Reverence or prejudice must not be suffered to give beauty or deformity to any of their opinions.

4. *Of Practice and Habits.*—We are born with faculties and powers capable almost of anything, such at least as would carry us farther than can easily be imagined : but it is only the exercise of those powers which gives us ability and skill in anything, and leads us towards perfection.

A middle-aged ploughman will scarce ever be brought to the carriage and language of a gentleman, though his body be as well-proportioned, and his joints as supple, and his natural parts not any way inferior. The legs of a dancing-master and the fingers of a musician fall as it were naturally, without thought or pains, into regular and admirable motions. Bid them change their parts, and they will in vain endeavour to produce like motions in the members not used to them, and it will require length of time and long practice to attain but some degrees of a like ability. What incredible and astonishing actions do we find rope-dancers and tumblers bring their bodies to ! Not but that sundry in almost all manual arts are as wonderful ; but I name those which the world takes notice of for such, because on that very account they give money to see them. All these admired motions, beyond the reach and almost conception of unpractised spectators, are nothing but the mere effects of use and industry in men whose bodies have nothing peculiar in them from those of the amazed lookers-on.

As it is in the body, so it is in the mind : practice makes it what it is ; and most even of those excellencies which are looked on as natural endowments, will be found, when examined into more narrowly, to be the product of exercise, and to be raised to that pitch only by repeated actions. Some men are remarked for pleasantness in raillery ; others for apologues and apposite diverting stories. This is apt to be taken for the effect of pure nature, and that the rather because it is not got by rules, and those who excel in either of them never purposely set themselves to the study of it as an art to be learnt.

But yet it is true, that at first some lucky hit, which took with somebody and gained him commendation, encouraged him to try again, inclined his thoughts and endeavours that way, till at last he insensibly got a facility in it, without perceiving how ; and that is attributed wholly to nature which was much more the effect of use and practice. I do not deny that natural disposition may often give the first rise to it, but that never carries a man far without use and exercise ; and it is practice alone that brings the powers of the mind, as well as those of the body, to their perfection.   Many a good poetic vein is buried under a trade, and never produces anything for want of improvement.[1]   We see the ways of discourse and reasoning are very different, even concerning the same matter, at court and in the university.   And he that will go but from Westminster-hall[2] to the Exchange will find a different genius and turn in their ways of talking ; and yet one cannot think that all whose lot fell in the city were born with different parts from those who were bred at the university or inns of court.

To what purpose all this but to show that the difference so observable in men's understandings and parts does not arise so much from their natural faculties as acquired habits.   He would be laughed at that should go about to make a fine dancer out of a country hedger at past fifty. And he will not have much better success who shall endeavour at that age to make a man reason well, or speak handsomely, who has never been used to it, though you should lay before him a collection of all the best precepts of logic or oratory.   Nobody is made anything by hearing of rules or laying them up in his memory ; practice must settle the habit of doing, without reflecting on the rule ; and you may as well hope to make a good painter or musician extempore, by a lecture and instruction in the arts of music and painting, as a coherent thinker or a strict reasoner by a set of rules showing him wherein right reasoning consists.[3]

[1] But cf. Thoughts, sec. 174.   [2] The Law Courts.
[3] Cf. Thoughts, sec. 188, and secs. 31, 43, 44 below.

This being so that defects and weakness in men's under standings, as well as other faculties, come from want of a right use of their own minds, I am apt to think the fault is generally mislaid upon nature, and there is often a complaint of want of parts when the fault lies in want of a due improvement of them. We see men frequently dexterous and sharp enough in making a bargain who if you reason with them about matters of religion, appear perfectly stupid.[1]

5. *Ideas.*—I will not here, in what relates to the right conduct and improvement of the understanding, repeat again the getting clear and determined ideas, and the employing our thoughts rather about them than about sounds put for them, nor of settling the signification of words which we use with ourselves in the search of truth, or with others in discoursing about it. Those hindrances of our understandings in the pursuit of knowledge I have sufficiently enlarged upon in another place,[2] so that nothing more needs here to be said of those matters.

6. *Principles.*—There is another fault that stops or misleads men in their knowledge which I have also spoken something of, but yet is necessary to mention here again, that we may examine it to the bottom and see the root it springs from, and that is, a custom of taking up with principles that are not self-evident, and very often not so much as true. It is not unusual to see men rest their opinions upon foundations that have no more certainty and solidity than the propositions built on them and embraced for their sake. Such foundations are these and the like, viz., the founders or leaders of my party are good men, and therefore their tenets are true ; it is the opinion of a sect that is erroneous, therefore it is false ; it hath been long received in the world, therefore it is true ; or, it is new, and therefore false.

These, and many the like, which are by no means the measures of truth and falsehood, the generality of men

[1] See sec. 28 and note thereon.
[2] Viz. in the *Essay concerning Human Understanding.* See particularly iii., chap. xi.

make the standards by which they accustom their under-standing to judge. And thus, they falling into a habit of determining of truth and falsehood by such wrong measures, it is no wonder they should embrace error for certainty, and be very positive in things they have no ground for.

There is not any who pretends to the least reason, but when any of these his false maxims are brought to the test, must acknowledge them to be fallible, and such as he will not allow in those that differ from him ; and yet after he is convinced of this you shall see him go on in the use of them, and the very next occasion that offers argue again upon the same grounds. Would one not be ready to think that men are willing to impose upon themselves, and mislead their own understandings, who conduct them by such wrong measures, even after they see they cannot be relied on ? But yet they will not appear so blameable as may be thought at first sight ; for I think there are a great many that argue thus in earnest, and do it not to impose on themselves or others. They are persuaded of what they say, and think there is weight in it, though in a like case they have been convinced there is none ; but men would be intolerable to themselves and contemptible to others if they should embrace opinions without any ground, and hold what they could give no manner of reason for. True or false, solid or sandy, the mind must have some foundation to rest itself upon, and, as I have remarked in another place,[1] it no sooner entertains any proposition, but it presently hastens to some hypothesis to bottom it on ; till then it is unquiet and unsettled. So much do our own very tempers dispose us to a right use of our understandings if we would follow, as we should, the inclinations of our nature.

In some matters of concernment, especially those of religion, men are not permitted to be always wavering and uncertain, they must embrace and profess some tenets or other ; and it would be a shame, nay a contradiction too heavy for any one's mind to lie constantly under, for

[1] *Cf. Essay*, i., chap. iii., sec. 24 *ff*.

him to pretend seriously to be persuaded of the truth of any religion, and yet not to be able to give any reason of his belief, or to say anything for his preference of this to any other opinion : and therefore they must make use of some principles or other, and those can be no other than such as they have and can manage ; and to say they are not in earnest persuaded by them, and do not rest upon those they make use of, is contrary to experience,[1] and [is] to allege that they are not misled, when we complain they are.

If this be so, it will be urged, why then do they not make use of sure and unquestionable principles, rather than rest on such grounds as may deceive them, and will, as is visible, serve to support error as well as truth ?

To this I answer, the reason why they do not make use of better and surer principles is because they cannot : but this inability proceeds not from want of natural parts (for those few, whose case that is, are to be excused) but for want of use and exercise. Few men are from their youth accustomed to strict reasoning, and to trace the dependence of any truth, in a long train of consequences, to its remote principles, and to observe its connexion ; and he that by frequent practice has not been used to this employment of his understanding, it is no more wonder that he should not, when he is grown into years, be able to bring his mind to it, than that he should not be on a sudden able to grave or design, dance on the ropes, or write a good hand, who has never practised either of them.

Nay, the most of men are so wholly strangers to this that they do not so much as perceive their want of it : they despatch the ordinary business of their callings by rote, as we say, as they have learnt it ; and if at any time they miss success, they impute it to anything rather than want of thought or skill, that[2] they conclude (because they know no better) they have in perfection : or if there be

---

[1] *Cf.* sec. 1, " All universally pay a ready submission " to their own ideas.

[2] *I.e.,* " which."

any subject that interest or fancy has recommended to
their thoughts, their reasoning about it is still after their
own fashion; be it better or worse, it serves their turns,
and is the best they are acquainted with; and therefore,
when they are led by it into mistakes and their business
succeeds accordingly, they impute it to any cross accident
or default of others, rather than to their own want of
understanding; that is what nobody discovers or complains of in himself. Whatsoever made his business to
miscarry, it was not want of right thought and judgment
in himself: he sees no such defect in himself, but is satisfied
that he carries on his designs well enough by his own
reasoning, or at least should have done, had it not been
for unlucky traverses[1] not in his power. Thus, being
content with this short and very imperfect use of his
understanding, he never troubles himself to seek out
methods of improving his mind, and lives all his life
without any notion of close reasoning in a continued connexion of a long train of consequences from sure foundations, such as is requisite for the making out and clearing
most of the speculative truths most men own to believe
and are most concerned in. Not to mention here what I
shall have occasion to insist on by and by more fully, viz.,
that in many cases it is not one series of consequences will
serve the turn, but many different and opposite deductions must be examined and laid together before a man
can come to make a right judgment of the point in
question.[2] What then can be expected from men that
neither see the want of any such kind of reasoning as this;
nor, if they do, know how to set about it, or could perform
it? You may as well set a countryman, who scarce
knows the figures and never cast[s] up a sum of three
particulars, to state a merchant's long account, and find
the true balance of it.

What then should be done in the case? I answer, we
should always remember what I said above, that the
faculties of our souls are improved and made useful to us
just after the same manner as our bodies are. Would

---

[1] Thwarting accidents.   [2] See p. 199.

you have a man write or paint, dance or fence well, or
perform any other manual operation dexterously and
with ease ; let him have ever so much vigour and activity,
suppleness and address naturally, yet nobody expects
this from him unless he has been used to it, and has
employed time and pains in fashioning and forming his
hand or outward parts to these motions.   Just so it is in
the mind ; would you have a man reason well, you must
use him to it betimes, exercise his mind in observing the
connexion of ideas and following them in train.[1]   Nothing
does this better than mathematics, which therefore I
think should be taught all those who have the time and
opportunity, not so much to make them mathematicians
as to make them reasonable creatures ; for though we all
call ourselves so because we are born to it if we please, yet
we may truly say, nature gives us but the seeds of it ; we
are born to be, if we please, rational creatures, but it is
use and exercise only that makes us so, and we are indeed
so no farther than industry and application has carried
us.   And therefore, in ways of reasoning which men
have not been used to, he that will observe the conclusions they take up must be satisfied they are not all
rational.

This has been the less taken notice of, because every one
in his private affairs uses some sort of reasoning or other,
enough to denominate him reasonable.   But the mistake
is, that he that is found reasonable in one thing is concluded to be so in all, and to think or to say otherwise is
thought so unjust an affront and so senseless a censure
that nobody ventures to do it.   It looks like the degra-
dation of a man below the dignity of his nature.   It is
true, that he that reasons well in any one thing, has a mind
naturally capable of reasoning well in others, and to the
same degree of strength and clearness, and possibly much
greater, had his understanding been so employed.   But
it is as true that he who can reason well to-day about one
sort of matters, cannot at all reason to-day about others,
though perhaps a year hence he may.   But wherever a

[1] *Cf. Thoughts*, sec. 188.

man's rational faculty fails him, and will not serve him to reason, there we cannot say he is rational, how capable soever he may be by time and exercise to become so.

Try in men of low and mean education who have never elevated their thoughts above the spade and the plough, nor looked beyond the ordinary drudgery of a day-labourer. Take the thoughts of such an one, used for many years to one track, out of that narrow compass he has been all his life confined to, you will find him no more capable of reasoning than almost a perfect natural.[1] Some one or two rules on which their conclusions immediately depend, you will find in most men have governed all their thoughts ; these, true or false, have been the maxims they have been guided by : take these from them and they are perfectly at a loss, their compass and pole-star then are gone, and their understanding is perfectly at a nonplus ; and therefore they either immediately return to their old maxims again, as the foundations to all truth to them, notwithstanding all that can be said to show their weakness ; or if they give them up to their reasons, they with them give up all truth, and farther inquiry, and think there is no such thing as certainty. For if you would enlarge their thoughts and settle them upon more remote and surer principles, they either cannot easily apprehend them, or, if they can, know not what use to make of them, for long deductions from remote principles are what they have not been used to and cannot manage.

What, then, can grown men never be improved or enlarged in their understandings ? I say not so, but this I think I may say, that it will not be done without industry and application, which will require more time and pains than grown men, settled in their course of life, will allow to it, and therefore very seldom is done. And this very capacity of attaining it by use and exercise only, brings us back to that which I laid down before, that it is only practice that improves our minds as well as bodies, and

[1] *I.e.*, idiot.

we must expect nothing from our understandings any farther than they are perfected by habits.[1]

The Americans are not all born with worse understandings than the Europeans, though we see none of them have such reaches in the arts and sciences. And among the children of a poor countryman, the lucky chance of education, and getting into the world, gives one infinitely the superiority in parts over the rest, who continuing at home had continued also just of the same size with his brethren.[2]

He that has to do with young scholars, especially in mathematics, may perceive how their minds open by degrees, and how it is exercise alone that opens them. Sometimes they will stick a long time at a part of a demonstration, not for want of will and application, but really for want of perceiving the connexion of two ideas that, to one whose understanding is more exercised, is as visible as anything can be. The same would be with a grown man beginning to study mathematics, the understanding for want of use often sticks in every plain way, and he himself that is so puzzled, when he comes to see the connexion, wonders what it was he stuck at in a case so plain.

7. *Mathematics.*—I have mentioned mathematics as a way to settle in the mind an habit of reasoning closely and in train ; not that I think it necessary that all men should be deep mathematicians, but that, having got the way of reasoning, which that study necessarily brings the mind to, they might be able to transfer it to other parts of knowledge as they shall have occasion. For in all sorts of reasoning every single argument should be managed as a mathematical demonstration ; the connexion and dependence of ideas should be followed, till the mind is brought to the source on which it bottoms, and observes the coherence all along, though in proofs of probability

[1] Sec. 4.

[2] The doctrine of heredity discountenances the notion that " the lucky chance of education" explains the child's superiority; and the modern scholarship system assumes the superiority to be prior to the education.

one such train is not enough to settle the judgment, as in demonstrative knowledge.

Where a truth is made out by one demonstration, there needs no farther inquiry ; but in probabilities, where there wants demonstration to establish the truth beyond doubt, there it is not enough to trace one argument to its source, and observe its strength and weakness, but all the arguments, after having been so examined on both sides, must be laid in balance one against another, and upon the whole the understanding determine its assent.

This is a way of reasoning the understanding should be accustomed to, which is so different from what the illiterate are used to, that even learned men sometimes seem to have very little or no notion of it. Nor is it to be wondered, since the way of disputing in the schools[1] leads them quite away from it, by insisting on one topical argument, by the success of which the truth or falsehood of the question is to be determined, and victory adjudged to the opponent or defendant ; which is all one, as if one should balance an account by one sum, charged and discharged, when there are an hundred others to be taken into consideration.

This, therefore, it would be well if men's minds were accustomed to, and that early ; that they might not erect their opinions upon one single view when so many others are requisite to make up the account, and must come into the reckoning before a man can form a right judgment. This would enlarge their minds and give a due freedom to their understandings, that they might not be led into error by presumption, laziness, or precipitancy ; for I think nobody can approve such a conduct of the understanding as should mislead it from truth, though it be ever so much in fashion to make use of it.[2]

To this perhaps it will be objected, that to manage the understanding as I propose would require every man to

[1] The allusion is to the dialectical exercises for degrees, which survived in the universities long after Locke's time. *Cf.* secs. 31, 43.
[2] *I.e.*, the " conduct," or method, in question.

be a scholar, and to be furnished with all the materials of knowledge and exercised in all the ways of reasoning. To which I answer, that it is a shame for those that have time and the means to attain knowledge, to want any helps or assistance for the improvement of their understandings that are to be got, and to such I would be thought here chiefly to speak. Those methinks, who, by the industry and parts of their ancestors, have been set free from a constant drudgery to their backs and their bellies, should bestow some of their spare time on their heads, and open their minds by some trials and essays, in all the sorts and matters of reasoning. I have before mentioned mathematics, wherein algebra gives new helps and views to the understanding. If I propose these, it is not, as I said, to make every man a thorough mathematician or a deep algebraist; but yet I think the study of them is of infinite use, even to grown men; first, by experimentally convincing them that to make any one reason well it is not enough to have parts wherewith he is satisfied and that serve him well enough in his ordinary course. A man in those studies will see, that however good he may think his understanding, yet in many things, and those very visible, it may fail him. This would take off that presumption that most men have of themselves in this part, and they would not be so apt to think their minds wanted no helps to enlarge them, that there could be nothing added to the acuteness and penetration of their understandings.

Secondly, the study of mathematics would show them the necessity there is in reasoning, to separate all the distinct ideas, and see the habitudes[1] that all those concerned in the present inquiry have to one another, and to lay by those which relate not to the proposition in hand, and wholly to leave them out of the reckoning. This is that which in other subjects besides quantity,[2] is what is absolutely requisite to just reasoning, though in them it is not so easily observed nor so carefully practised. In those parts of knowledge where it is thought demon-

[1] Relations.   [2] The subject-matter of mathematics.

stration has nothing to do, men reason as it were in the lump ; and if, upon a summary and confused view, or upon a partial consideration, they can raise the appearance of a probability, they usually rest content, especially if it be in a dispute where every little straw is laid hold on, and everything that can but be drawn in any way to give colour to the argument is advanced with ostentation. But that mind is not in a posture to find the truth that does not distinctly take all the parts asunder, and omitting what is not at all to the point, draw a conclusion from the result of all the particulars which any way influence it. There is another no less useful habit to be got by an application to mathematical demonstrations, and that is, of using the mind to a long train of consequences : but having mentioned that already, I shall not again here repeat it.

As to men whose fortunes and time are narrower, what may suffice them is not of that vast extent as may be imagined, and so comes not within the objection.

Nobody is under an obligation to know every thing. Knowledge and science in general is the business only of those who are at ease and leisure. Those who have particular callings ought to understand them, and it is no unreasonable proposal, nor impossible to be compassed, that they should think and reason right about what is their daily employment. This one cannot think them incapable of, without levelling them with the brutes and charging them with a stupidity below the rank of rational creatures.

8. *Religion.*—Besides his particular calling for the support of this life, every one has a concern in a future life, which he is bound to look after. This engages his thoughts in religion, and here it mightily lies upon him to understand and reason right. Men, therefore, cannot be excused from understanding the words and framing the general notions relating to religion right. The one day of seven, besides other days of rest, allows in the christian world time enough for this, (had they no other idle hours), if they would but make use of these vacancies from their daily labour, and apply themselves to an

improvement of knowledge with as much diligence as they often do to a great many other things that are useless, and had but those[1] that would enter them, according to their several capacities, in a right way to this knowledge.   The original make of their minds is like that of other men, and they would be found not to want understanding fit to receive the knowledge of religion if they were a little encouraged and helped in it as they should be.   For there are instances of very mean people who have raised their minds to a great sense and understanding of religion ; and though these have not been so frequent as could be wished, yet they are enough to clear that condition of life from a necessity of gross ignorance, and to show that more might be brought to be rational creatures and christians, (for they can hardly be thought really to be so who, wearing the name, know not so much as the very principles of that religion,) if due care were taken of them.   For, if I mistake not, the peasantry lately in France (a rank of people under a much heavier pressure of want and poverty than the day-labourers in England)[2] of the reformed religion understood it much better and could say more for it than those of a higher condition among us.

But if it shall be concluded that the meaner sort of people must give themselves up to brutish stupidity in the things of their nearest concernment, which I see no reason for, this excuses not those of a freer fortune and education, if they neglect their understandings, and take no care to employ them as they ought and set them right in the knowledge of those things for which principally they were given them.   At least those whose plentiful fortunes allow them the opportunities and helps of improvement are not so few, but that it might be hoped great advancements might be made in knowledge of all kinds, especially in that of the greatest concern and largest views, if men would make a right use of their faculties and study their own understandings.

[1] *I.e.*, if they had but teachers.
[2] Locke is speaking from personal experience.   When in France, he took careful note of the condition of the peasantry.

9. *Ideas.*—Outward corporeal objects that constantly importune our senses and captivate our appetites, fail not to fill our heads with lively and lasting ideas of that kind. Here the mind needs not to be set upon getting greater store ; they offer themselves fast enough, and are usually entertained in such plenty and lodged so carefully, that the mind wants room or attention for others that it has more use and need of. To fit the understanding, therefore, for such reasoning as I have been above speaking of, care should be taken to fill it with moral and more abstract ideas ; for these not offering themselves to the senses, but being to be framed to the understanding, people are generally so neglectful of a faculty they are apt to think wants nothing, that I fear most men's minds are more unfurnished with such ideas than is imagined.[1] They often use the words, and how can they be suspected to want the ideas ? What I have said in the third book of my essay[2] will excuse me from any other answer to this question. But to convince people of what moment it is to their understandings to be furnished with such abstract ideas, steady and settled in them, give me leave to ask how any one shall be able to know whether he be obliged to be just, if he has not established ideas in his mind of obligation and of justice, since knowledge consists in nothing but the perceived agreement or disagreement of those ideas ? and so of all others the like which concern our lives and manners. And if men do find a difficulty to see the agreement or disagreement of two angles which lie before their eyes unalterable in a diagram, how utterly impossible will it be to perceive it in ideas that have no other sensible object to represent them to the mind but sounds, with which they have no manner of conformity, and therefore had need to be clearly settled in the mind themselves, if we would make any clear judgment about

---

[1] The criticism applies to an undue prolongation in education of what may be called the perceptual stage, that is, "sense-training," "observation," and "kindergarten methods" generally. *Cf.* p. 186.

[2] *Concerning Human Understanding*, chaps. ix., x., xi.

them ?   This therefore, is one of the first things the mind should be employed about in the right conduct of the understanding, without which it is impossible it should be capable of reasoning right about those matters.   But in these, and all other ideas, care must be taken that they harbour no inconsistencies, and that they have a real existence where real existence is supposed, and are not mere chimeras[1] with a supposed existence.

10. *Prejudice.*—Every one is forward to complain of the prejudices that mislead other men or parties, as if he were free and had none of his own.   This being objected on all sides, it is agreed that it is a fault and an hindrance to knowledge.   What now is the cure ?   No other but this, that every man should let alone other[s'] prejudices and examine his own.   Nobody is convinced of his by the accusation of another ; he recriminates by the same rule, and is clear.   The only way to remove this great cause of ignorance and error out of the world is, for every one impartially to examine himself.   If others will not deal fairly with their own minds, does that make my errors truths ? or ought it to make me in love with them and willing to impose on myself ?   If others love cataracts in their eyes, should that hinder me from couching[2] of mine as soon as I can ?   Every one declares against blindness, and yet who almost is not fond of that which dims his sight, and keeps the clear light out of his mind, which should lead him into truth and knowledge ?   False or doubtful positions, relied upon as unquestionable maxims, keep those in the dark from truth who build on them. Such are usually the prejudices imbibed from education, party, reverence, fashion, interest, &c.   This is the mote which every one sees in his brother's eye, but never regards the beam in his own.   For who is there almost that is ever brought fairly to examine his own principles, and see whether they are such as will bear the trial ?   But yet this should be one of the first things every one

---

[1] Idle fancies, whose existence is only supposed, not actual.
[2] The surgical operation for removing a cataract.

should set about, and be scrupulous in, who would rightly
conduct his understanding in the search of truth and
knowledge.

To those who are willing to get rid of this great hindrance of knowledge (for to such only I write), to those
who would shake off this great and dangerous impostor,
prejudice, who dresses up falsehood in the likeness of truth,
and so dexterously hoodwinks men's minds as to keep
them in the dark with a belief that they are more in the
light than any that do not see with their eyes, I shall offer
this one mark whereby prejudice may be known. He
that is strongly of any opinion must suppose (unless he be
self-condemned) that his persuasion is built upon good
grounds, and that his assent is no greater than what the
evidence of the truth he holds forces him to, and that
they are arguments, and not inclination or fancy, that
make him so confident and positive in his tenets. Now
if, after all his profession, he cannot bear any opposition
to his opinion, if he cannot so much as give a patient
hearing, much less examine and weigh the arguments on
the other side, does he not plainly confess it is prejudice
governs him ? and it is not the evidence of truth, but some
lazy anticipation, some beloved presumption that he
desires to rest undisturbed in. For if what he holds be,
as he gives out, well fenced with evidence, and he sees it
to be true, what need he fear to put it to the proof ? If
his opinion be settled upon a firm foundation, if the
arguments that support it and have obtained his assent
be clear, good, and convincing, why should he be shy to
have it tried whether they be proof or not ? He whose
assent goes beyond this evidence, owes this excess of his
adherence only to prejudice ; and does in effect own it
when he refuses to hear what is offered against it,
declaring thereby that it is not evidence he seeks,
but the quiet enjoyment of the opinion he is fond of,
with a forward condemnation of all that may stand in
opposition to it, unheard and unexamined ; which,
what is it but prejudice ? " qui æquum statuerit, parte
inaudita altera, etiamsi æquum statuerit, haud æquus

fuerit."[1] He that would acquit himself in this case as a
lover of truth, not giving way to any pre-occupation or
bias that may mislead him, must do two things that are
not very common nor very easy.

11. *Indifferency.*—First, he must not be in love with
any opinion, or wish it to be true till he knows it to be so,
and then he will not need to wish it ; for nothing that is
false can deserve our good wishes, nor a desire that it
should have the place and force of truth ; and yet nothing
is more frequent than this. Men are fond of certain
tenets upon no other evidence but respect and custom,
and think they must maintain them or all is gone, though
they have never examined the ground they stand on,
nor have ever made them out to themselves : or can make
them out to others : we should contend earnestly for the
truth, but we should first be sure that it is truth, or else
we fight against God, who is the God of truth, and do the
work of the devil, who is the father and propagator of
lies ; and our zeal, though ever so warm, will not excuse
us, for this is plainly prejudice.

12. *Examine.*—Secondly, he must do that which he will
find himself very averse to, as judging the thing unnecessary, or himself incapable of doing it. He must try
whether his principles be certainly true or not, and how
far he may safely rely upon them. This, whether fewer
have the heart or the skill to do, I shall not determine,
but this I am sure is that which every one ought to do
who professes to love truth, and would not impose upon
himself, which is a surer way to be made a fool of than by
being exposed to the sophistry of others. The disposition
to put any cheat upon ourselves works constantly, and
we are pleased with it, but are impatient of being bantered
or misled by others. The inability I here speak of, is not

---

[1] That is, a man has but small claim to be thought just who
decides upon the justice of a cause without hearing the other side,
even though he decides rightly. Fowler (Locke's *Conduct of the
Understanding*) quotes Seneca's *Medea*, 199, 200 :

> " Qui statuit aliquid parte inaudita altera,
> Æquum licet statuerit, haud aequus fuit."

any natural defect that makes men incapable of examining their own principles. To such, rules of conducting their understandings are useless; and that is the case of very few. The great number is of those whom the ill habit of never exerting their thoughts has disabled; the powers of their minds are starved by disuse and have lost that reach and strength which nature fitted them to receive from exercise. Those who are in a condition to learn the first rules of plain arithmetic, and could be brought to cast up an ordinary sum, are capable of this, if they had but accustomed their minds to reasoning; but they that have wholly neglected the exercise of their understandings in this way, will be very far at first from being able to do it, and as unfit for it as one unpractised in figures to cast up a shop-book, and perhaps think it as strange to be set about it. And yet it must nevertheless be confessed to be a wrong use of our understandings to build our tenets (in things where we are concerned to hold the truth) upon principles that may lead us into error. We take our principles at hap-hazard upon trust, and without ever having examined them, and then believe a whole system upon a presumption that they are true and solid: and what is all this but childish, shameful, senseless credulity?

In these two things, viz., an equal indifferency for all truth (I mean the receiving it, the love of it, as truth, but not loving it for any other reason, before we know it to be true) and in the examination of our principles, and not receiving any for such, nor building on them, till we are fully convinced as rational creatures of their solidity, truth, and certainty, consists that freedom of the understanding which is necessary to a rational creature, and without which it is not truly an understanding. It is conceit, fancy, extravagance, anything rather than understanding, if it must be under the constraint of receiving and holding opinions by the authority of anything but their own, not fancied, but perceived evidence. This was rightly called imposition, and is of all other the worst and most dangerous sort of it. For we impose upon ourselves, which is the strongest imposition of all others, and we impose

upon ourselves in that part which ought with the greatest
care to be kept free from all imposition.   The world is apt
to cast great blame on those who have an indifferency [1] for
opinions, especially in religion.   I fear this is the foundation of great error and worse consequences.   To be indifferent which of two opinions is true, is the right temper
of the mind that preserves it from being imposed on, and
disposes it to examine with that indifferency till it has
done its best to find the truth ; and this is the only direct
and safe way to it.   But to be indifferent whether we
embrace falsehood or truth is the great road to error.
Those who are not indifferent which opinion is true are
guilty of this ; they suppose, without examining, that
what they hold is true, and then think they ought to be
zealous for it.   Those, it is plain by their warmth and
eagerness, are not indifferent for their own opinions, but
methinks are very indifferent whether they be true or
false ; since they cannot endure to have any doubts raised
or objections made against them, and it is visible they
never have made any themselves, and so never having
examined them, know not, nor are concerned, as they
should be, to know whether they be true or false.

   These are the common and most general miscarriages
which I think men should avoid or rectify in a right
conduct of their understandings, and should be particularly taken care of in education.   The business whereof
in respect of knowledge, is not, as I think, to perfect a
learner in all or any one of the sciences, but to give his
mind that freedom, that disposition, and those habits
that may enable him to attain any part of knowledge he
shall apply himself to, or stand in need of, in the future
course of his life.[2]

   This, and this only, is well principling, and not the
instilling a reverence and veneration for certain dogmas
under the specious title of principles, which are often so
remote from that truth and evidence which belongs to
principles, that they ought to be rejected as false and
erroneous ; and often cause men so educated when they

[1] Impartiality.   [2] *Cf. Thoughts*, secs. 31-33, 75.

come abroad into the world and find they cannot maintain the principles so taken up and rested in, to cast off all principles, and turn perfect sceptics, regardless of knowledge and virtue.

There are several weaknesses and defects in the understanding, either from the natural temper of the mind, or ill habits taken up, which hinder it in its progress to knowledge. Of these there are as many, possibly, to be found, if the mind were thoroughly studied, as there are diseases of the body, each whereof clogs and disables the understanding to some degree, and therefore deserves to be looked after and cured. I shall set down some few to excite men, especially those who make knowledge their business, to look into themselves, and observe whether they do not indulge some weaknesses, allow some miscarriages in the management of their intellectual faculty which is prejudicial to them in the search of truth.

13. *Observations.*—Particular matters of fact are the undoubted foundations on which our civil and natural knowledge is built : the benefit the understanding makes of them is to draw from them conclusions which may be as standing rules of knowledge, and consequently of practice. The mind often makes not that benefit it should of the information it receives from the accounts of civil or natural historians, by being too forward or too slow in making observations on the particular facts recorded in them.

There are those who are very assiduous in reading, and yet do not much advance their knowledge by it. They are delighted with the stories that are told, and perhaps can tell them again, for they make all they read nothing but history[1] to themselves ; but not reflecting on it, not making to themselves observations from what they read, they are very little improved by all that crowd of particulars that either pass through or lodge themselves in their understandings. They dream on in a constant course of reading and cramming themselves ; but not digesting anything, it produces nothing but a heap of crudities.

[1] That is, narrative and not principles.

14

If their memories retain well, one may say, they have the materials of knowledge, but like those for building they are of no advantage if there be no other use made of them but to let them lie heaped up together. Opposite to these there are others, who lose the improvement they should make of matters of fact by a quite contrary conduct. They are apt to draw general conclusions and raise axioms from every particular they meet with. These make as little true benefit of history as the other ; nay, being of forward and active spirits, receive more harm by it, it being of worse consequence to steer one's thoughts by a wrong rule than to have none at all, error doing to busy men much more harm than ignorance to the slow and sluggish. Between these, those seem to do best who, taking material and useful hints, sometimes from single matters of fact, carry them in their minds to be judged of by what they shall find in history to confirm or reverse their imperfect observations, which may be established into rules fit to be relied on, when they are justified by a sufficient and wary induction of particulars. He that makes no such reflection, on what he reads, only loads his mind with a rhapsody of tales, fit in winter nights for the entertainment of others ; and he that will improve every matter of fact into a maxim, will abound in contrary observations that can be of no other use but to perplex and pudder[1] him if he compares them, or else to misguide him if he gives himself up to the authority of that which for its novelty or for some other fancy best pleases him.[2]

14. *Bias*.—Next to these we may place those who suffer their own natural tempers and passions they are possessed with to influence their judgments, especially of men and things that may any way relate to their present circumstances and interest. Truth is all simple, all pure, will bear no mixture of anything else with it. It is rigid and inflexible to any by-interests, and so should the understanding be, whose use and excellency lies in conforming itself to it. To think of everything just as it is in itself,

---

[1] " Pother," " bother."
[2] Topic continued in secs. 20, 24 42.

is the proper business of the understanding, though it be not that which men always employ it to. This all men at first hearing allow is the right use every one should make of his understanding. Nobody will be at such an open defiance with common sense, as to profess that we should not endeavour to know and think of things as they are in themselves ; and yet there is nothing more frequent than to do the contrary ; and men are apt to excuse themselves, and think they have reason to do so, if they have but a pretence that it is for God, or a good cause ; that is, in effect, for themselves, their own persuasion or party : for those in their turns the several sects of men, especially in matters of religion, entitle God and a good cause. But God requires not men to wrong or misuse their faculties for him, nor to lie to others or themselves for his sake, which they purposely do who will not suffer their understandings to have right conceptions of the things proposed to them, and designedly restrain themselves from having just thoughts of every thing, as far as they are concerned to inquire. And as for a good cause, that needs not such ill helps ; if it be good, truth will support it, and it has no need of fallacy or falsehood.

15. *Arguments.*—Very much of kin to this is the hunting after arguments to make good one side of a question, and wholly to neglect and refuse those which favour the other side. What is this but wilfully to misguide the understanding, and is so far from giving truth its due value, that it wholly debases it : [to] espouse opinions that best comport with their power, profit, or credit, and then seek arguments to support them ? Truth lighted upon this way, is of no more avail to us than error, for what is so taken up by us may be false as well as true ; and he has not done his duty who has thus stumbled upon truth in his way to preferment.

There is another but more innocent way of collecting arguments very familiar among bookish men, which is to furnish themselves with the arguments they meet with pro and con in the questions they study. This helps them not to judge right nor argue strongly, but only to talk copiously on either side without being steady and settled in their own judgments. For such arguments gathered from other men's thoughts, floating only in the memory, are there ready indeed to supply copious talk with some appearance of reason, but are far from helping us to judge right. Such variety of arguments only distract[s] the understanding that relies on them, unless it has gone farther than such a superficial way of examining ; this is to quit truth for appearance, only to serve our vanity. The sure and only way to get true knowledge, is to form in our minds clear settled notions of things, with names annexed to those determined ideas.[1]   These we are to consider with their several relations and habitudes, and not amuse ourselves with floating names and words of indetermined signification which we can use in several senses to serve a turn. It is in the perception of the habitudes and respects our ideas have one to another that real knowledge consists, and when a man once perceives how far they agree or disagree one with another, he will be able to judge of what other people say, and will not need to be led by the arguments of others, which are many of them nothing but plausible sophistry. This will teach him to state the question right, and see whereon it turns, and thus he will stand upon his own legs, and know by his own understanding. Whereas by collecting and learning arguments by heart, he will be but a retainer to others ; and when any one questions the foundations they are built upon, he will be at a nonplus,[2] and be fain to give up his implicit knowledge.[3]

16. *Haste.*—Labour for labour-sake is against nature. The understanding, as well as all the other faculties, chooses always the shortest way to its end, would presently[4] obtain the knowledge it is about, and then set upon some new inquiry. But this, whether laziness or haste, often misleads it and makes it content itself with

---

[1] P. 184, *note.*   [2] Will be unable to proceed.
[3] "Knowledge," so called, which he cannot make explicit; "second-hand or implicit knowledge," sec. 24.
[4] *I.e.,* at once.

improper ways of search, and such as will not serve the turn : sometimes it rests upon testimony, when testimony of right has nothing to do,[1] because it is easier to believe than to be scientifically instructed : sometimes it contents itself with one argument, and rests satisfied with that as it were a demonstration, whereas the thing under proof is not capable of demonstration, and therefore must be submitted to the trial of probabilities, and all the material arguments pro and con be examined and brought to a balance.   In some cases the mind is determined by probable topics in inquiries where demonstration may be had. All these, and several others, which laziness, impatience, custom, and want of use and attention lead men into, are misapplications of the understanding in the search of truth.   In every question the nature and manner of the proof it is capable of should be considered, to make our inquiry such as it should be.   This would save a great deal of frequently misemployed pains, and lead us sooner to that discovery and possession of truth we are capable of. The multiplying variety of arguments, especially frivolous ones, such as are all that are merely verbal, is not only lost labour, but cumbers the memory to no purpose, and serves only to hinder it from seizing and holding of the truth in all those cases which are capable of demonstration. In such a way of proof, the truth and certainty is seen, and the mind fully possesses itself of it ; when in the other way of assent it only hovers about it, is amused with uncertainties.   In this superficial way, indeed, the mind is capable of more variety of plausible talk, but is not enlarged, as it should be, in its knowledge.   It is to this same haste and impatience of the mind also, that a not due tracing of the arguments to their true foundation is owing ; men see a little, presume a great deal, and so jump to the conclusion.   This is a short way to fancy and conceit, and (if firmly embraced) to opinionatry,[2]

[1] When in strictness the matter does not call for testimony, but for demonstration.

[2] *I.e.*, obstinate and unreasonable adherence to one's own opinion. See sec. 26.

but is certainly the farthest way about to knowledge. For he that will know, must by the connexion of the proofs see the truth and the ground it stands on ; and therefore if he has for haste skipt over what he should have examined, he must begin and go over all again, or else he will never come to knowledge.[1]

17. *Desultory.*—Another fault of as ill consequence as this, which proceeds also from laziness, with a mixture of vanity, is the skipping from one sort of knowledge to another. Some. men's tempers are quickly weary of one thing. Constancy and assiduity is what they cannot bear ; the same study long continued in is as intolerable to them, as the appearing long in the same clothes or fashion is to a court-lady.

18. *Smattering.*—Others, that they may seem universally knowing, get a little smattering in everything. Both these may fill their heads with superficial notions of things, but are very much out of the way of attaining truth or knowledge.

19. *Universality.*—I do not here speak against the taking a taste of every sort of knowledge ; it is certainly very useful and necessary to form the mind ; but then it must be done in a different way and to a different end. Not for talk and vanity to fill the head with shreds of all kinds, that he who is possessed of such a frippery [2] may be able to match the discourses of all he shall meet with, as if nothing could come amiss to him, and his head was so well stored a mazagine, that nothing could be proposed which he was not master of, and was readily furnished to entertain any one on. This is an excellency indeed, and a great one too, to have a real and true knowledge in all or most of the objects of contemplation. But it is what the mind of one and the same man can hardly attain unto ; and the instances are so few of those who have in any measure approached towards it, that I know not whether they are to be proposed as examples in the

---

[1] See sec. 25.
[2] A " rag-fair." *Cf. Thoughts*, sec. 193, on " fitting one's self for conversation."

ordinary conduct of the understanding. For a man to understand fully the business of his particular calling in the commonwealth, and of religion, which is his calling as he is a man in the world, is usually enough to take up his whole time,[1] and there are few that inform themselves in these, which is every man's proper and peculiar business, so to the bottom as they should do. But though this be so, and there are very few men that extend their thoughts towards universal knowledge; yet I do not doubt but if the right way were taken, and the methods of inquiry were ordered as they should be, men of little business and great leisure might go a great deal farther in it than is usually done. To turn to the business in hand ; the end and use of a little insight in those parts of knowledge which are not a man's proper business, is to accustom our minds to all sorts of ideas, and the proper ways of examining their habitudes and relations. This gives the mind a freedom, and the exercising the understanding in the several ways of inquiry and reasoning which the most skilful have made use of, teaches the mind sagacity and wariness, and a suppleness to apply itself more closely and dexterously to the bents and turns of the matter in all its researches. Besides, this universal taste of all the sciences, with an indifferency before the mind is possessed with any one in particular, and grown into love and admiration of what is made its darling, will prevent another evil very commonly to be observed in those who have from the beginning been seasoned only by one part of knowledge. Let a man be given up to the contemplation of one sort of knowledge, and that will become everything. The mind will take such a tincture from a familiarity with that object, that everything else, how remote soever, will be brought under the same view. A metaphysician will bring plowing and gardening immediately to abstract notions, the history of nature shall signify nothing to him. An alchemist, on the contrary,

[1] These two constitute Locke's conception of the education of persons outside the leisured class. See Introduction ; also sec. 8, above.

shall reduce divinity to the maxims of his laboratory : explain morality by sal,[1] sulphur and mercury, and allegorize the scripture itself, and the sacred mysteries thereof, into the philosopher's stone. And I heard once a man who had a more than ordinary excellency in music seriously accommodate Moses's seven days of the first week to the notes of music, as if from thence had been taken the measure and method of the creation. It is of no small consequence to keep the mind from such a possession, which I think is best done by giving it a fair and equal view of the whole intellectual world, wherein it may see the order, rank, and beauty of the whole, and give a just allowance to the distinct provinces of the several sciences in the due order and usefulness of each of them.

If this be that which old men will not think necessary, nor be easily brought to, it is fit at least that it should be practised in the breeding of the young. The business of education, as I have already observed,[2] is not, as I think, to make them perfect in any one of the sciences, but so to open and dispose their minds as may best make them capable of any when they shall apply themselves to it. If men are for a long time accustomed only to one sort or method of thoughts, their minds grow stiff in it, and do not readily turn to another. It is therefore to give them this freedom that I think they should be made to look into all sorts of knowledge, and exercise their understandings in so wide a variety and stock of knowledge. But I do not propose it as a variety and stock of knowledge, but a variety and freedom of thinking ; as an increase of the powers and activity of the mind, not as an enlargement of its possessions.

20. *Reading.*—[3] This is that which I think great readers are apt to be mistaken in. Those who have read of every thing are thought to understand every thing too ; but it is not always so. Reading furnishes the mind only with materials of knowledge, it is thinking makes what we read ours. We are of the ruminating kind, and it is

[1] Salt.   [2] Sec. 12.   [3] See secs. 13, 24, 42.

not enough to cram our selves with a great load of collections ; unless we chew them over again they will not give us strength and nourishment. There are indeed in some writers visible instances of deep thoughts, close and acute reasoning, and ideas well pursued. The light these would give would be of great use if their reader would observe and imitate them ; all the rest at best are but particulars fit to be turned into knowledge ; but that can be done only by our own meditation and examining the reach, force, and coherence of what is said, and then as far as we apprehend and see the connexion of ideas, so far it is ours ; without that, it is but so much loose matter floating in our brain. The memory may be stored, but the judgment is little better, and the stock of knowledge not increased by being able to repeat what others have said, or produce the arguments we have found in them. Such a knowledge as this is but knowledge by hearsay, and the ostentation of it is at best but talking by rote, and very often upon weak and wrong principles. For all that is to be found in books is not built upon true foundations, nor always rightly deduced from the principles it is pretended to be built on. Such an examen as is requisite to discover that, every reader's mind is not forward to make, especially in those who have given themselves up to a party, and only hunt for what they can scrape together that may favour and support the tenets of it. Such men wilfully exclude themselves from truth, and from all true benefit to be received by reading. Others of more indifferency[1] often want attention and industry. The mind is backward in itself to be at the pains to trace every argument to its original, and to see upon what basis it stands and how firmly ; but yet it is this that gives so much the advantage to one man more than another in reading. The mind should by severe rules be tied down to this, at first, uneasy task ; use and exercise will give it facility. So that those who are accustomed to it readily, as it were with one cast of the eye, take a view of the argument, and

[1] Impartiality.

presently,[1] in most cases, see where it bottoms. Those who have got this faculty, one may say, have got the true key of books, and the clue to lead them through the mizmaze[2] of variety of opinions and authors to truth and certainty. This young beginners should be entered in, and showed the use of, that they might profit by their reading. Those who are strangers to it will be apt to think it too great a clog in the way of men's studies, and they will suspect they shall make but small progress if, in the books they read, they must stand to examine and unravel every argument, and follow it step by step up to its original.

I answer, this is a good objection, and ought to weigh with those whose reading is designed for much talk and little knowledge, and I have nothing to say to it. But I am here inquiring into the conduct of the understanding in its progress towards knowledge ; and to those who aim at that I may say, that he who fair and softly goes steadily forward in a course that points right, will sooner be at his journey's end than he that runs after every one he meets, though he gallop all day full speed.

To which let me add, that this way of thinking on and profiting by what we read will be a clog and rub to any one only in the beginning : when custom and exercise have made it familiar, it will be despatched on most occasions without resting or interruption in the course of our reading. The motions and views of a mind exercised that way are wonderfully quick, and a man used to such sort of reflections sees as much at one glimpse as would require a long discourse to lay before another, and make out in an entire and gradual deduction. Besides that, when the first difficulties are over, the delight and sensible advantage it brings mightily encourages and enlivens the mind in reading, which without this is very improperly called study.

21. *Intermediate Principles.*—As a help to this, I think it may be proposed, that for the saving the long progression of the thoughts to remote and first principles in every

---

[1] *I.e.*, at once.   [2] *I.e.*, maze ; *cf.* " tee-total."

case, the mind should provide it[1] several stages ; that is to say, intermediate principles which it might have recourse to in the examining those positions that come in its way. These, though they are not self-evident principles, yet if they had been made out from them by a wary and unquestionable deduction, may be depended on as certain and infallible truths, and serve as unquestionable truths to prove other points depending on them by a nearer and shorter view than [by] remote and general maxims.[2] These may serve as landmarks to show what lies in the direct way of truth, or is quite beside it. And thus mathematicians do, who do not in every new problem run it back to the first axioms, through all the whole train of intermediate propositions. Certain theorems that they have settled to themselves upon sure demonstration, serve to resolve to them multitudes of propositions which depend on them, and are as firmly made out from thence as if the mind went afresh over every link of the whole chain that ties them to first self-evident principles. Only in other sciences great care is to be taken that they establish those intermediate principles with as much caution, exactness, and indifferency as mathematicians use in the settling any of their great theorems. When this is not done, but men take up the principles in this or that science upon credit, inclination, interest, &c., in haste, without due examination and most unquestionable proof, they lay a trap for themselves, and, as much as in them lies, captivate their understandings, to mistake falsehood and error.

[1] " It " is equivalent to " the progression, or course, of the thoughts," " the flow of thought." The mind should provide several stages for the course of thought.

[2] *Cf.* Bacon, *Novum Organum*, I. civ. " Nor can we suffer the understanding to jump and fly from particulars to remote and most general axioms . . . and thus prove and make out their intermediate axioms according to the supposed unshaken truth of the former. . . . We can then only augur well for the sciences, when the ascent shall proceed by a true scale and successive steps, without interruption, or breach, from particulars to the lesser axioms, thence to the intermediate (rising one above the other), and lastly to the most general."

22. *Partiality.*—As there is a partiality to opinions, which, as we have already observed, is apt to mislead the understanding, so there is often a partiality to studies which is prejudicial also to knowledge and improvement. Those sciences which men are particularly versed in they are apt to value and extol, as if that part of knowledge which every one has acquainted himself with were that alone which was worth the having, and all the rest were idle and empty amusements, comparatively of no use or importance.   This is the effect of ignorance and not knowledge, the being vainly puffed up with a flatulency arising from a weak and narrow comprehension.   It is not amiss that every one should relish the science that he has made his peculiar study ; a view of its beauties and a sense of its usefulness carries a man on with the more delight and warmth in the pursuit and improvement of it.   But the contempt of all other knowledge, as if it were nothing in comparison of law or physic, of astronomy or chemistry,[1] or perhaps some yet meaner part of knowledge wherein I have got some smattering or am somewhat advanced, is not only the mark of a vain or little mind, but does this prejudice in the conduct of the understanding, that it coops it up within narrow bounds, and hinders it looking abroad into other provinces of the intellectual world, more beautiful possibly, and more fruitful than that which it had till then laboured in, wherein it might find, besides new knowledge, ways or hints whereby it might be enabled the better to cultivate its own.

23. *Theology.*—There is indeed one science (as they are now distinguished) incomparably above all the rest, where

[1] Chemistry was a favourite study with the seventeenth-century *amateur*.   Anthony Wood says that in 1663 he and " John Lock " were members of a private chemistry club, or class, at Oxford. " This J. L. was a man of a turbulent spirit, clamorous and never contented.   The club wrote and took notes from the mouth of their master, who sate at the upper end of a table, but the said J. Lock scorned to do it ; so that while every man besides of the club were writing, he would be prating and troublesome." (Clark, *Life and Times of Anthony Wood*, vol. i., p. 472.) Not everything can be accepted which Wood says of a political opponent.

it is not by corruption narrowed into a trade or faction
for mean or ill ends and secular interests ; I mean theology,
which, containing the knowledge of God and his creatures,
our duty to him and our fellow-creatures, and a view of
our present and future state, is the comprehension of all
other knowledge directed to its true end ; i.e., the honour
and veneration of the Creator and the happiness of mankind. This is that noble study which is every man's
duty, and every one that can be called a rational creature
is capable of. The works of nature and the words of
revelation display it to mankind in characters so large and
visible, that those who are not quite blind may in them
read and see the first principles and most necessary parts
of it ; and from thence, as they have time and industry,
may be enabled to go on to the more abstruse parts of it,
and penetrate into those infinite depths filled with the
treasures of wisdom and knowledge. This is that science
which would truly enlarge men's minds, were it studied
or permitted to be studied everywhere with that freedom,
love of truth, and charity which it teaches, and were not
made, contrary to its nature, the occasion of strife,
faction, malignity, and narrow impositions. I shall say
no more here of this, but that it is undoubtedly a wrong
use of my understanding to make it the rule and measure
of another man's, a use which it is neither fit for nor
capable of.

24. *Partiality.*[1]—This partiality, where it is not permitted an authority to render all other studies insignificant
or contemptible, is often indulged so far as to be relied
upon and made use of in other parts of knowledge to
which it does not at all belong, and wherewith it has no
manner of affinity. Some men have so used their heads
to mathematical figures, that giving a preference to the
methods of that science, they introduce lines and diagrams
into their study of divinity or politic[2] inquiries, as if
nothing could be known without them ; and others
accustomed to retired speculations run natural philosophy
into metaphysical notions and the abstract generalities

---

[1] Continuation of sec. 22, 23 being a digression.   [2] Political.

of logic ; and how often may one meet with religion and
morality treated of in the terms of the laboratory, and
thought to be improved by the methods and notions of
chemistry ? But he that will take care of the conduct of
his understanding, to direct it right to the knowledge of
things, must avoid those undue mixtures, and not by a
fondness for what he has found useful and necessary in
one, transfer it to another science, where it serves only to
perplex and confound the understanding. It is a certain
truth that " res nolunt male administrari ;"[1] it is no less
certain " res nolunt male intelligi."[2] Things themselves
are to be considered as they are in them selves, and then
they will show us in what way they are to be understood.
For to have right conceptions about them we must bring
our understandings to the inflexible natures and unalterable relations of things, and not endeavour to bring things
to any preconceived notions of our own.

There is another partiality very commonly observable
in men of study, no less prejudicial or ridiculous than the
former, and that is a fantastical and wild attributing all
knowledge to the ancients alone, or to the moderns. This
raving upon antiquity in matter of poetry, Horace has
wittily described and exposed in one of his satires.[3] The
same sort of madness may be found in reference to all the
other sciences. Some will not admit an opinion not
authorized by men of old, who were then all giants in
knowledge. Nothing is to be put into the treasury of
truth or knowledge which has not the stamp of Greece or
Rome upon it, and since their days[4] will scarce allow that
men have been able to see, think or write. Others, with a
like extravagancy, contemn all that the ancients have left
us, and being taken with the modern inventions and discoveries, lay by all that went before, as if whatever is
called old must have the decay of time upon it, and truth
too were liable to mould and rottenness. Men I think
have been much the same for natural endowments in all

[1] Affairs will not suffer themselves to be badly administered.
[2] Affairs will not submit to be misunderstood.
[3] *Epistles*, bk. ii., ep. 1, 34 *ff*.   [4] *Subaud.* " some."

times. Fashion, discipline, and education have put
eminent differences in the ages of several countries, and
made one generation much differ from another in arts
and sciences : but truth is always the same ; time alters it
not, nor is it the better or worse for being of ancient or
modern tradition. Many were eminent in former ages of
the world for their discovery and delivery of it ; but
though the knowledge they have left us be worth our study,
yet they exhausted not all its treasure ; they left a great
deal for the industry and sagacity of after-ages, and so
shall we. That was once new to them which any one
now receives with veneration for its antiquity, nor was it
the worse for appearing as a novelty ; and that which is
now embraced for its newness, will to posterity be old,
but not thereby be less true or less genuine. There is
no occasion on this account to oppose the ancients and
the moderns to one another, or to be squeamish on either
side.[1] He that wisely conducts his mind in the pursuit
of knowledge, will gather what lights and get what helps
he can from either of them, from whom they are best to be
had, without adoring the errors or rejecting the truths
which he may find mingled in them.

Another partiality may be observed in some to vulgar,
in others to heterodox tenets ; some are apt to conclude
that what is the common opinion cannot but be true ; so
many men's eyes they think cannot but see right ; so
many men's understandings of all sorts cannot be deceived ;
and therefore will not venture to look beyond the received
notions of the place and age, nor have so presumptuous a
thought as to be wiser than their neighbours. They are
content to go with the crowd, and so go easily, which they
think is going right, or at least serves them as well. But
however " vox populi vox Dei " has prevailed as a maxim,
yet I do not remember wherever God delivered his oracles

[1] A characteristic attitude towards the controversy then raging
concerning the respective merits of ancient and modern learning.
Up to 1693, Perrault and Fontenelle in France, and Temple in
England had been prominent in the discussion ; Bentley and Swift
were the most notable contributors at a later date. See A.
Guthkelch's *The Battle of the Books*, etc., 1908.

by the multitude, or nature, truths by the herd.   On the other side, some fly all common opinions as either false or frivolous.   The title of many-headed beast is a sufficient reason to them to conclude that no truths of weight or consequence can be lodged there.   Vulgar opinions are suited to vulgar capacities, and adapted to the ends of those that govern.   He that will know the truth of things must leave the common and beaten track, which none but weak and servile minds are satisfied to trudge along continually in.   Such nice palates relish nothing but strange notions quite out of the way : whatever is commonly received has the mark of the beast on it, and they think it a lessening to them to hearken to it or receive it : their mind runs only after paradoxes ; these they seek, these they embrace, these alone they vent, and so as they think distinguish themselves from the vulgar.   But common or uncommon are not the marks to distinguish truth or falsehood, and therefore should not be any bias to us in our inquiries. We should not judge of things by men's opinions, but of opinions by things.   The multitude reason but ill, and therefore may be well suspected, and cannot be relied on, nor should be followed as a sure guide ; but philosophers who have quitted the orthodoxy of the community and the popular doctrines of their countries have fallen into as extravagant and as absurd opinions as ever common reception countenanced.   It would be madness to refuse to breathe the common air or quench one's thirst with water, because the rabble use them to these purposes ; and if there are conveniences of life which common use reaches not, it is not reason to reject them because they are not grown into the ordinary fashion of the country, and every villager doth not know them.

Truth, whether in or out of fashion, is the measure of knowledge and the business of the understanding ; whatsoever is besides that, however authorized by consent or recommended by rarity, is nothing but ignorance or something worse.

Another sort of partiality there is, whereby men impose upon themselves ; and by it make their reading little useful to themselves ; I mean the making use of the opinions of writers and laying stress upon their authorities wherever they find them to favour their own opinions.

There is nothing almost has done more harm to men dedicated to letters than giving the name of study to reading,[1] and making a man of great reading to be the same with a man of great knowledge, or at least to be a title of honour.   All that can be recorded in writing are only facts or reasonings.   Facts are of three sorts : (1) Merely of natural agents observable in the ordinary operations of bodies one upon another, whether in the visible course of things left to themselves, or in experiments made by them,[2] applying agents and patients to one another after a peculiar and artificial manner. (2) Of voluntary agents, more especially the actions of men in society, which makes civil and moral history. (3) Of opinions.

In these three consists, as it seems to me, that which commonly has the name of learning ; to which perhaps some may add a distinct head of critical writings, which indeed at bottom is nothing but matter of fact, and resolves itself into this, that such a man or set of men used such a word or phrase in such a sense, *i.e.*, that they made such sounds the marks of such ideas.[3]

Under reasonings I comprehend all the discoveries of general truths made by human reason, whether found by intuition, demonstration, or probable deductions.   And this is that which is, if not alone knowledge (because the truth or probability of particular propositions may be known too), yet is, as may be supposed, most properly the business of those who pretend to improve their understandings and make themselves knowing by reading.

Books and reading are looked upon to be the great helps of the understanding and instruments of knowledge, as it must be allowed that they are ; and yet I beg leave to question whether these do not prove an hindrance to many, and keep several bookish men from attaining to

[1] See secs. 13, 20.   [2] *I.e.*, " by means of them."
[3] Characteristic of Locke to ignore *æsthetic* criticism.

15

solid and true knowledge. This I think I may be permitted to say, that there is no part wherein the understanding needs a more careful and wary conduct than in the use of books ; without which they will prove rather innocent amusements than profitable employments of our time, and bring but small additions to our knowledge.

There is not seldom to be found, even amongst those who aim at knowledge, who[1] with an unwearied industry employ their whole time in books, who scarcely allow themselves time to eat or sleep, but read, and read, and read on, yet make no great advances in real knowledge, though there be no defect in their intellectual faculties to which their little progress can be imputed. The mistake here is, that it is usually supposed that by reading, the author's knowledge is transfused into the reader's understanding ; and so it is, but not by bare reading, but by reading and understanding what he writ. Whereby I mean, not barely comprehending what is affirmed or denied in each proposition (though that great readers do not always think themselves concerned precisely to do), but to see and follow the train of his reasonings, observe the strength and clearness of their connexion, and examine upon what they bottom. Without this a man may read the discourses of a very rational author, writ in a language and in propositions that he very well understands, and yet acquire not one jot of his knowledge ; which consisting only in the perceived, certain, or probable connexion of the ideas made use of in his reasonings, the reader's knowledge is no farther increased than he perceives that ; so much as he sees of this connexion, so much he knows of the truth or probability of that author's opinions.

All that he relies on without this perception he takes upon trust, upon the author's credit, without any knowledge of it at all. This makes me not at all wonder to see some men so abound in citations and build so much upon authorities, it being the sole foundation on which they bottom most of their own tenets ; so that in effect they

[1] That is, " There are . . . to be found . . . [those] who with an unwearied," etc. *Cf. sunt . . . qui.*

have but a second-hand or implicit[1] knowledge, *i.e.*, are in the right if such an one from whom they borrowed it were in the right in that opinion which they took from him ; which indeed is no knowledge at all. Writers of this or former ages may be good witnesses of matters of fact which they deliver, which we may do well to take upon their authority ; but their credit can go no farther than this ; it cannot at all affect the truth and falsehood of opinions which have no other sort of trial but reason and proof, which they themselves made use of to make themselves knowing ; and so must others too that will partake in their knowledge. Indeed it is an advantage that they have been at the pains to find out the proofs and lay them in that order that may show the truth or probability of their conclusions ; and for this we owe them great acknowledgments for saving us the pains in searching out those proofs which they have collected for us, and which possibly after all our pains we might not have found, nor been able to have set them in so good a light as that which they left them us in. Upon this account we are mightily beholden to judicious writers of all ages for those discoveries and discourses they have left behind them for our instruction, if we know how to make a right use of them, which is not to run them over in an hasty perusal, and perhaps lodge their opinions or some remarkable passages in our memories ; but to enter into their reasonings, examine their proofs, and then judge of the truth or falsehood, probability or improbability of what they advance ; not by any opinion we have entertained of the author, but by the evidence he produces and the conviction he affords us, drawn from things themselves. Knowing is seeing, and if it be so, it is madness to persuade ourselves that we do so by another man's eyes, let him use ever so many words to tell us that what he asserts is very visible. Till we ourselves see it with our own eyes and perceive it by our own understandings, we are as much in the dark and as void of knowledge as before, let us believe any learned author as much as we will.[2]

---

[1] *Cf.* sec. 15, second paragraph.   [2] See *Introduction*, p. 8.

Euclid and Archimedes are allowed to be knowing and to have demonstrated what they say ; and yet whoever shall read over their writings without perceiving the con nexion of their proofs, and seeing what they show, though he may understand all their words, yet he is not the more knowing : he may believe indeed, but does not know what they say, and so is not advanced one jot in mathematical knowledge by all his reading of those approved mathematicians.[1]

25. *Haste*.[2]—The eagerness and strong bent of the mind after knowledge, if not warily regulated, is often a hindrance to it.   It still presses into farther discoveries and new objects, and catches at the variety of knowledge ; and therefore often stays not long enough on what is before it to look into it as it should, for haste to pursue what is yet out of sight.   He that rides post through a country may be able from the transient view to tell how in general the parts lie, and may be able to give some loose description of here a mountain and there a plain, here a morass and there a river, woodland in one part and savannahs in another.   Such superficial ideas and observations as these he may collect in galloping over it ; but the more useful observations of the soil, plants, animals, and inhabitants, with their several sorts and properties, must necessarily escape him ; and it is seldom men ever discover the rich mines without some digging.   Nature commonly lodges her treasure and jewels in rocky ground.   If the matter be knotty and the sense lies deep, the mind must

---

[1] " The great Mr. Locke was the first who became a Newtonian philosopher without the help of geometry; for having asked Mr. Huygens whether all the mathematical propositions in Sir Isaac's *Principia* were true, and being told he might depend upon their certainty, he took them for granted, and carefully examined the reasonings and corollaries drawn from them, became master of all the Physics, and was fully convinced of the great discoveries contained in that book: thus also he read the *Optics* with pleasure, acquainting himself with everything in them that was not merely mathematical.   This I was told several times by Sir Isaac Newton himself " (J. T. Desaguliers, *A Course of Experimental Philosophy* (1734), vol. i., preface.

[2] See sec. 16.

stop and buckle to it, and stick upon it with labour and thought and close contemplation, and not leave it till it has mastered the difficulty and got possession of truth. But here care must be taken to avoid the other extreme ; a man must not stick at every useless nicety, and expect mysteries of science in every trivial question or scruple that he may raise. He that will stand to pick up and examine every pebble that comes in his way, is as unlikely to return enriched and loaden with jewels, as the other that travelled full speed. Truths are not the better nor the worse for their obviousness or difficulty, but their value is to be measured by their usefulness and tendency. Insignificant observations should not take up any of our minutes, and those that enlarge our view and give light towards farther and useful discoveries, should not be neglected, though they stop our course and spend some of our time in a fixed attention.

There is another haste that does often and will mislead the mind, if it be left to itself and its own conduct. The understanding is naturally forward, not only to learn its knowledge by variety (which makes it skip over one to get speedily to another part of knowledge), but also eager to enlarge its views by running too fast into general observations and conclusions without a due examination of particulars enough whereon to found those general axioms. This seems to enlarge their stock, but it is of fancies, not realities ; such theories, built upon narrow foundations, stand but weakly, and if they fall not of themselves, are at least very hardly to be supported against the assaults of opposition. And thus men being too hasty to erect to themselves general notions and ill-grounded theories, find themselves deceived in their stock of knowledge when they come to examine their hastily assumed maxims themselves, or to have them attacked by others. General observations drawn from particulars are the jewels of knowledge, comprehending great store in a little room ; but they are therefore to be made with the greater care and caution, lest if we take counterfeit for true our loss and shame be the greater, when our stock comes to a severe

scrutiny.[1] One or two particulars may suggest hints of
inquiry, and they do well to take those hints ; but if they
turn them into conclusions, and make them presently
general rules, they are forward indeed, but it is only to
impose on themselves by propositions assumed for truths
without sufficient warrant.   To make such observations
is, as has been already remarked, to make the head a
magazine of materials which can hardly be called knowledge, or at least it is but like a collection of lumber not
reduced to use or order ; and he that makes everything
an observation has the same useless plenty and much
more falsehood mixed with it.   The extremes on both
sides are to be avoided, and he will be able to give the
best account of. his studies who keeps his understanding
in the right mean[2] between them.

    26. *Anticipation.*—Whether it be a love of that which
brings the first light and information to their minds, and
want of vigour and industry to inquire ; or else that men
content themselves with any appearance of knowledge,
right or wrong, which when they have once got they will
hold fast ; this is visible, that many men give themselves
up to the first anticipations of their minds, and are very
tenacious of the opinions that first possess them ; they
are as often fond of their first conceptions as of their
first-born, and will by no means recede from the judgment
they have once made, or any conjecture or conceit which
they have once entertained.   This is a fault in the conduct of the understanding, since this firmness or rather
stiffness of the mind is not from[3] an adherence to truth,
but a submission to prejudice.   It is an unreasonable
homage paid to prepossession, whereby we show a
reverence not to (what we pretend to seek) truth, but
what by haphazard we chance to light on, be it what it
will.   This is visibly a preposterous use of our faculties,
and is a downright prostituting of the mind to resign it
thus and put it under the power of the first comer.   This
can never be allowed or ought to be followed as a right

---

[1] Verification is an essential procedure in the inductive method.
[2] Not necessarily the *mathematical* mean.   [3] *I.e.*, owing to.

way to knowledge, till the understanding (whose business
it is to conform itself to what it finds in the objects without) can by its own opinionatry[1] change that, and make
the unalterable nature of things comply with its own
hasty determinations, which will never be. Whatever we
fancy, things keep their course, and the habitudes, correspondence, and relations keep the same to one another.

27. *Resignation.*—Contrary to these, but by a like
dangerous excess on the other side, are those who always
resign their judgment to the last man they heard or read.
Truth never sinks into these men's minds nor gives any
tincture to them, but chameleon-like, they take the colour
of what is laid before them, and, as soon, lose and resign
it to the next that happens to come in their way. The
order wherein opinions are proposed or received by us is
no rule of their rectitude, nor ought to be a cause of their
preference. First or last in this case is the effect of
chance, and not the measure of truth or falsehood. This
every one must confess, and therefore should in the pursuit of truth keep his mind free from the influence of any
such accidents. A man may as reasonably draw cuts[2]
for his tenets, regulate his persuasion by the cast of a
die, as take it up for its novelty, or retain it because it
had his first assent and he was never of another mind.
Well-weighed reasons are to determine the judgment ;
those the mind should be always ready to hearken and
submit to, and by their testimony and suffrage[3] entertain
or reject any tenet indifferently, whether it be a perfect
stranger or an old acquaintance.

28. *Practice.*—Though the faculties of the mind are
improved by exercise, yet they must not be put to a
stress beyond their strength. " Quid valeant humeri,
quid ferre recusent,"[4] must be made the measure of every

---

[1] See sec. 16.   [2] Draw lots; "toss up."
[3] *Suffragium*, decision marked by casting a vote.
[4] " What the shoulders are strong enough for, and what they
refuse to bear " (Horace, *Ars Poetica*, 39). The analogy between
muscular and mental activity, weak as it is, has been greatly over-
pressed. Muscles can be isolated by the anatomist's knife ; mental
powers are only discriminated by logical analysis, that is, by a

one's understanding who has a desire not only to perform well, but to keep up the vigour of his faculties and
not to balk his understanding by what is too hard for it.
The mind by being engaged in a task beyond its strength,
like the body strained by lifting at a weight too heavy,
has often its force broken, and thereby gets an unaptness
or an aversion to any vigorous attempt ever after. A
sinew cracked seldom recovers its former strength, or at
least the tenderness of the sprain remains a good while
after, and the memory of it longer, and leaves a lasting
caution in the man not to put the part quickly again to
any robust employment. So it fares in the mind once
jaded by an attempt above its power ; it either is disabled for the future, or else checks at any vigorous under-
taking ever after, at least is very hardly brought to exert
its force again on any subject that requires thought and
meditation. The understanding should be brought to
the difficult and knotty parts of knowledge, that try the
strength of thought and a full bent of the mind, by insensible degrees ; and in such a gradual proceeding nothing
is too hard for it.   Nor let it be objected that such a slow
progress will never reach the extent of some sciences.
It is not to be imagined how far constancy will carry a
man ; however, it is better walking slowly in a rugged
way than to break a leg and be a cripple.   He that begins
with the calf may carry the ox, but he that will at first
go to take up an ox may so disable himself as not to be
able to lift up a calf after that.   When the mind by
insensible degrees has brought itself to attention and close
thinking, it will be able to cope with difficulties and master
them without any prejudice to itself, and then it may go
on roundly.   Every abstruse problem, every intricate
question, will not baffle, discourage, or break it.   But
though putting the mind unprepared upon an unusual

---

process of abstraction. " Faculties," not being real entities of the
kind to which muscles belong, are not capable of such very special
exercise as can be applied, for example, to the biceps.   The contrary opinion is responsible for much bad pedagogy.   See secs. (first
paragraph) 29, 31, and *Some Thoughts*, sec. 176.

stress that may discourage or damp it for the future ought to be avoided, yet this must not run it by an over-great shyness of difficulties into a lazy sauntering about ordinary and obvious things that demand no thought or application. This debases and enervates the understanding, makes it weak and unfit for labour. This is a sort of hovering about the surface of things without any insight into them or penetration ; and when the mind has been once habituated to this lazy recumbency and satisfaction on the obvious surface of things, it is in danger to rest satisfied there and go no deeper, since it cannot do it without pains and digging. He that has for some time accustomed himself to take up with what easily offers itself at first view, has reason to fear he shall never reconcile himself to the fatigue of turning and tumbling things in his mind to discover their more retired and more valuable secrets.

It is not strange that methods of learning which scholars have been accustomed to in their beginning and entrance upon the sciences should influence them all their lives, and be settled in their minds by an over-ruling reverence ; especially if they be such as universal use has established. Learners must at first be believers, and their master's rules having been once made axioms to them, it is no wonder they should keep that dignity, and by the authority they have once got, mislead those who think it sufficient to excuse them if they go out of their way in a well-beaten track.

29. *Words.*—I have copiously enough spoken of the abuse of words in another place,[1] and therefore shall upon this reflection, that the sciences are full of them, warn those that would conduct their understandings right not to take any term, howsoever authorized by the language of the schools, to stand for anything till they have an idea of it. A word may be of frequent use and great credit with several authors, and be by them made use of as if it stood for some real being ; but yet, if he that reads cannot frame any distinct idea of that being, it is cer-

---

[1] *Essay on the Human Understanding*, iii., especially chaps. x., xi.

tainly to him a mere empty sound without a meaning, and he learns no more by all that is said of it or attributed to it than if it were affirmed only of that bare empty sound. They who would advance in knowledge, and not deceive and swell themselves with a little articulated air, should lay down this as a fundamental rule, not to take words for things, nor suppose that names in books signify real entities in nature, till they can frame clear and distinct ideas of those entities. It will not perhaps be allowed, if I should set down " substantial forms " and " intentional species," as such that may justly be suspected to be of this kind of insignificant[1] terms. But this I am sure, to one that can form no determined ideas of what they stand for, they signify nothing at all ; and all that he thinks he knows about them is to him so much knowledge about nothing, and amounts at most but to be a learned ignorance. It is not without all reason supposed that there are many such empty terms to be found in some learned writers, to which they had recourse to etch[2] out their systems, where their understandings could not furnish them with conceptions from things. But yet I believe the supposing of some realities in nature answering those and the like words, have much perplexed some and quite misled others in the study of nature. That which in any discourse signifies, " I know not what," should be considered " I know not when." Where men have any conceptions, they can, if they are never so abstruse or abstracted, explain them and the terms they use for them.[3] For our conceptions being nothing but ideas, which are all made up of simple ones, if they cannot give us the ideas their words stand for it is plain they have none. To what purpose can it be to hunt after his conceptions who has none, or none distinct ? He that knew not what he himself meant by a learned term, cannot make us know anything by his use of it, let us

---

[1] *I.e.*, meaningless. The phrases belong to the Peripatetic as opposed to the Corpuscular philosophy. See *Thoughts*, sec. 193.

[2] *I.e.*, to eke.

[3] See sec. 31, " He that has settled in his mind," etc., and sec. 32.

beat our heads about it never so long. Whether we are able to comprehend all the operations of nature and the manners of them, it matters not to inquire ; but this is certain, that we can comprehend no more of them than we can distinctly conceive, and therefore to obtrude terms where we have no distinct conceptions, as if they did contain, or rather conceal something, is but an artifice of learned vanity to cover a defect in an hypothesis or our understandings. Words are not made to conceal, but to declare and show something ; where they are by those who pretend to instruct otherwise used, they conceal indeed something ; but that that they conceal is nothing but the ignorance, error, or sophistry of the talker, for there is in truth nothing else under them.

30. *Wandering.*—That there is a constant succession and flux of ideas in our minds I have observed in the former part of this essay, and every one may take notice of it in himself. This, I suppose, may deserve some part of our care in the conduct of our understandings ; and I think it may be of great advantage if we can, by use, get that power over our minds, as to be able to direct that train of ideas, that so, since there will new ones perpetually come into our thoughts by a constant succession, we may be able by choice so to direct them, that none may come in view but such as are pertinent to our present inquiry, and in such order as may be most useful to the discovery we are upon ; or, at least, if some foreign and unsought ideas will offer themselves, that yet we might be able to reject them and keep them from taking off our minds from its present pursuit, and hinder them from running away with our thoughts quite from the subject in hand. This is not, I suspect, so easy to be done as perhaps may be imagined ; and yet, for aught I know, this may be, if not the chief, yet one of the great differences that carry some men in their reasoning so far beyond others, where they seem to be naturally of equal parts.[1] A proper and

[1] Experiment seems to show that intellectual differences between man and man greatly depend upon differences in power of attention, of concentration of mind.

effectual remedy for this wandering of thoughts I would be glad to find. He that shall propose such an one would do great service to the studious and contemplative part of mankind, and perhaps help unthinking men to become thinking. I must acknowledge that hitherto I have discovered no other way to keep our thoughts close to their business, but the endeavouring as much as we can, and by frequent attention and application, getting the habit of attention and application. He that will observe children will find that even when they endeavour their utmost, they cannot keep their minds from straggling. The way to cure it, I am satisfied, is not angry chiding or beating, for that presently fills their heads with all the ideas that fear, dread, or confusion can offer to them. To bring back gently their wandering thoughts, by leading them into the path and going before them in the train they should pursue, without any rebuke, or so much as taking notice (where it can be avoided) of their roving, I suppose, would sooner reconcile and inure them to attention than all these rougher methods, which more distract their thought, and hindering the application they would promote, introduce a contrary habit.[1]

31. *Distinction.*—Distinction and division are (if I mistake not the import of the words) very different things ; the one[2] being the perception of a difference that nature has placed in things ; the other,[3] our making a division where there is yet none ; at least if it may be permitted to consider them in this sense, I think I may say of them, that one[2] of them is the most necessary and conducive to true knowledge that can be ; the other,[3] when too much made use of, serves only to puzzle and confound the understanding. To observe every the least difference that is in things argues a quick and clear sight, and this keeps the understanding steady and right in its way to knowledge. But though it be useful to discern every variety that is to be found in nature, yet it is not convenient to consider every difference that is in things, and divide

[1] See *Thoughts*, sec. 167.   [2] *Sc.* division.
[3] *Sc.* distinction.   See *Thoughts*, close of sec. 195.

them into distinct classes under every such difference.[1]
This will run us, if followed, into particulars (for every
individual has something that differences it from another),
and we shall be able to establish no general truths, or else
at least shall be apt to perplex the mind about them.
The collection of several things into several classes gives
the mind more general and larger views, but we must
take care to unite them only in that,[2] and so far as they
do agree, for so far they may be united under the consideration; for entity [3] itself, that comprehends all things,
as general as it is, may afford us clear and rational conceptions.   If we would weigh and keep in our minds what
it is we are considering, that would best instruct us when
we should or should not branch into farther distinctions,
which are to be taken only from a due contemplation of
things ; to which there is nothing more opposite than the
art of verbal distinctions made at pleasure in learned
and arbitrarily invented terms, to be applied at a venture,
without comprehending or conveying any distinct notions ;
and so altogether fitted to artificial talk or empty noise
in dispute, without any clearing of difficulties or advance
in knowledge.   Whatsoever subject we examine and
would get knowledge in, we should, I think, make as
general and as large as it will bear ; nor can there be any
danger of this, if the idea of it be settled and determined :
for if that be so, we shall easily distinguish it from any
other idea, though comprehended under the same name.
For it is to fence against the entanglements of equivocal
words, and the great art of sophistry which lies in them,
that distinctions have been multiplied and their use
thought so necessary.   But had every distinct abstract idea
a distinct known name, there would be little need of these
multiplied scholastic distinctions, though there would be
nevertheless as much need still of the mind's observing
the differences that are in things, and discriminating them
thereby one from another.   It is not therefore the right
way to knowledge to hunt after and fill the head with

---

[1] A truth commonly defied by writers on English grammar.
[2] *Subaud.*, "they agree."   [3] Being.

abundance of artificial and scholastic distinctions, wherewith learned men's writings are often filled : we sometimes
find what they treat of so divided and subdivided that
the mind of the most attentive reader loses the sight of it,
as it is more than probable the writer himself did ; for
in things crumbled into dust it is in vain to affect or
pretend order, or expect clearness. To avoid confusion
by too few or too many divisions, is a great skill in thinking
as well as writing, which is but the copying our thoughts ;
but what are the boundaries of the mean between the
two vicious excesses on both hands, I think is hard to
set down in words : clear and distinct ideas[1] is [*sic*] all
that I yet know able to regulate it. But as to verbal
distinctions received and applied to common terms, *i.e.*,
equivocal words,[2] they are more properly, I think, the
business of criticisms and dictionaries than of real knowledge and philosophy, since they for the most part explain
the meaning of words, and give us their several significa-
tions. The dexterous management of terms, and being
able to fend[3] and prove with them, I know has and does
pass in the world for a great part of learning ; but it is
learning distinct from knowledge, for knowledge consists
only in perceiving the habitudes and relations of ideas
one to another, which is done without words ; the inter-
vention of a sound helps nothing to it. And hence we see
that there is least use of distinctions where there is most
knowledge, I mean in mathematics, where men have determined ideas without[4] known names to them, and so there
being no room for equivocations, there is no need of
distinctions. In arguing, the opponent uses as comprehensive and equivocal terms as he can, to involve his
adversary in the doubtfulness of his expressions : this is

[1] *Essay*, ii., chap. xxix.; *Thoughts*, sec. 195, *note* on concluding
words of section.
[2] The fact that terms are common, or general, renders them
equivocal on occasion.
[3] Ward off (an opponent). The disputations so familiar in the
universities of his day were Locke's pet aversion. See sec. 43
[4] So the text reads, but the fact seems to require "with": see
next page.

expected, and therefore the answerer on his side makes it his play to distinguish as much as he can, and thinks he can never do it too much ; nor can he indeed in that way wherein victory may be had without truth and without knowledge. This seems to me to be the art of disputing. Use your words as captiously as you can in your arguing on one side, and apply distinctions as much as you can on the other side to every term, to nonplus your opponent ; so that in this sort of scholarship, there being no bounds set to distinguishing, some men have thought all acuteness to have lain in it, and therefore in all they have read or thought on, their great business has been to amuse themselves with distinctions, and multiply to themselves divisions ; at least, more than the nature of the thing required. There seems to me, as I said, to be no other rule for this but a due and right consideration of things as they are in themselves. He that has settled in his mind determined ideas, with names affixed to them, will be able both to discern their differences one from another, which is really distinguishing ; and where the penury of words affords not terms answering every distinct idea, will be able to apply proper distinguishing terms to the comprehensive and equivocal names he is forced to make use of.[1] This is all the need I know of distinguishing terms, and in such verbal distinctions each term of the distinction, joined to that whose signification it distinguishes, is but a distinct name for a distinct idea. Where they are so, and men have clear and distinct conceptions that answer their verbal distinctions, they are right, and are pertinent as far as they serve to clear anything in the subject under consideration. And this is that which seems to me the proper and only measure of distinctions and divisions ; which he that will conduct his understanding right must not look for in the acuteness of invention nor the authority of writers, but will find only in the consideration of things themselves, whether he is led into it by his own meditations or the information of books.

An aptness to jumble things together wherein can be

_____

[1] See sec. 29.

found any likeness, is a fault in the understanding on the other side which will not fail to mislead it, and by thus lumping of things, hinder the mind from distinct and accurate conceptions of them.

32. *Similes.*—To which let me here add another near of kin to this, at least in name, and that is letting the mind, upon the suggestion of any new notion, run immediately after similes to make it the clearer to itself; which, though it may be a good way and useful in the explaining our thoughts to others, yet it is by no means a right method to settle true notions of anything in ourselves, because similes always fail in some part, and come short of that exactness which our conceptions should have to things if we would think aright.[1] This indeed makes men plausible talkers, for those are always most acceptable in discourse who have the way to let their thoughts into other men's minds with the greatest ease and facility ; whether these thoughts are well formed and correspond with things matters not ; few men care to be instructed but at an easy rate. They who in their discourse strike the fancy, and take the hearers' conceptions along with them as fast as their words flow, are the applauded talkers, and go for the only men of clear thoughts. Nothing contributes so much to this as similes, whereby men think they themselves understand better, because they are the better understood. But it is one thing to think right, and another thing to know the right way to lay our thoughts before others with advantage and clearness, be they right or wrong. Well-chosen similes, metaphors, and allegories, with method and order, do this the best of anything, because being taken from objects already known and familiar to the understanding, they are conceived as fast as spoken, and the correspondence being concluded, the thing they are brought to explain and elucidate is thought to be understood too. Thus fancy passes for knowledge, and what is prettily said is mistaken for solid. I say not this to decry

[1] Locke's own similes of " blank paper " and " wax " might be retorted upon him. See sec. 2 *note.*

metaphor, or with design to take away that ornament of speech ; my business here is not with rhetoricians and orators,[1] but with philosophers and lovers of truth, to whom I would beg leave to give this one rule whereby to try whether in the application of their thoughts to anything for the improvement of their knowledge, they do in truth comprehend the matter before them really such as it is in itself. The way to discover this is to observe whether, in the laying it before themselves or others, they make use only of borrowed representations and ideas foreign to the things which are applied to it by way of accommodation, as bearing some proportion or imagined likeness to the subject under consideration. Figured and metaphorical expressions do well to illustrate more abstruse and unfamiliar ideas which the mind is not yet thoroughly accustomed to, but then they must be made use of to illustrate ideas that we already have, not to paint to us those which we yet have not. Such borrowed and allusive ideas may follow real and solid truth, to set it off when found, but must by no means be set in its place and taken for it. If all our search has yet reached no farther than simile and metaphor, we may assure ourselves we rather fancy than know, and have not yet penetrated into the inside and reality of the thing, be it what it will, but content ourselves with what our imaginations, not things themselves, furnish us with.

33. *Assent.*—In the whole conduct of the understanding, there is nothing of more moment than to know when and where, and how far to give assent, and possibly there is nothing harder. It is very easily said, and nobody questions it, that giving and withholding our assent and the degrees of it should be regulated by the evidence which things carry with them ; and yet we see men are not the better for this rule ; some firmly embrace doctrines upon slight grounds, some upon no grounds, and some contrary to appearance : some admit of certainty,

---

[1] But men who " have business " with rhetoricians should bear Locke's warning in mind.

and are not to be moved in what they hold ; others waver in everything, and there want not those that reject all as uncertain. What then shall a novice, an inquirer, a stranger do in the case ? I answer, use his eyes. There is a correspondence in things, and agreement and dis- agreement in ideas, discernible in very different degrees, and there are eyes in men to see them if they please ; only their eyes may be dimmed or dazzled, and the dis- cerning sight in them impaired or lost. Interest and passion dazzle ; the custom of arguing on any side, even against our persuasions, dims the understanding, and makes it by degrees lose the faculty of discerning clearly between truth and falsehood, and so of adhering to the right side. It is not safe to play with error and dress it up to ourselves or others in the shape of truth. The mind by degrees loses its natural relish of real solid truth, is reconciled insensibly to anything that can be dressed up into any feint[1] appearance of it ; and if the fancy be allowed the place of judgment at first in sport, it after- wards comes by use to usurp it, and what is recommended by this flatterer (that studies but to please) is received for good. There are so many ways of fallacy, such arts of giving colours, appearances, and resemblances by this court-dresser, the fancy, that he who is not wary to admit nothing but truth itself, very careful not to make his mind subservient to anything else, cannot but be caught. He that has a mind to believe, has half assented already ; and he that by often arguing against his own sense im- poses falsehood on others, is not far from believing him- self. This takes away the great distance there is be- twixt truth and falsehood ; it brings them almost together, and makes it no great odds, in things that approach so near, which you take ; and when things are brought to that pass, passion, or interest, &c., easily, and without being perceived, determine which shall be the right.

34. *Indifferency.*[2]—I have said above that we should keep a perfect indifferency for all opinions, not wish any of them true, or try to make them appear so, but being

---

[1] Feigned.   [2] Impartiality. See sec. 11.

indifferent, receive and embrace them according as evidence, and that alone, gives the attestation of truth. They that do thus, *i.e.*, keep their minds indifferent to opinions, to be determined only by evidence, will always find the understanding has perception enough to distinguish between evidence and no evidence, betwixt plain and doubtful ; and if they neither give nor refuse their assent but by that measure, they will be safe in the opinions they have. Which being perhaps but few, this caution will have also this good in it, that it will put them upon considering, and teach them the necessity of examining more than they do ; without which the mind is but a receptacle of inconsistencies, not the storehouse of truths. They that do not keep up this indifferency in themselves for all but truth, not supposed, but evidenced in themselves, put coloured spectacles before their eyes, and look on things through false glasses, and then think themselves excused in following the false appearances which they themselves put upon them. I do not expect that by this way the assent should in every one be proportioned to the grounds and clearness wherewith every truth is capable to be made out, or that men should be perfectly kept from error ; that is more than human nature can by any means be advanced to ; I aim at no such unattainable privilege : I am only speaking of what they should do, who would deal fairly with their own minds, and make a right use of their faculties in the pursuit of truth ; we fail them[1] a great deal more than they fail us. It is mismanagement more than want of abilities that men have reason to complain of, and which they actually do complain of in those that differ from them. He that by indifferency for all but truth, suffers not his assent to go faster than his evidence, nor beyond it, will learn to examine, and examine fairly instead of presuming, and nobody will be at a loss or in danger for want of embracing those truths which are necessary in his station and circumstances. In any other way but this all the world are born to orthodoxy ; they imbibe at first

[1] *I.e.*, our faculties.

the allowed opinions of their country and party, and so
never questioning their truth, not one of an hundred ever
examines. They are applauded for presuming they are
in the right. He that considers, is a foe to orthodoxy,
because possibly he may deviate from some of the received
doctrines there. And thus men, without any industry
or acquisition of their own, inherit local truths (for it is
not the same everywhere) and are inured to assent without evidence. This influences farther than is thought,
for what one of an hundred of the zealous bigots in all
parties ever examined the tenets he is so stiff in, or ever
thought it his business or duty so to do ? It is suspected
of lukewarmness to suppose it necessary, and a tendency
to apostacy to go about it. And if a man can bring his
mind once to be positive and fierce for positions whose
evidence he has never once examined, and that in matters
of greatest concernment to him, what shall keep him from
this short and easy way of being in the right in cases of
less moment ? Thus we are taught to clothe our minds
as we do our bodies, after the fashion in vogue, and it is
accounted fantasticalness, or something worse, not to do
so. This custom (which who dares oppose ?) makes the
short-sighted, bigots, and the warier, sceptics, as far as
it prevails : and those that break from it are in danger of
heresy : for taking the whole world, how much of it doth
truth and orthodoxy possess together ? Though it is by
the last alone (which has the good luck to be everywhere)
that error and heresy are judged of : for argument and
evidence signify nothing in the case, and excuse no where,
but are sure to be borne down in all societies by the
infallible orthodoxy of the place. Whether this be the
way to truth and right assent, let the opinions that take
place and prescribe in the several habitable parts of the
earth declare. I never saw any reason yet why truth
might not be trusted on its own evidence : I am sure if
that be not able to support it there is no fence against
error ; and then truth and falsehood are but names that
stand for the same things. Evidence therefore is that by
which alone every man is (and should be) taught to

regulate his assent, who is then, and then only, in the right way when he follows it.

Men deficient in knowledge are usually in one of these three states : either wholly ignorant, or as doubting of some proposition they have either embraced formerly, or are at present inclined to ; or lastly, they do with assurance hold and profess without ever having examined and being convinced by well-grounded arguments.

The first of these are in the best state of the three, by having their minds yet in their perfect freedom and indifferency, the likelier to pursue the truth better, having no bias yet clapped on to mislead them.

35. For ignorance with an indifferency for truth is nearer to it than opinion with ungrounded inclination, which is the great source of error ; and they are more in danger to go out of the way who are marching under the conduct of a guide[1] that it is a hundred to one will mislead them, than he that has not yet taken a step, and is likelier to be prevailed on to inquire after the right way. The last of the three sorts are in the worst condition of all ; for if a man can be persuaded and fully assured of anything for a truth, without having examined, what is there that he may not embrace for truth ? and if he has given himself up to believe a lie, what means is there left to recover one who can be assured without examining ? To the other two, this I crave leave to say, that as he that is ignorant is in the best state of the two, so he should pursue truth in a method suitable to that state ; i.e., by inquiring directly into the nature of the thing itself, without minding the opinions of others, or troubling himself with their questions or disputes about it ; but to see what he himself can, sincerely searching after truth, find out. He that proceeds upon other principles in his inquiry into any sciences, though he be resolved to examine them and judge of them freely, does yet at least put himself on that side, and post himself in a party which he will not quit till he be beaten out : by which the mind is insensibly

[1] Viz., inclination.

engaged to make what defence [1] it can, and so is unawares biassed. I do not say but a man should embrace some opinion when he has examined, else he examines to no purpose; but the surest and safest way is to have no opinion at all till he has examined, and that without any the least regard to the opinions or systems of other men about it. For example, were it my business to understand physic, would not the safe and readier way be to consult nature herself, and inform myself in the history of diseases and their cures, than espousing the principles of the dogmatists, methodists, or chemists, to engage in all the disputes concerning either of those systems, and suppose it to be true, till I have tried what they can say to beat me out of it? Or, supposing that Hippocrates,[2] or any other book, infallibly contains the whole art of physic; would not the direct way be to study, read, and consider that book, weigh and compare the parts of it to find the truth, rather than espouse the doctrines of any party? who, though they acknowledge his authority, have already interpreted and wire-drawn all his text to their own sense; the tincture whereof when I have imbibed, I am more in danger to misunderstand his true meaning, than if I had come to him with a mind unprepossessed by doctors and commentators of my sect; whose reasonings, interpretation, and language which I have been used to, will of course make all chime that way, and make another, and perhaps the genuine, meaning of the author seem harsh, strained, and uncouth to me. For words having naturally none of their own, carry that signification to the hearer that he is used to put upon them, whatever be the sense of him that uses them. This, I think, is visibly so; and if it be, he that begins to have any doubt of any of his tenets, which he received without examination, ought as much as he can, to put himself wholly into this state of ignorance in reference to that question; and throwing wholly by all his former notions, and the opinions

---

[1] Edition of 1706: the 1812 edition reads, "difference."

[2] Hippocrates, a great Greek physician of the fifth century B.C. It is probable that by the "other book" Locke means the Bible, but not, of course, as a text-book of medicine.

of others, examine, with a perfect indifferency, the question in its source, without any inclination to either side or any regard to his or others' unexamined opinions. This I own is no easy thing to do ; but I am not inquiring the easy way to opinion, but the right way to truth, which they must follow who will deal fairly with their own understandings and their own souls.

36. *Question.*—The indifferency that I here propose will also enable them to state the question right which they are in doubt about, without which they can never come to a fair and clear decision of it.

37. *Perseverance.*—Another fruit from this indifferency, and the considering things in themselves abstract[1] from our own opinions and other men's notions and discourses on them, will be, that each man will pursue his thoughts in that method which will be most agreeable to the nature of the thing, and to his apprehension of what it suggests to him, in which he ought to proceed with regularity and constancy, until he come to a well-grounded resolution wherein he may acquiesce. If it be objected that this will require every man to be a scholar, and quit all his other business and betake himself wholly to study, I answer, I propose no more to any one than he has time for. Some men's state and condition require no great extent of knowledge ; the necessary provision for life swallows the greatest part of their time. But one man's want of leisure is no excuse for the oscitancy[2] and ignorance of those who have time to spare ; and every one has enough to get as much knowledge as is required and expected of him, and he that does not that, is in love with ignorance, and is accountable for it.

38. *Presumption.*—The variety of distempers in men's minds is as great as of those in their bodies ; some are epidemic, few escape them ; and every one too, if he would look into himself, would find some defect of his particular genius. There is scarce any one without some idiosyncrasy that he suffers by. This man presumes upon his parts, that they will not fail him at time of need ;

[1] *I.e.*, abstracted.   [2] Yawning.

and so thinks it superfluous labour to make any provision beforehand. His understanding is to him like Fortunatus's purse,[1] which is always to furnish him, without ever putting anything into it beforehand ; and so he sits still satisfied, without endeavouring to store his understanding with knowledge. It is the spontaneous product of the country, and what need of labour in tillage ? Such men may spread their native riches before the ignorant ; but they were best not come to stress and trial with the skilful. We are born ignorant of everything. The superficies of things that surround them make impressions on the negligent, but nobody penetrates into the inside without labour, attention, and industry. Stones and timber grow of themselves, but yet there is no uniform pile with symmetry and convenience to lodge in without toil and pains. God has made the intellectual world harmonious and beautiful without us ; but it will never come into our heads all at once ; we must bring it home piecemeal, and there set it up by our own industry, or else we shall have nothing but darkness and a chaos within, whatever order and light there be in things without us.

39. *Despondency.*—On the other side, there are others that depress their own minds, despond at the first difficulty, and conclude that the getting an insight in any of the sciences, or making any progress in knowledge farther than serves their ordinary business, is above their capacities. These sit still, because they think they have not legs to go ; as the others I last mentioned do, because they think they have wings to fly, and can soar on high when they please. To these latter one may for answer apply the proverb, " Use legs and have legs." Nobody knows what strength of parts he has till he has tried them. And of the understanding one may most truly say, that its force is greater generally than it thinks, till it is put to it. " Viresque acquirit eundo."[2]

And therefore the proper remedy here is but to set the

[1] Fortune at his request gave Fortunatus an inexhaustible purse, which proved his ruin.

[2] " And it gathers strength in the going " (*Æneid*, iv. 175). On this section, *cf. Thoughts*, sec. 195.

mind to work, and apply the thoughts vigorously to the business ; for it holds in the struggles of the mind as in those of war, " dum putant se vincere vicere."[1] A persuasion that we shall overcome any difficulties that we meet with in the sciences seldom fails to carry us through them. Nobody knows the strength of his mind, and the force of steady and regular application, till he has tried. This is certain, he that sets out upon weak legs, will not only go farther, but grow stronger too than one who, with a vigorous constitution and firm limbs, only sits still.

Something of kin to this men may observe in themselves, when the mind frights itself (as it often does) with anything reflected on in gross, and transiently viewed confusedly and at a distance. Things thus offered to the mind carry the show of nothing but difficulty in them, and are thought to be wrapt up in impenetrable obscurity. But the truth is, these are nothing but spectres that the understanding raises to itself to flatter its own laziness. It sees nothing distinctly in things remote and in a huddle ; and therefore concludes too faintly, that there is nothing more clear to be discovered in them. It is but to approach nearer, and that mist of our own raising that enveloped them will remove ; and those that in that mist appeared hideous giants not to be grappled with, will be found to be of the ordinary and natural size and shape. Things that in a remote and confused view seem very obscure, must be approached by gentle and regular steps ; and what is most visible, easy, and obvious in them first considered. Reduce them into their distinct parts ; and then in their due order bring all that should be known concerning every one of those parts into plain and simple questions ; and then what was thought obscure, perplexed, and too hard for our weak parts, will lay itself open to the understanding in a fair view, and let the mind into that which before[2] it was awed with, and kept at a distance from, as wholly mysterious. I appeal to

[1] " They conquered as long as they believed they were conquering," (Liv., ii. 64).
[2] Previously.

my reader's experience, whether this has never happened to him, especially when, busy on one thing, he has occasionally reflected on another. I ask him whether he has never thus been scared with a sudden opinion of mighty difficulties, which yet have vanished, when he has seriously and methodically applied himself to the consideration of this seeming terrible subject ; and there has been no other matter of astonishment left, but that he amused himself with so discouraging a prospect of his own raising, about a matter which in the handling was found to have nothing in it more strange nor intricate than several other things which he had long since, and with ease, mastered. This experience would teach us how to deal with such bugbears another time, which should rather serve to excite our vigour than enervate our industry. The surest way for a learner in this, as in all other cases, is not to advance by jumps and large strides ; let that which he sets himself to learn next be indeed the next, *i.e.*, as nearly conjoined with what he knows already as is possible ; let it be distinct, but not remote from it ; let it be new, and what he did not know before, that the understanding may advance ; but let it be as little at once as may be, that its advances may be clear and sure.[1]   All the ground that it gets this way it will hold.   This distinct gradual growth in knowledge is firm and sure ; it carries its own light with it in every step of its progression in an easy and orderly train ;[2] than which there is nothing of more use to the understanding.   And though this perhaps may seem a very slow and lingering way to knowledge, yet I dare confidently affirm, that whoever will try it in himself, or any one he will teach, shall find the advances greater in this method, than they would in the same space of time have been in any other he could have taken.   The greatest part of true knowledge lies in a distinct perception of things in themselves distinct. And some men give more clear light and knowledge by the bare distinct stating of a question, than others by talking of it in gross, whole hours together.   In this, they

[1] See *Thoughts*, sec. 180.   [2] Sequence.

who so state a question, do no more but separate and dis-
entangle the parts of it one from another, and lay them,
when so disentangled, in their due order. This often,
without any more ado, resolves the doubt, and shows the
mind where the truth lies. The agreement or disagreement of the ideas in question, when they are once separated
and distinctly considered, is, in many cases, presently
perceived, and thereby clear and lasting knowledge
gained,[1] whereas things in gross taken up together, and
so lying together in confusion, can produce in the mind
but a confused, which in effect is no, knowledge ; or at
least, when it comes to be examined and made use of, will
prove little better than none. I therefore take the liberty
to repeat here again what I have said elsewhere,[2] that in
learning anything, as little should be proposed to the
mind at once as is possible ; and, that being understood
and fully mastered, to proceed to the next adjoining part,
yet unknown, simple, unperplexed proposition, belonging
to the matter in hand, and tending to the clearing what is
principally designed.[3]

40. *Analogy.*[4]—Analogy is of great use to the mind in
many cases, especially in natural philosophy ; and that
part of it chiefly which consists in happy and successful
experiments. But here we must take care that we keep
ourselves within that wherein the analogy consists. For
example : the acid oil of vitriol is found to be good in such
a case, therefore the spirit of nitre or vinegar may be
used in the like case. If the good effect of it be owing
wholly to the acidity of it, the trial may be justified ;

[1] *Cf. Thoughts*, sec. 195, at close.

[2] See sec. 28, and *Thoughts*, secs. 167, 180, 195.

[3] Save for differences of punctuation, this is the reading of the
editions of 1706 and 1714. The following emendation is suggested :
" and, that being understood and fully mastered, to proceed to the
next adjoining part yet unknown ; [to state] what is belonging to
the matter in hand as simple, unperplexed proposition [s, and so]
tending to clear it, [is] what is principally designed." The reader
will remember that the *Conduct* is a posthumous publication.

[4] Analogy (ἀναλογία, proportion) is an inference from resemblance,
or partial identity : A and B are alike in possessing the qualities
x, y, z ; A has the quality *l* and, by analogy, B also has it.

but if there be something else besides the acidity in the oil of vitriol, which produces the good we desire in the case, we mistake that for analogy which is not, and suffer our understanding to be misguided by a wrong supposition of analogy where there is none.

41. *Association.*—Though I have, in the second book of my Essay concerning Human Understanding,[1] treated of the association of ideas ; yet having done it there historically, as giving a view of the understanding in this as well as its several other ways of operating, rather than designing there to inquire into the remedies that ought to be applied to it ; it will, under this latter consideration, afford other matter of thought to those who have a mind to instruct themselves thoroughly in the right way of conducting their understandings : and that the rather, because this, if I mistake not, is as frequent a cause of mistake and error in us as perhaps anything else that can be named ; and is a disease of the mind as hard to be cured as any, it being a very hard thing to convince any one that things are not so, and naturally so, as they constantly appear to him.

By this one easy and unheeded miscarriage of the understanding, sandy and loose foundations become infallible principles, and will not suffer themselves to be touched or questioned ; such unnatural connexions become by custom as natural to the mind as [that] sun and light, fire and warmth go together, and so seem to carry with them as natural an evidence as self-evident truths themselves. And where then shall one with hopes of success begin the cure ? Many men firmly embrace falsehood for truth ; not only because they never thought otherwise, but also because, thus blinded as they have been from the beginning, they never could think otherwise ; at least without a vigour of mind able to contest the empire of habit, and look into its own principles ; a freedom which few men have the notion of in themselves, and fewer are allowed the practice of by others ; it being the great art and business of the teachers and guides in most sects to suppress,

1 Chap. xxxiii.

as much as they can, this fundamental duty which every man owes himself, and is the first steady step towards right and truth in the whole train of his actions and opinions. This would give one reason to suspect, that such teachers are conscious to themselves of the falsehood or weakness of the tenets they profess, since they will not suffer the grounds whereon they are built to be examined ; whereas those who seek truth only, and desire to own and propagate nothing else, freely expose their principles to the test ; are pleased to have them examined ; give men leave to reject them if they can ; and if there be anything weak and unsound in them, are willing to have it detected, that they themselves, as well as others, may not lay any stress upon any received proposition beyond what the evidence of its truths will warrant and allow.

There is, I know, a great fault among all sorts of people of principling their children and scholars ; which at least, when looked into, amounts to no more but making them imbibe their teacher's notions and tenets by an implicit faith, and firmly to adhere to them whether true or false. What colours may be given to this, or of what use it may be when practised upon the vulgar, destined to labour, and given up to the service of their bellies, I will not here inquire. But as to the ingenuous part of mankind, whose condition allows them leisure, and letters, and inquiry after truth, I can see no other right way of principling them, but to take heed, as much as may be, that in their tender years, ideas that have no natural cohesion come not to be united in their heads ; and that this rule be often inculcated to them to be their guide in the whole course of their lives and studies, viz., that they never suffer any ideas to be joined in their understandings in any other or stronger combination than what their own nature[1] and correspondence give them ; and that they often examine those that they find linked together in their minds, whether this association of ideas be from the visible agreement that is in the ideas themselves, or from

[1] *I.e.*, the nature of the ideas.

the habitual and prevailing custom of the mind joining them thus together in thinking.

This is for caution against this evil, before it be thoroughly riveted by custom in the understanding; but he that would cure it when habit has established it, must nicely observe the very quick and almost imperceptible motions of the mind in its habitual actions. What I have said in another place[1] about the change of the ideas of sense into those of judgment may be proof of this. Let any one, not skilled in painting, be told when he sees bottles and tobacco-pipes, and other things so painted, as they are in some places shown, that he does not see protuberances, and you will not convince him but by the touch; he will not believe that by an instantaneous legerdemain of his own thoughts, one idea is substituted for another. How frequent instances may one meet with of this in the arguings of the learned, who not seldom, in two ideas that they have been accustomed to join in their minds, substitute one for the other; and I am apt to think, often without perceiving it themselves! This, whilst they are under the deceit of it, makes them incapable of conviction, and they applaud themselves as zealous champions for truth, when indeed they are contending for error. And the confusion of two different ideas, which a customary connexion of them in their minds hath made to them almost one, fills their head with false views, and their reasonings with false consequences.

42. *Fallacies.*—Right understanding consists in the discovery and adherence to truth, and that in the perception of the visible or probable agreement or disagreement of ideas, as they are affirmed and denied one of another. From whence it is evident, that the right use and conduct of the understanding, whose business is purely truth and nothing else, is, that the mind should be kept in a perfect indifferency, not inclining to either side, any farther than evidence settles it by knowledge, or the over-balance

[1] *Essay*, ii., chap. ix.: "We are farther to consider concerning perception, that the ideas we received by sensation are often by grown people altered by the judgment without our taking notice of it," *etc.*

of probability gives it the turn of assent and belief ; but yet it is very hard to meet with any discourse wherein one may not perceive the author not only maintain (for that is reasonable and fit) but inclined and biassed to one side of the question, with marks of a desire that that should be true. If it be asked me, how authors who have such a bias and lean to it may be discovered ; I answer, by observing how in their writings or arguings they are often led by their inclinations to change the ideas of the question, either by changing the terms, or by adding and joining others to them, whereby the ideas under consideration are so varied as to be more serviceable to their purpose, and to be thereby brought to an easier and nearer agreement, or more visible and remoter disagreement one with another. This is plain and direct sophistry ; but I am far from thinking that wherever it is found it is made use of with design to deceive and mislead the readers. It is visible that men's prejudices and inclinations by this way impose often upon themselves ; and their affection for truth, under their prepossession in favour of one side, is the very thing that leads them from it. Inclination suggests and slides into their discourse favourable terms, which introduce favourable ideas ; till at last by this means that is concluded clear and evident, thus dressed up, which, taken in its native state, by making use of none but the precise determined ideas, would find no admittance at all. The putting these glosses on what they affirm, these, as they are thought, handsome, easy, and graceful explications of what they are discoursing on, is so much the character of what is called and esteemed writing well, that it is very hard to think that authors will ever be persuaded to leave what serves so well to propagate their opinions, and procure themselves credit in the world, for a more jejune and dry way of writing, by keeping to the same terms precisely annexed to the same ideas ; a sour and blunt stiffness tolerable in mathematicians only, who force their way, and make truth prevail by irresistible demonstration.

But yet if authors cannot be prevailed with to quit the

looser, though more insinuating ways of writing; if they will not think fit to keep close to truth and instruction by unvaried terms and plain unsophisticated arguments; yet it concerns readers not to be imposed on by fallacies and the prevailing ways of insinuation. To do this,[1] the surest and most effectual remedy is to fix in the mind the clear and distinct ideas of the question stripped of words; and so likewise in the train of argumentation, to take up the author's ideas, neglecting his words, observing how they connect or separate those in question. He that does this will be able to cast off all that is superfluous; he will see what is pertinent, what coherent, what is direct to, what slides by the question. This will readily show him all the foreign ideas in the discourse, and where they were brought in; and though they perhaps dazzled the writer, yet he will perceive that they give no light nor strength to his reasonings.

This, though it be the shortest and easiest way of reading[2] books with profit, and keeping one's self from being misled by great names or plausible discourses; yet it being hard and tedious to those who have not accustomed themselves to it, it is not to be expected that every one (amongst those few who really pursue truth) should this way guard his understanding from being imposed on by the wilful, or at least undesigned sophistry, which creeps into most of the books of argument. They that write against their conviction, or that, next to them, are resolved to maintain the tenets of a party they were engaged in, cannot be supposed to reject any arms that may help to defend their cause, and therefore such should be read with the greatest caution. And they who write for opinions they are sincerely persuaded of and believe to be true, think they may so far allow themselves to indulge their laudable affection to truth, as to permit their esteem of it to give it the best colours, and set it off with the best expressions and dress they can, thereby to gain it the easiest entrance into the minds of their readers, and fix it deepest there.

[1] *I.e.*, to prevent this imposition.   [2] See sec. 20.

One of those being the state of mind we may justly suppose most writers to be in, it is fit their readers, who apply to them for instruction, should not lay by that caution which becomes a sincere pursuit of truth, and should make them always watchful against whatever might conceal or misrepresent it. If they have not the skill of representing to themselves the author's sense by pure ideas separated from sounds, and thereby divested of the false lights[1] and deceitful ornaments of speech ; this yet they should do, they should keep the precise question steadily in their minds, carry it along with them through the whole discourse, and suffer not the least alteration in the terms, either by addition, subtraction, or substituting any other. This every one can do who has a mind to it ; and he that has not a mind to it, it is plain, makes his understanding only the warehouse of other men's lumber ; I mean false and unconcluding[2] reasonings, rather than a repository of truth for his own use, which will prove substantial, and stand him in stead, when he has occasion for it. And whether such an one deals fairly by his own mind, and conducts his own understanding right, I leave to his own understanding to judge.

43. *Fundamental Verities.*—The mind of man being very narrow, and so slow in making acquaintance with things, and taking in new truths, that no one man is capable, in a much longer life than ours, to know all truths ; it becomes our prudence, in our search after knowledge, to employ our thoughts about fundamental and material questions, carefully avoiding those that are trifling, and not suffering ourselves to be diverted from our main even purpose, by those that are merely incidental. How much of many young men's time is thrown away in purely logical inquiries[3] I need not mention. This is no better than if a man, who was to be a painter, should spend all his time in examining the threads of the several cloths he is to paint upon, and counting the hairs of each pencil

---

[1] Wreckers' beacons.   [2] Inconclusive.
[3] *Cf.* secs. 7, 31, 44, and *Thoughts*, secs. 166, 188, 189.

and brush he intends to use in the laying on of his colours. Nay, it is much worse than for a young painter to spend his apprenticeship in such useless niceties ; for he, at the end of all his pains to no purpose, finds that it is not painting, nor any help to it, and so is really to no purpose ; whereas men designed for scholars have often their heads so filled and warmed with disputes on logical questions, that they take those airy useless notions for real and substantial knowledge, and think their understandings so well furnished with science, that they need not look any farther into the nature of things, or descend to the mechanical drudgery of experiment and inquiry. This is so obvious a mismanagement of the understanding, and that in the professed way to knowledge, that it could not be passed by ; to which might be joined abundance of questions, and the way of handling of them in the schools.[1] What faults in particular of this kind every man is or may be guilty of would be infinite to enumerate ; it suffices to have shown that superficial and slight discoveries, and observations that contain nothing of moment in themselves, nor serve as clues to lead us into farther knowledge, should not be thought worth our searching after.

There are fundamental truths that lie at the bottom, the basis upon which a great many others rest, and in which they have their consistency. These are teeming truths, rich in store, with which they furnish the mind, and, like the lights of heaven, are not only beautiful and entertaining in themselves, but give light and evidence to other things, that without them could not be seen or known. Such is that admirable discovery[2] of Mr. Newton, that all bodies gravitate to one another, which may be counted as the basis of natural philosophy ; which, of what use it is to the understanding of the great frame of our solar system, he has to the astonishment of the learned world shown ; and how much farther it would guide us in other things, if rightly pursued, is not yet known.

---

[1] *I.e.*, in the formal exercises of the universities. An examination or course of study is still termed a "school" at Oxford and elsewhere.

[2] First made public in his *Principia*, 1687.

Our Saviour's great rule, that " we should love our neighbour as ourselves," is such a fundamental truth for the regulating human society, that I think by that alone one might without difficulty determine all the cases and doubts in social morality.[1] These and such as these are the truths we should endeavour to find out, and store our minds with. Which leads me to another thing in the conduct of the understanding that is no less necessary, viz. :

44. *Bottoming.*—To accustom ourselves, in any question proposed, to examine and find out upon what it bottoms. Most of the difficulties that come in our way, when well considered and traced, lead us to some proposition, which, known to be true, clears the doubt, and gives an easy solution of the question ; whilst topical and superficial arguments, of which there is store to be found on both sides, filling the head with variety of thoughts, and the mouth with copious discourse, serve only to amuse the understanding, and entertain company, without coming to the bottom of the question, the only place of rest and stability for an inquisitive mind, whose tendency is only to truth and knowledge.

For example, if it be demanded whether the grand seignior[2] can lawfully take what he will from any of his people ? This question cannot be resolved without coming to a certainty whether all men are naturally equal, for upon that it turns ; and that truth well settled in the understanding, and carried in the mind through the various debates concerning the various rights of men in society, will go a great way in putting an end to them, and showing on which side the truth is.

45. *Transferring of Thoughts.*—There is scarcely anything more for the improvement of knowledge, for the ease of life, and the despatch of business, than for a man to be able to dispose of his own thoughts ; and there is

[1] " I am never to act otherwise than so that I could also will that my maxim should become a universal law " (*Kant*).

[2] The Turkish Sultan. In 1690, Locke (*Two Treatises of Government*) had maintained that man is born with a title to perfect freedom and uncontrolled enjoyment of all the rights and privileges of the law of nature.

scarcely anything harder in the whole conduct of the understanding than to get a full mastery over it. The mind, in a waking man, has always some object that it applies itself to ; which, when we are lazy or unconcerned, we can easily change, and at pleasure transfer our thoughts to another, and from thence to a third, which has no relation to either of the former. Hence men forwardly conclude, and frequently say, nothing is so free as thought, and it were well it were so ; but the contrary will be found true in several instances ; and there are many cases wherein there is nothing more resty and ungovernable than our thoughts ; they will not be directed what objects to pursue, nor be taken off from those they have once fixed on, but run away with a man in the pursuit of those ideas they have in view, let him do what he can.

I will not here mention again what I have above taken notice of, how hard it is to get the mind, narrowed by a custom of thirty or forty years' standing to a scanty collection of obvious and common ideas, to enlarge itself to a more copious stock, and grow into an acquaintance with those that would afford more abundant matter of useful contemplation ; it is not of this I am here speaking. The inconveniency I would here represent, and find a remedy for, is the difficulty there is sometimes to transfer our minds from one subject to another, in cases where the ideas are equally familiar to us.

Matters that are recommended to our thoughts by any of our passions, take possession of our minds with a kind of authority, and will not be kept out or dislodged ; but as if the passion that rules were for the time the sheriff of the place, and came with all the posse,[1] the understanding is seized and taken with the object it introduces, as if it had a legal right to be alone considered there. There is scarce anybody I think of so calm a temper who hath not some time found this tyranny on his understanding, and suffered under the inconvenience of it.

---

[1] The " posse comitatus," or body of persons summoned by the sheriff of the county (comitatus) to help him in maintaining order and securing obedience to the King's writ.

Who is there almost whose mind, at some time or other, love or anger, fear or grief, has not so fastened to some clog that it could not turn itself to any other object ? I call it a clog, for it hangs upon the mind so as to hinder its vigour and activity in the pursuit of other contemplations ; and advances itself little or not at all in the knowledge of the thing which it so closely hugs and constantly pores on. Men thus possessed are sometimes as if they were so in the worse sense, and lay under the power of an enchantment. They see not what passes before their eyes, hear not the audible discourse of the company, and when by any strong application to them they are roused a little, they are like men brought to themselves from some remote region ; whereas in truth they come no farther than their secret cabinet within, where they have been wholly taken up with the puppet, which is for that time appointed for their entertainment. The shame that such dumps cause to well-bred people, when it carries them away from the company, where they should bear a part in the conversation, is a sufficient argument that it is a fault in the conduct of our understanding not to have that power over it as to make use of it to those purposes and on those occasions wherein we have need of its assistance. The mind should be always free and ready to turn itself to the variety of objects that occur, and allow them as much consideration as shall for that time be thought fit. To be engrossed so by one object as not to be prevailed on to leave it for another that we judge fitter for our contemplation, is to make it of no use to us. Did this state of mind remain always so, every one would, without scruple, give it the name of perfect madness ; and whilst it does last, at whatever intervals it returns, such a rotation of thoughts about the same object no more carries us forward towards the attainment of knowledge, than getting upon a mill-horse whilst he jogs on in his circular track would carry a man a journey.

I grant something must be allowed to legitimate passions and to natural inclinations. Every man, besides occasional affections, has beloved studies, and those the mind will more closely stick to ; but yet it is best that it should be always at liberty, and under the free disposal of the man, and to act how and upon what he directs. This we should endeavour to obtain unless we would be content with such a flaw in our understanding, that sometimes we should be, as it were, without it ;[1] for it is very little better than so in cases where we cannot make use of it to those purposes we would, and which stand in present need of it.

But before fit remedies can be thought on for this disease we must know the several causes of it, and thereby regulate the cure, if we will hope to labour with success.

One we have already instanced in, whereof all men that reflect have so general a knowledge, and so often an experience in themselves, that nobody doubts of it. A prevailing passion so pins down our thoughts to the object and concern of it, that a man passionately in love cannot bring himself to think of his ordinary affairs, or a kind mother, drooping under the loss of a child, is not able to bear a part as she was wont in the discourse of the company, or conversation of her friends.

But though passion be the most obvious and general, yet it is not the only cause that binds up the understanding, and confines it for the time to one object, from which it will not be taken off.

Besides this, we may often find that the understanding, when it has a while employed itself upon a subject which either chance or some slight accident offered to it, without the interest or recommendation of any passion, works itself into a warmth, and by degrees gets into a career, wherein, like a bowl down a hill, it increases its motion by going, and will not be stopped or diverted ; though, when the heat is over, it sees all this earnest application was about a trifle not worth a thought, and all the pains employed about it lost labour.

There is a third sort, if I mistake not, yet lower than this ; it is a sort of childishness, if I may so say, of the understanding, wherein, during the fit, it plays with and dandles some insignificant puppet to no end, nor with

---

[1] *I.e.*, our understanding.

any design at all, and yet cannot easily be got off from it. Thus some trivial sentence, or a scrap of poetry, will sometimes get into men's heads, and make such a chiming there, that there is no stilling of it ; no peace to be obtained, nor attention to anything else, but this impertinent guest will take up the mind and possess the thoughts in spite of all endeavours to get rid of it. Whether every one hath experimented[1] in themselves this troublesome intrusion of some frisking ideas which thus importune the understanding, and hinder it from being better employed, I know not. But persons of very good parts, and those more than one, I have heard speak and complain of it themselves. The reason I have to make this doubt, is from what I have known in a case something of kin to this, though much odder, and that is of a sort of visions that some people have lying quiet, but perfectly awake, in the dark, or with their eyes shut. It is a great variety of faces, most commonly very odd ones, that appear to them in a train[2] one after another ; so that having had just the sight of the one, it immediately passes away to give place to another, that the same instant succeeds, and has as quick an exit as its leader ; and so they march on in a constant succession ; nor can any one of them by any endeavour be stopped or restrained beyond the instant of its appearance, but is thrust out by its follower, which will have its turn. Concerning this fantastical phenomenon I have talked with several people, whereof some have been perfectly acquainted with it, and others have been so wholly strangers to it that they could hardly be brought to conceive or believe it. I knew a lady of excellent parts, who had got past thirty without having ever had the least notice of any such thing ; she was so great a stranger to it, that when she heard me and another talking of it, could scarcely forbear thinking we bantered her ; but some time after, drinking a large dose of dilute tea (as she was ordered by a physician) going to bed, she told us at next meeting, that she had now experimented[1] what our discourse had much ado

[1] *I.e.*, experienced.   [2] *I.e.*, in succession.

to persuade her of. She had seen a great variety of faces in a long train, succeeding one another, as we had described ; they were all strangers and intruders, such as she had no acquaintance with before, nor sought after then ; and as they came of themselves, they went too ; none of them stayed a moment, nor could be detained by all the endeavours she could use, but went on in their solemn procession, just appeared and then vanished. This odd phenomenon seems to have a mechanical cause, and to depend upon the matter and motion of the blood or animal spirits.[1]

When the fancy is bound by passion, I know no way to set the mind free and at liberty to prosecute what thoughts the man would make choice of, but to allay the present passion, or counterbalance it with another ; which is an art to be got by study, and acquaintance with the passions.

Those who find themselves apt to be carried away with the spontaneous current of their own thoughts, not excited by any passion or interest, must be very wary and careful in all the instances of it to stop it, and never humour their minds in being thus triflingly busy. Men know the value of their corporeal liberty, and therefore suffer not willingly fetters and chains to be put upon them. To have the mind captivated is, for the time, certainly the greater evil of the two, and deserves our utmost care and endeavours to preserve the freedom of our better part. In this case our pains will not be lost ; striving and struggling will prevail, if we constantly on all such occasions make use of it. We must never indulge these trivial attentions of thought ; as soon as we find the mind makes itself a business of nothing, we should immediately disturb and check it, introduce new and more serious considerations, and not leave till we have beaten it off

---

[1] A reference to the ancient opinion that only the veins contained blood, while the arteries during life were filled with a fluid of extreme tenuity, the "animal spirits." The whole of the preceding paragraph is interesting, as exhibiting Locke's use of the comparative method in the study of psychology.

from the pursuit it was upon. This, at first, if we have let the contrary practice grow to an habit, will perhaps be difficult ; but constant endeavours will by degrees prevail, and at last make it easy. And when a man is pretty well advanced, and can command his mind off at pleasure from incidental and undesigned pursuits, it may not be amiss for him to go on farther, and make attempts upon meditations of greater moment, that at the last he may have a full power over his own mind, and be so fully master of his own thoughts as to be able to transfer them from one subject to another, with the same ease that he can lay by anything he has in his hand, and take something else that he has a mind to in the room of it. This liberty of mind is of great use both in business and study, and he that has got it will have no small advantage of ease and despatch in all that is the chosen and useful employment of his understanding.

The third and last way which I mentioned the mind to be sometimes taken up with, I mean the chiming of some particular words or sentence in the memory, and, as it were, making a noise in the head, and the like, seldom happens but when the mind is lazy, or very loosely and negligently employed. It were better indeed to be without such impertinent and useless repetitions : any obvious idea, when it is roving carelessly at a venture, being of more use, and apter to suggest something worth consideration, than the insignificant buzz of purely empty sounds. But since the rousing of the mind, and setting the understanding on work with some degree of vigour, does for the most part presently set it free from these idle companions, it may not be amiss whenever we find ourselves troubled with them, to make use of so profitable a remedy that is always at hand.

INDEX

266

Rational creature, 28, 33, 39, 196, 201 *f.*, 207, 221
Rationalism, 9, 11
Readers, great, 216, 225 *f.*
Reading, 115 *ff.*, 209, 216 *ff.*, 225 *ff.*, 256
" Real knowledge," 8, 16 *f.*, 127, 138
Reason, 28, 30 *ff.*, 35, 38, 159, 184 *f.*, 187
  miscarriages of, 184 *f.*, 208
Reasoning, 64, 184, 194 *ff.*, 215, 225, 257
  trains of, 194 *f.*, 198, 201
Records, 225, 227
Recreation, 57, 166, 171
Reflection, 7, 44, 216 *f.*
Religion, 201 *f.*, 208
Religious belief, 193 *f.*
  controversy, 188
  instruction, 19, 120, 123 *n.*, 169
Renascence, 4
Reputation, 33, 40 *f.*, 43, 151
Research, 227
Resignation, 231
Restraint, 32 *f.*, 37, 48
Revelation, 159
Reverence, 99
Rewards, 37 *ff.*
Reynard the Fox, 120
Rhetoric, 2, 12, 153 *f.*, 241
Rich, Jeremiah, 124
Riding, 16, 166
  post, 228
Ripe for employment. 152
Rochow, 17
Rod, the, 15, 33, 36 *f.*, 39
Rome, 222
Rope-dancers, 190, 194
Rote, 120, 123, 130, 175 *ff.*
Rousseau, 11, 39 *n.*, 120 *n.*
Royal Oak lottery, 117, 119
Royal Society, the, 1, 162 *n.*
Rule, the Golden, 259
Rules, 44 *ff.*, 191

Sanctius (Sanchez), 129
Sauntering, 76, 96 *ff.*, 173
Savannah, 228
Saviour, our, 259
Scepticism, 9
Scheibler, 76

Scholar, 163, 200, 258
Schools, 1 *ff.*, 15, 52, 69, 74, 138, 142
Science, 10
Scioppius (Schoppe), 129
Sectarianism, 184 *ff.*, 211, 217, 246, 252 *f.*, 256
Self-denial, 28, 30 *f.*, 35, 38 *f.*
Seneca, 76
Sense-impressions, 7, 203
Senses, instruction by the, 15, 127, 186, 203
Sequence, 250 *f.*
Servants, 41 *f.*, 46, 48 *f.*, 70, 85, 93
Severity, 32, 34 *f.*, 37
Shame, 36, 40 *ff.*, 61, 168
Sheriff, 260
Short-hand, 124
Similes, 240 *f.*
Smattering, 214
Solon, 29
Some Thoughts concerning Education, 4, 12 *f.*, 21 *ff.*
  original draft of, 21
  translations of, 13
Some Thoughts concerning Reading and Study, 12, 18
Sophistry, 235, 237, 255 *f.*
Spectres, 160
Spelling, 118
Spencer, Herbert, 39 *n.*
Spirits, 106, 159 *ff.*, 185
Squire Western, 3
St Jerome, *Epistle to Laeta,* 132 *n.*, 180
Standards, 192
Standpoints, different, 185
Sternhold, 114 *n.*
Strauchius, 150
Study, 12, 214, 217, 225
  men of, 185, 211, 222
"Substantial forms," 234
Sugar-plums, 30, 37

Tabula rasa, the, 6, 11, 183 *n.*
Talk, 212 *ff.*, 218, 237, 240, 259
Task, 56, 58, 97, 115
Temper (temperament), 82 *f.*, 97, 108, 130, 166, 179, 193, 214
Testimony, 213. See Evidence
Theatrum Historicum (Helwig), 150 *n.*

Themes, 139
Theology, 16, 220
Theory, educational, 5, 11
Theory of the Earth (Burnet), 161 *n.*
Things as they are in themselves, 39 *ff.*, 245, 253
Thinking, 216, 260
Trade, 169, 172
Transferring of thoughts, 259 *ff.*
Translations, 133, 138
Travel, 3, 12, 175 *ff.*
Truth, 108, 187, 199, 206, 210 *f.*, 224, 227, 229, 241 *f.*, 244, 258 *f.*
Truths, local, 244
Tully (Marcus Tullius Cicero), 127, 151, 153 *f.*
Tumblers, 190
Turkish Sultan, the, 259 *n.*
Turning, 169
Tutor, 70 *ff.*, 115, 145 *f.*, 164, 177
private, 3, 36, 44, 47

Understanding, the, 181 *ff.*, 192
defects of, 209 *ff.*, 221, 229 *f.*, 247, 252, 258, 261 *ff.*
right, 254
Universality (omniscience), 214 *ff.*
Universities, 1, 4, 187, 191
Utility as educational principle, 14, 16, 76 *f.*, 166

Vagary, 80
Variety of mental endowment, 133
Varnishing, 173

Verses, 141 *f.*
Verulam, 182
Vices, 38, 46, 48
Virgil, 151
Virtue, 5, 28, 31, 33, 35, 38 *f.*, 41, 43, 54, 105, 145, 151, 168
Visions, a sort of, 263 *f.*
Voiture, 156
Voltaire, 9 *f.*
"Vox populi," 223
Vulgar, the, 253
opinion, 223 *f.*

Wandering of thought, 130, 132, 235 *f.*
Westminster, 2 *f.*
Hall, 191
Whipping, 66 *ff.*
Whitehall, 188
Will, 181
Wisdom, 105, 109, 168
Wood-work, 170
Words, 233 *ff.*, 246
Working schools, 19
World, entering the, 73 *ff.*, 177
the intellectual, 248
Worthington, Dr. John, 122
Writing, 123, 194, 255
Writings, 225

Xerxes, 144

Zedlitz, 17

PRINTED IN ENGLAND BY J. B. PEACE, M.A.
AT THE CAMBRIDGE UNIVERSITY PRESS

For EU product safety concerns, contact us at Calle de José Abascal, 56–1°, 28003 Madrid, Spain or eugpsr@cambridge.org.

www.ingramcontent.com/pod-product-compliance
Ingram Content Group UK Ltd.
Pitfield, Milton Keynes, MK11 3LW, UK
UKHW010346140625
459647UK00010B/869